Intention, Supremacy and the Theories of Judicial Review

In the late 1980s, a vigorous debate began about how we may best justify, in constitutional terms, the English courts' jurisdiction to judicially review the exercise of public power derived from an Act of Parliament. Two rival theories emerged in this debate, the *ultra vires* theory and the common law theory. The debate between the supporters of these two theories has never satisfactorily been resolved and has been criticised as being futile. Yet, the debate raises some fundamental questions about the constitution of the United Kingdom, particularly: the relationship between Parliament and the courts; the nature of parliamentary supremacy in the contemporary constitution; and the possibility and validity of relying on legislative intent.

This book critically analyses the *ultra vires* and common law theories and argues that neither offers a convincing explanation for the courts' judicial review jurisdiction. Instead, the author puts forward the theory that parliamentary supremacy – and, in turn, the relationship between Parliament and the courts – is not absolute and does not operate in a hard and fast way but, rather, functions in a more flexible way and that the courts will balance particular Acts of Parliament against competing statutes or principles. McGarry argues that this new conception of parliamentary supremacy leads to an alternative theory of judicial review which significantly differs from both the *ultra vires* and common law theories.

This book will be of great interest to students and scholars of UK public law.

John McGarry is a Reader in Law at Edge Hill University, UK.

Intention, Supremacy and the Theories of Judicial Review

John McGarry

LONDON AND NEW YORK

First published 2017
by Routledge
2 Park Square, Milton Park, Abingdon, Oxon OX14 4RN

and by Routledge
711 Third Avenue, New York, NY 10017

First issued in paperback 2018

Routledge is an imprint of the Taylor & Francis Group, an informa business

© 2017 John McGarry

The right of John McGarry to be identified as author of this work has been asserted by him in accordance with sections 77 and 78 of the Copyright, Designs and Patents Act 1988.

All rights reserved. No part of this book may be reprinted or reproduced or utilised in any form or by any electronic, mechanical, or other means, now known or hereafter invented, including photocopying and recording, or in any information storage or retrieval system, without permission in writing from the publishers.

Trademark notice: Product or corporate names may be trademarks or registered trademarks, and are used only for identification and explanation without intent to infringe.

British Library Cataloguing in Publication Data
A catalogue record for this book is available from the British Library

Library of Congress Cataloging in Publication Data
Names: McGarry, John (Law teacher), author.
Title: Intention, supremacy and the theories of judicial review / John McGarry.
Description: New York, NY : Routledge, 2016. | Includes bibliographical references and index.
Identifiers: LCCN 2016008643| ISBN 9781138856011 (hbk) | ISBN 9781315719986 (ebk)
Subjects: LCSH: Judicial review--Great Britain. | Ultra vires--Great Britain. | Separation of powers--Great Britain. | Jurisdiction--Great Britain.
Classification: LCC KD4645 .M34 2016 | DDC 347.41/012--dc23
LC record available at http://lccn.loc.gov/2016008643

ISBN 13: 978-1-138-60661-6 (pbk)
ISBN 13: 978-1-138-85601-1 (hbk)

Typeset in ITC Galliard by
Servis Filmsetting Ltd, Stockport, Cheshire

For Clare, Joe, Joan and Ken

Contents

Permissions	ix
Acknowledgements	x
Table of cases	xi
Table of statutes	xv

1   Introduction   1
   Bibliography 5

2   Philosophical hermeneutics   6
   Philosophical hermeneutics 6
   Understanding and intention 7
   Application and interpretation 10
   Tradition and prejudice 16
   Gadamer and Dworkin 19
   Language 23
   Bibliography 26

**3   The *ultra vires* theory and the common law theory of judicial
   review**   28
   The ultra vires *theory 30*
   The common law theory 34
   Summary 38
   Bibliography 40

4   Themes of the debate   42
   Conceptions of parliamentary sovereignty 42
   Review of non-statutory power 55
   The rule of law 58
   Ouster clauses 62
   The structural coherence of the ultra vires *theory 68*
   Conclusion 72
   Bibliography 74

viii *Contents*

5 Immanent critique and the theories of judicial review   77
Immanent critique 77
Values underlying the two theories 80
Comparison: theories and practice 84
Conclusion 104
Bibliography 107

6 The principle of parliamentary sovereignty   110
Parliamentary sovereignty as a principle 110
Potential criticisms 124
Conclusion 130
Bibliography 131

7 The constitutional legitimacy of judicial review   133
The constitutional legitimacy of judicial review 133
The standards of good administration 136
Conclusion 140
Bibliography 142

Index   143

Permissions

I am grateful to the publishers of the following works for kindly granting me permission to reproduce extracts from them:

Forsyth C F (ed), (2000), *Judicial Review and the Constitution* (Hart Publishing, an imprint of Bloomsbury Publishing Plc) – reproduced by permission of Bloomsbury Publishing Plc

Forsyth C F and Elliott M C, 'The Legitimacy of Judicial Review' [2003] *Public Law* 286 – reproduced by permission of THOMSON REUTERS (PROFESSIONAL) UK LIMITED

Gadamer H-G (D G Marshall and Joel Weinsheimer trs) (1989), *Truth and Method* (2nd edn, Bloomsbury Academic, an imprint of Bloomsbury Publishing Plc) – reproduced by permission of Bloomsbury Publishing Plc

Jowell J L, 'Of Vires and Vacuums: The Constitutional Context of Judicial Review' [1999] *Public Law* 448 – reproduced by permission of THOMSON REUTERS (PROFESSIONAL) UK LIMITED

Jowell J L, 'Parliamentary Sovereignty Under the New Constitutional Hypothesis' [2006] *Public Law* 562 – reproduced by permission of THOMSON REUTERS (PROFESSIONAL) UK LIMITED

Oliver D, 'Common Values in Public and Private Law and the Public/Private Divide' [1997] *Public Law* 630 – reproduced by permission of THOMSON REUTERS (PROFESSIONAL) UK LIMITED

Lord Woolf of Barnes, '*Droit Public* – English Style' [1995] *Public Law* 57 – reproduced by permission of THOMSON REUTERS (PROFESSIONAL) UK LIMITED

Acknowledgements

I would first like to thank the staff at Routledge for commissioning the book, for their help and advice about its content, for guiding me through the different stages of the publication process and for tolerating my deadline stretching. In particular, I am grateful to Annabelle Harris, Olivia Manley, Damian Mitchell and Mark Sapwell.

Next, I would like to thank Michael Salter and Andrew Harries who supervised the PhD on which this monograph is based. Both were patient, encouraging and generous with their time, help and support. I am also indebted to Shaun Mills and Ian Donnison for their helpful suggestions when this project was in its early stages. I also thank the University of Central Lancashire who provided me with a bursary to pay the tuition fees for the PhD.

I thank my colleagues at Edge Hill University for their help, support and advice. In particular, I thank Robert Collinson, Maggi Eastwood, Peter Langford, Sharon McAvoy, Richard Parrish, Adam Pendlebury and Franco Rizzuto. I would also like to acknowledge numerous students who, through their conversations and questions, have helped me to clarify things. I am also grateful to Edge Hill for providing the funds to buy me out of teaching for one semester to enable me to complete this book.

I am extremely grateful to my friends who have supplied me with the welcome distractions of, among other things, badminton, insobriety and curries and, in some cases, endured my bad temper, especially David Horman, Allan and Zoe Gibbs-Monaghan, Alison Haughton, Phillipa Malone, Alex Muir, Gavin Muir, Gemma Shiels and Phil McNabb.

Finally, I thank my family, Clare, Joe, Joan and Ken. As ever, Clare and Joe deserve, and have, the greatest share of my thanks – for tolerating my working on this when I should have been with them and for putting up with my mardiness. I love them both very much and I would not have completed this without their patience and help; I am more grateful than I can adequately express.

Table of cases

Agriculture, Horticultural and Forestry Industry Training Board v Aylesbury Mushrooms Ltd [1972] 1 WLR 190 29

Anisminic Ltd v Foreign Compensation Commission [1969] 2 AC 147 .... 62, 64, 65, 66, 102, 115, 122, 141

Associated Provincial Picture Houses Ltd v Wednesbury Corporation [1948] 1 KB 223...29

Aston Cantlow and Wilmcote with Billesley Parochial Church Council v Wallbank [2003] UKHL 37, [2004] 1 AC 546...87

AXA General Insurance Ltd and others v HM Advocate and others [2011] UKSC 46, [2012] 1 AC 868..70, 99, 124

Benkharbouche v Embassy of the Republic of Sudan [2015] EWCA Civ 33, [2015] 3 WLR 301 ....54, 121

Black-Clawson International Ltd. v Papierwerke Waldhof-Aschaffenburg A.G. [1975] AC 591... 45, 47

Boddington v British Transport Police [1999] 2 AC 143 ....34, 53, 67

British Oxygen Co Ltd v Minister of Technology [1971] AC 610 29

Cart v The Upper Tribunal [2011] UKSC 28, [2012] 1 AC 663......................67

Council of Civil Service Unions v Minister for the Civil Service [1985] AC 374 .....29, 37

Duport Steel v Sirs [1980] 1 WLR 142 61

E v Secretary of State for the Home Department [2004] EWCA Civ 49, [2004] QB 1044 67

Ellen St Estates v Minister of Health [1934] 1 KB 590.....................................113

Entick v Carrington (1765) 19 St. Tr. 1030...28

Ghaidan v Godin-Mendoza [2004] UKHL 30, [2004] 2 AC 557 127

HM Treasury v Ahmed and others (No. 2) [2010] UKSC 5, [2012] 2 AC 534 .....70, 71

Inland Revenue Commissioners v National Federation of Self-Employed and Small Businesses Ltd. [1982] AC 617 ....90, 91, 96, 98, 99–100

International Transport Roth GmbH and others v Secretary of State for the Home Department [2002] EWCA Civ 158, [2003] QB 728 .... 61, 116, 119, 123

JB v Switzerland [2001] ECHR 31827/96...118

Khawaja v Home Secretary [1984] AC 74 115

Lloyd v McMahon [1987] AC 625 14

M v Home Office [1994] 1 AC 377...45

Mawdsley v Chief Constable of the Cheshire Constabulary [2003] EWHC 1586 118

Macarthys v Smith [1979] ICR 785...115

Magnor and St Melens Rural District Council v Newport Corporation [1952] AC 189..47

xii *Table of case*

Marbury v Madison 1 Cranch 137 (1803) **30, 32**
Mass Energy Ltd v Birmingham City Council [1994] Env LR 298 .... **86**
Nagarajan v London Regional Transport [2000] 1 AC 501 .... **139**
Nairn v University of Saint Andrews [1909] AC 147 .... **120**
O'Reilly and Others v Mackman and Others [1983] 2 AC 237 .... **67, 89**
Padfield v Minister of Agriculture [1968] 2 WLR 92 .... **138**
Poplar Housing and Regeneration Community Association Ltd v Donoghue
    [2001] EWCA Civ 595, [2002] QB 48 .... **83**
Pyx Granite Co v Ministry of Housing and Local Government [1960] AC 260 ..... **115**
Racal Communications, Re [1981] AC 374 .... **67**
R (Agnello) v Hounslow LBC [2003] EWHC 3112 (Admin), [2004] LLR. 268 ... **86**
R (Alconbury Developments Ltd and others) v Secretary of State for the
    Environment, Transport and the Regions [2001] UKHL 23, [2003] 2 AC
    295 .... **58, 67**
R (Beer) v Hampshire Farmer's Market Ltd [2003] EWCA Civ 1056, [2004],
    1 WLR 233 .... **86, 88**
R (Bulger) v Secretary of State for the Home Department [2001] EWHC Admin
    119, [2001] 3 All ER 449 .... **97**
R (Cart) v Upper Tribunal [2009] EWHC 3052 (Admin), [2010] 2 WLR
    1012 .... **116**
R (Chandler) v Secretary of State for Children, Schools and Families [2009]
    EWCA Civ 1011, [2010] PTSR 749 .... **97, 98**
R (Cowl and others) v Plymouth City Council (Practice Note) [2001] EWCA Civ
    1935, [2002] 1 WLR 803 .... **89**
R (Feakins) v Secretary of State for the Environment, Food and Rural Affairs
    [2003] EWCA Civ 1546, [2004] 1 WLR 1761 .... **98**
R (Gentle) v Prime Minister [2006] EWCA Civ 1078 .... **90**
R (HS2 Action Alliance Ltd and others) v Secretary of State for Transport [2014]
    UKSC 3, [2014] 1 WLR 324 .... **114**
R (Hurley and Moore) v Secretary of State for Business Innovation and Skills
    [2012] EWHC 201 (Admin), [2012] HRLR 13 .... **71**
R (Jackson) v Attorney-General [2005] EWCA Civ 126, [2005] QB 579 .... **119**
R (Jackson) v Attorney-General [2005] UKHL 56, [2006] 1 AC 262 ... **54, 63, 116,**
    117, 119, 124, 126, 135
R (Lumba) v Secretary of State for the Home Department (JUSTICE and another
    intervening) [2011] UKSC 12, [2012] 1 AC 245 .... **67**
R (M) v School Organisation Committee, Oxford CC. [2001] EWHC Admin
    245 .... **95**
R (Prolife Alliance) v British Broadcasting Corporation [2003] UKHL 23,
    [2004] 1 AC 185 .... **61**
R (Sivasubramaniam) v Wandsworth County Court [2002] EWCA Civ 1738,
    [2003] 1 WLR 475 .... **89, 116**
R (T) v Greater Manchester Chief Constable and others [2013] EWCA Civ 25,
    [2013] 1 WLR 2515 .... **70**
R (Wright) v Secretary of State for Health [2009] UKHL 3, [2009] 1 AC 739 ...... **84**
R v A (No 2) [2001] UKHL 25, [2002] 1 AC 45 .... **83**
Riggs v Palmer 115 N.Y. 506; 22 N.E. 188 (1889) **22, 112**
R v Advertising Standards Authority, ex p Insurance Services (1990) 9 Tr LR
    169 .... **87**
R v Chief Rabbi of the United Congregations of Great Britain and the
    Commonwealth, ex p Wachmann [1992] 1 WLR 1036 .... **87**
R v Cornwall County Council, ex p Huntington and another [1992] 3 All ER
    566 .... **63**

Table of cases xiii

R v *Criminal Injuries Compensation Board, ex p A* [1999] 2 AC 330 67
R v *Criminal Injuries Compensation Board, ex p Lain* [1967] 2 QB 864 .... **86, 87**
R v *Department of Education and Employment, ex p Begbie* [2000] 1 WLR
   1115..**117**
R v *Director of the Serious Fraud Office, ex p Johnson* [1993] COD 58 97
R v *Disciplinary Committee of the Jockey Club, ex p Aga Khan* [1993] 1 WLR
   909...**85, 86, 87**
R v *Disciplinary Committee of the Jockey Club, ex p Massingberd-Mundy* [1993]
   2 All ER 207 ....**88**
R v *Felixstowe Justices, ex p Leigh* [1987] QB 582 ....**96**
R v *Football Association Ltd, ex p Football League Ltd* [1993] 2 All ER 833.... **87, 88**
R v *Hillingdon LBC, ex p Pulhofer* [1986] AC 484..**69**
R v *Inland Revenue Commissioners, ex p Preston* [1985] AC 835 ....**89**
R v *Inspectorate of Pollution, ex p Greenpeace (No. 2)* [1994] 4 All ER 329 ....**100**
R v *London Metal Exchange, ex p Albatross Warehousing BV* (QBD, 30 March
   2000) **88**
R v *Lord Chancellor, ex p Witham* [1998] QB 575 .... **80, 111, 112, 116**
R v *Lord President of the Privy Council, ex p Page* [1993] AC 682.................. **34, 67**
R v *Lord Saville of Newdigate and others, ex p A and others* [2000] 1 WLR
   1855..**117**
R v *Medical Appeal Tribunal, ex p Gilmore* [1957] 1 QB 574............................**116**
R v *Ministry of Defence, ex p Smith* [1996] QB 517 ....**117**
R v *Monopolies and Mergers Commission, ex p Argyll Group Plc* [1986] 1 WLR
   763.. **69, 96**
R v *Monopolies and Mergers Commission, ex p South Yorkshire Passenger
   Transport Authority* [1993] 1 WLR 23..**67**
R v *Panel on Take-overs and Mergers, ex p Datafin and another* [1987] QB
   815...**56, 85, 86, 87, 88, 94**
R v *Panel on Take-overs and Mergers, ex p Guinness* [1990] 1 QB 146 .... **56, 91**
R v *Parliamentary Commissioner for Standards, ex p Al Fayed* [1998] 1 WLR
   669... **61, 122**
R v *Provincial Court of the Church in Wales, ex p Williams* [1998] EWHC
   Admin 998 ....**90**
R v *Secretary of State for Employment, ex p Equal Opportunities Commission and
   Another* [1995] 1 AC 1...**54**
R v *Secretary of State for Foreign and Commonwealth Affairs, ex parte Rees-Mogg*
   [1994] QB 552 ....**97**
R v *Secretary of State for Foreign and Commonwealth Affairs, ex p World
   Development Movement Ltd* [1995] 1 WLR 386 ....**95, 98, 100**
R v *Secretary of State for the Home Department, ex p Abdi* [1996] 1 WLR 298 ......**34**
R v *Secretary of State for the Home Department, ex p Anderson and Taylor* [2002]
   UKHL 46, [2003] 1 AC 837...**83–84**
R v *Secretary of State for the Home Department, ex p Brind* [1991] 1 AC 696......**116**
R v *Secretary of State for the Home Department, ex p Doody and Others* [1994] 1
   AC 531 ....**14**
R v *Secretary of State for the Home Department, ex p Fire Brigades Union and
   Others* [1995] 2 AC 513 ....**60**
R v *Secretary of State for the Home Department, ex p Leech* [1994] QB 198 ....**120**
R v *Secretary of State for the Home Department, ex p McQuillan* [1995] 4 All ER
   400..**116**
R v *Secretary of State for the Home Department, ex p Pierson* [1998] AC 539.........**34**
R v *Secretary of State for the Home Department, ex p Hosenball* [1977] 1 WLR
   766..**14**

xiv   *Table of case*

R v Secretary of State for the Home Department, ex p Ruddock and Others [1987]
1 WLR 1482 ....**95**

R v Secretary of State for the Home Department, ex p Simms and Another [2000]
2 AC 115... **116, 117**

R v Secretary of State for the Home Department, ex p Swati [1986] 1 All ER 717 ...**89**

R v Secretary of State for Social Services, ex p Child Poverty Action Group [1990]
2 QB 540 ....**100**

R v Secretary of State for Trade and Industry, ex p Greenpeace Ltd [2000] Env
LR 221 ....**95**

R v Secretary of State for Transport, ex p Factortame and Others (No 2) [1991]
1 AC 603....................................**9, 28, 54, 113–114, 121, 122, 123, 140**

R v Somerset County Council and ARC Southern Limited, ex p Dixon [1998]
Env. LR 111 .... **92, 96**

R v Somerset County Council, ex p Fewings and others [1995] 1 WLR 1037 ....**29**

R v Swale Borough Council, ex p Royal Society for the Protection of Birds [1991]
1 PLR 6..**95**

S (A Minor) v Knowsley Borough Council and others [2004] EWHC 491 (Fam),
[2004] 2 FLR 716...**93**

Sharma v Brown-Antoine [2006] UKPC 57, [2007] 1 WLR 780 ....**90**

Straatspresident en andere v United Democratic Front en 'n ander 1988(4) S.A.
830(A) **66**

Terry v Huntington (1668) Hardr. 480 ....**67**

Thoburn v Sunderland City Council [2002] EWHC 195 (Admin), [2003] QB
151..**113, 114, 117, 123, 126, 135**

Vauxhall Estates v Liverpool Corporation [1932] 1 KB 733 ....**113**

Vine v National Dock Labour Board [1957] AC 488 ....**29**

Walton v Scottish Ministers [2012] UKSC 44, [2013] PTSR 51 .... **97, 99**

Table of statutes

Civil Procedure Act 1997
  s 2 95
Criminal Justice and Courts Act
  2015
  s 84 ....90, 103
Disability Discrimination Act
  1995 139
Equal Pay Act 1970 139
European Communities Act
  1972 .... 113, 114, 115, 121,
                           139, 140
Foreign Compensation Act 1950 ...102,
                                     122
  s 4(4) 62
Human Rights Act 1998 ....28, 83,
                   85, 96, 101, 123, 139
  s 3(1) 83
  s 4(2) 28
  s 4(3) 28
  s 6(1) 28, 85, 96
  s 6(3)(b) 86
  s 6(5) 86
  s 7 .... 28, 85, 96
Hunting Act 2004 119
Merchant Shipping Act 1988 ....9, 54,
                          113–114, 122
Parliament Act 1911 119
Parliament Act 1949 119
Race Relations Act 1976 139
Road Traffic Act 1988
  s 172 118
Senior Courts Act 1981 ....96, 101
  s 31(2A) 103, 104
  s 31(2B) 103, 104
  s 31(2C) 104
  s 31(3) 11, 88, 95, 96,
                           98, 100, 101

  s 31(3C) 89
  s 31(3D) 90
  s 31(3E) 90
  s 31(6) 93, 94
  s 130 ....80–81, 111
Sex Discrimination Act 1975 139
State Immunity Act 1978 ....54, 121
Supreme Court Act 1981 111

Statutory instruments

Civil Procedure Rules, SI
  1998/3132 .... 37, 95, 98
  54A PD 8.4 89
  54A PD 8.5 89
  CPR 3.1 95
  CPR 54 37
  CPR 54.1 86
  CPR 54.2 29
  CPR 54.3 29
  CPR 54.4 88
  CPR 54.5 ....93, 95
The Public Contracts Regulations
  2015, SI 2015/102 ....95, 105

European Legislation, Conventions and Treaties

European Convention on Human
  Rights and Fundamental
  Freedoms 116, 125, 139
  Art 6 118
European Union Charter of
  Fundamental Human Rights 54,
                                     121

1 Introduction

In 1987, Dawn Oliver published an article entitled: 'Is the *Ultra Vires* Rule the Basis of Judicial Review?'[1] This explored the way in which we justify the supervisory jurisdiction of the English courts. It followed a number of cases in which the judicial review jurisdiction seemed to have 'burst through its logical boundaries'[2] as apparently delineated by the *ultra vires* theory. Since then there have been numerous publications[3] and at least one conference[4] examining this issue. Despite this academic interest, some commentators question the utility of this debate. The claim is that it is a 'largely semantic tussle'[5] which is 'sterile'[6] and 'pointless'.[7]

It is surely the case, however, that identifying the basis of court action is valuable, both practically and theoretically. The theoretical foundation on which the courts base their jurisdiction will affect the manner in which they reach their

---

1 Dawn Oliver, 'Is the *Ultra Vires* Rule the Basis of Judicial Review?' [1987] *PL* 543.
2 HWR Wade, 'Judicial Review of Ministerial Guidance' (1986) 102 *LQR* 173,175. The comment was made with regard to a number of cases where the courts have reviewed 'non-statutory rules' exercised in pursuit of 'non-statutory powers'.
3 Including: Christopher F Forsyth, 'Of Fig Leaves and Fairy Tales: The Ultra Vires Doctrine, the Sovereignty of Parliament and Judicial Review' [1996] *CLJ* 122; Paul P Craig, 'Ultra Vires and the Foundations of Judicial Review' [1998] *CLJ* 63; Mark C Elliott, 'The Ultra Vires Doctrine in a Constitutional Setting: Still the Central Principle of Administrative Law' [1999] *CLJ* 129; Mark C Elliott, *The Constitutional Foundations of Judicial Review* (Hart Publishing 2001); TRS Allan, 'Constitutional Dialogue and the Justification of Judicial Review' (2003) 23 *OJLS* 563; Christopher F Forsyth and Mark C Elliott, 'The Legitimacy of Judicial Review' [2003] *PL* 286; Lori A Ringhand, 'Fig Leaves, Fairy Tales, and Constitutional Foundations: Debating Judicial Review in Britain' (2005) 43(3) *Columbia Journal of Transnational Law* 865; John Chu, 'One Controversy, Two Jurisdictions: A Comparative Evaluation of the Ultra Vires and Common Law Theories of Judicial Review' [2009] *JR* 347; TRS Allan, *The Sovereignty of Law: Freedom, Constitution, and Common Law* (OUP 2013) Chapter Six.
4 Cambridge, 22 May 1999. The papers given are contained in Christopher F Forsyth (ed), *Judicial Review and the Constitution* (Hart Publishing 2000).
5 TRS Allan, 'The Constitutional Foundations of Judicial Review: Conceptual Conundrum or Interpretative Inquiry?' [2002] *CLJ* 87, 101.
6 ibid.
7 ibid 123.

2 Intention, Supremacy and Judicial Review

decisions and the substance of those decisions. This will, in turn, govern the way in which lawyers frame their arguments before court.

In addition, identifying the theoretical basis underlying judicial review enables us to evaluate the degree to which any particular decision is consistent with that basis and thereby provide a means of assessing the propriety of the decision. Furthermore, the debate teaches us 'much about the British constitution', highlighting 'the interaction of fundamental legal principles'.[8] This will be seen throughout the following work where engagement with the debate encourages us to reconsider the relationship between Parliament and the courts and between common law principles of legality and the doctrine of parliamentary sovereignty,[9] including the degree to which the courts adhere to the assumed intention of, or legislation enacted by, Parliament. As Chu writes, the 'fundamental issues' identified in the debate are important because they 'inform the definition and clarification of the relationship between the judiciary and the other branches of government'.[10]

Indeed, it is the fact that the debate has largely centred on this aspect of the UK constitution – the relationship between Parliament and the courts – that makes it so interesting and worthwhile. For the most part, it is this that divides the supporters of the two alternative theories generally proffered as providing the constitutional legitimacy for judicial review: the *ultra vires* theory and the common law theory. Disagreement centres on the question of how the judicial supervision of public power granted by a sovereign legislature may be explicated. The proponents of the *ultra vires* theory argue that we must assume that the review of such power is intended by Parliament. They state that, without this assumption, the supervision of such power would amount to a breach of parliamentary supremacy. Supporters of the alternative common law theory contend that judicial review is exercised by virtue of a common law jurisdiction to supervise public power and that justification by reference to parliamentary intent is not necessary.

In the following work, I subject these two theories to critical analysis. This involves examining both the theories themselves and the debate that has taken place between the supporters of each. It also involves using immanent critique to evaluate the degree to which the theories match the practice of review. Such a critique is appropriate because it is implicit in any theory that it should correspond to the activity for which it is given as an explanation and, what is more, it is inherent in the arguments advanced by the proponents of both theories that they coincide with judicial review in reality.

I follow this analysis by proposing an alternative justification for judicial review. This is based on a novel conception of parliamentary sovereignty – one that

---

8 Allan, *The Sovereignty of Law* (n 3) 209. Indeed, Allan ascribes to the participants in the debate the ambition of 'seeking to improve our grasp of constitutional theory', ibid 211.

9 Also known as legislative sovereignty or supremacy; these terms will be used synonymously throughout the text.

10 Chu, 'One Controversy, Two Jurisdictions' (n 3) para 2.

Introduction 3

operates in a way which differs from that assumed in either the *ultra vires* or common law theories. I argue that this alternative justification, and the conception of sovereignty on which it is based, is better able to account for the relationship between Parliament and the courts and for the operation of judicial review.

The research is underpinned by philosophical hermeneutics. Philosophical hermeneutics reflects on the process of understanding. Among other things, it claims that understanding also involves interpretation and application and that, when attempting to understand a text, artwork or law, we cannot and should not attempt to divine the intention of its creator. This rejection of authorial and legislative intention has obvious implications for the present work which, in part, analyses two alternative theories which differ in the reliance they place on the intention of the Parliament. Indeed, adopting philosophical hermeneutics as my methodology provides me with a range of assumptions and concepts by which I evaluate the *ultra vires* and common law theories. It also guides my development of an alternative justification for judicial review and the conception of parliamentary supremacy on which it is based.

Chapter Two describes this methodology. I give an account of the main aspects of philosophical hermeneutics, justify its adoption as the methodology for this work and illustrate the way in which it will guide the research undertaken in this book.

In Chapter Three, I delineate and examine the *ultra vires* and common law theories and the rationales on which they are based. In so doing, I identify the assumptions – both explicit and implicit – underlying these theories.

Chapter Four explores the main themes of the debate between the supporters of the *ultra vires* and common law theories and considers the differences and similarities that exist between the two. In particular, I investigate: the way in which parliamentary sovereignty is understood in the two theories; the validity of relying on parliamentary intent in the *ultra vires* theory; the use made of the doctrine of the rule of law; the way in which the courts' treatment of ouster clauses and of non-statutory public power is explained; and the structural coherence of the *ultra vires* theory.

In Chapter Five, I use immanent critique to gauge the extent to which the two competing theories match the practice of review. Immanent critique attempts to evaluate the degree to which a practice aligns with the values which are claimed to underlie and justify it. It is used here to assess the degree to which the *ultra vires* and common law theories match judicial review in practice. I begin with a brief account of immanent critique. I then identify the principles underlying the two theories. I use these principles to undertake the critique and evaluate the degree to which the practice of judicial review coincides with the two theories. I examine six aspects of review: the extent of the judicial review jurisdiction; the permission stage; the time limits for bringing a claim; the sufficient interest requirement; the courts' treatment of ouster clauses; and the discretionary nature of remedies.

In Chapter Six, I follow the analysis undertaken in the previous three chapters and argue that parliamentary supremacy functions in a different way to that assumed in either the *ultra vires* or common law theory: that it operates as a

4   *Intention, Supremacy and Judicial Review*

Dworkinian principle rather than a rule. I also consider some potential criticisms of this conception of parliamentary sovereignty.

In the final chapter, I examine the implications for justifying the judicial review jurisdiction in the light of the alternative conception of parliamentary sovereignty suggested in Chapter Six. I also explore the way in which the standards of good administration – breach of which may found a claim in judicial review – are developed by the courts and the direct and indirect influence of legislation on the exercise of the supervisory jurisdiction.

Bibliography

Allan TRS, 'Constitutional Dialogue and the Justification of Judicial Review' (2003) 23 *Oxford Journal of Legal Studies* 563

— 'The Constitutional Foundations of Judicial Review: Conceptual Conundrum or Interpretative Inquiry?' [2002] *Cambridge Law Journal* 87

— *The Sovereignty of Law: Freedom, Constitution, and Common Law* (OUP 2013)

Chu J, 'One Controversy, Two Jurisdictions: A Comparative Evaluation of the Ultra Vires and Common Law Theories of Judicial Review' [2009] *Judicial Review* 347

Craig P P, 'Ultra Vires and the Foundations of Judicial Review' [1998] *Cambridge Law Journal* 63

Elliott M C, 'The Ultra Vires Doctrine in a Constitutional Setting: Still the Central Principle of Administrative Law' [1999] *Cambridge Law Journal* 129

— *The Constitutional Foundations of Judicial Review* (Hart Publishing 2001)

Forsyth C F, 'Of Fig Leaves and Fairy Tales: The Ultra Vires Doctrine, the Sovereignty of Parliament and Judicial Review' [1996] *Cambridge Law Journal* 122

— (ed), *Judicial Review and the Constitution* (Hart Publishing 2000)

— and Elliott M C, 'The Legitimacy of Judicial Review' [2003] *Public Law* 286

Oliver D, 'Is the *Ultra Vires* Rule the Basis of Judicial Review?' [1987] *Public Law* 543

Ringhand L A, 'Fig Leaves, Fairy Tales, and Constitutional Foundations: Debating Judicial Review in Britain' (2005) 43(3) *Columbia Journal of Transnational Law* 865

Wade HWR, 'Judicial Review of Ministerial Guidance' (1986) 102 *Law Quarterly Review* 173

2 Philosophical hermeneutics

The analysis in this book and the conclusions I make are informed by a framework of assumptions and concepts derived from philosophical hermeneutics. This chapter provides an account of philosophical hermeneutics. I draw, predominantly, on the work of Gadamer and on those who have commented on, and further developed, his work.

I begin with a brief outline of philosophical hermeneutics and a justification of its use as a methodological approach. I follow this with five sections which elucidate different aspects of philosophical hermeneutics and explain why they are relevant for the present work: understanding and intention; application and interpretation; tradition and prejudice; Gadamer and Dworkin; and language.

The first of these explains how, for Gadamer, the meaning of a text or historical event is not synonymous with the meaning intended by the author of that text or the participant in that historical event. It is, rather, contingent on the situatedness of the person attempting to understand. Indeed, as will be seen in the third section, application and interpretation are integral parts of understanding and, therefore, understanding is always a productive activity. Application is guided by experience which is not merely a matter of time but is also qualitative and is characterised by a willingness to learn from new situations. In the fourth section, I examine the conditioning force of tradition and prejudice in Gadamer's account of understanding. I should be clear that he uses the word 'prejudice' in a non-derogatory way; for him, it merely refers to the pre-judgements which are a necessary part of all understanding. In the fifth section, the similarity between Gadamer and Dworkin, and the use that will be made of the latter's work, will be noted. Finally, I look at the pre-eminence that Gadamer ascribes to language in understanding and at his description of a genuine dialogue which is epitomised by an endeavour to reach a common understanding.

Philosophical hermeneutics

Hermeneutics is the art of interpretive understanding.[1] It is necessary when understanding is not immediate, when mediation is required to assimilate the

---

1 Jean Grondin, *Introduction to Philosophical Hermeneutics* (Joel Weinshiemer tr, Yale University Press 1994) x, 7.

initially strange into the already familiar. Gadamer's philosophical hermeneutics is, among other things, a reflection on how the process of coming to an understanding occurs. It applies to understanding whether it occurs in the natural or social sciences, art, literature, philosophy, history or law. In short, the contention is that philosophical hermeneutics can account for *all* understanding and this, therefore, amounts to a claim that it is universal.[2]

Moreover, as Gadamer occasionally makes plain,[3] and as will be evident throughout this chapter, hermeneutic understanding is often exemplified by legal understanding.[4] This indicates that it is an appropriate methodology to adopt when evaluating the way in which judicial review may be legitimated. More particularly, it is Gadamer's rejection of authorial and, by implication, legislative intention which means that his work is of particular relevance here. This is because the debate about the constitutional legitimacy of judicial review considers the validity of, and extent to which, reliance on the intention of Parliament is legitimate.

Understanding and intention

I begin by explaining that, for Gadamer, if we want to understand a work of art or a text, it should not be our goal to identify the meaning intended by the artist or author in creating their work. Similarly, if we wish to understand a historical event, our aim should not be to ascertain the intention of the historical actors in that event. Gadamer therefore rejects the approach whereby the aim is to achieve a reproduction of the author's intention in writing a text; the approach whereby one attempts to place 'oneself within the whole framework of the author, [thereby achieving] an appreciation of the "inner origin" of the composition of a work, a re-creation of the creative act'.[5]

In the first place, Gadamer argues that it is not possible to re-create the creative process in this way. We cannot understand the intended meaning of, say, an author because we will be differently situated, both temporally and culturally, than that author: 'Reconstructing the original circumstances, like all restoration,

---

2 This is clear throughout Gadamer's work; for particular examples see: the introductions to the first and second editions of *Truth and Method*: Hans-Georg Gadamer, *Truth and Method* (D G Marshall and Joel Weinsheimer trs, 2nd edn, Sheed and Ward 1989) xxi–xxv, xxvii–xxxviii (respectively); Hans-Georg Gadamer, 'On the Scope and Function of Hermeneutical Reflection' (G B Hess and R E Palmer trs) in David E Linge (ed), *Philosophical Hermeneutics* (University of California Press 1976) 18; Foreword by Gadamer in Grondin, *Introduction to Philosophical Hermeneutics* (ibid) ix–xi. However, Gadamer also writes: '"hermeneutic" philosophy . . . does not understand itself to be an "absolute" position' (quoted in *Introduction to Philosophical Hermeneutics* 121). Rather, it is likely that, in this context, the claim to universality is simply an assertion that hermeneutic understanding is not confined to a particular field of knowledge.

3 *Truth and Method* (n 2) 38, 308–309, 539, 537.

4 Kenneth Henley, 'Protestant Hermeneutics and the Rule of Law: Gadamer and Dworkin' (1990) 3 *Ratio Juris* 14, 15.

5 *Truth and Method* (n 2) 187 (citation omitted).

8 *Intention, Supremacy and Judicial Review*

is a futile undertaking in view of the historicity of our being'.[6] As will be described below, our understanding is necessarily conditioned by our history, by our experiences and by the tradition we inhabit. These influences will be different for author and interpreter. For instance, both will be differently experienced, not least in the fact that the latter will have experienced the work – and perhaps the whole body of work – of the former.

The interpreter will also have experience of the subsequent impact of the work. The interpreter of Shakespeare cannot 'un-experience' either the work or its impact to put himself in the same position as this playwright when he was originally creating it. Indeed, any attempt to re-create the creative moment will necessarily be governed by a situatedness which inevitably differs from that of the artist at that moment. This means that, 'What is reconstructed . . . is not the original. In its continuance in an estranged state it acquires only a derivative, cultural existence'.[7] It is, therefore, not possible for the interpreter to understand, in a pristine 'as is' manner, the meaning intended by the author when creating the work.

Second, even if such re-creation was possible, Gadamer argues that is not desirable. This is for a number of reasons. For instance, to restrict our interpretation of, say, a text to that meant by its author would be to limit our understanding. Words are capable of conveying meanings in ways and in situations that may not have been conceived of, or intended by, those who framed them. Because of this, 'a hermeneutics that regarded understanding as reconstructing the original would be no more than handing on a dead meaning'.[8] This can be clearly seen in the application of laws. If the meaning of a statute is restricted to the intention of those who framed it (leaving aside for the moment the argument given above that access to such intention is not possible) this may prevent it from being applied in situations where it could and should be.

Hart has implicitly recognised this, pointing out that laws are made by 'men not gods' and that,

> It is a feature of the human predicament (and so of the legislative one) that we labour under two connected handicaps whenever we seek to regulate, unambiguously and in advance, some sphere of conduct by means of general standards to be used without further official direction on particular occasions. The first handicap is our relative ignorance of fact: the second is our relative ignorance of aim.[9]

Those who make laws are not capable of foreseeing all the situations where these measures could be applied and are, therefore, incapable of foreseeing all the

---

6 ibid 167.

7 ibid.

8 ibid.

9 HLA Hart, *The Concept of Law* (3rd edn, OUP 2012) 128. Ekins makes a related point here: 'in making explicit what may otherwise be conveyed by impliciture or implicatur the legislator, like any other speaker, risks failing to say part of what he otherwise intends to mean', Richard Ekins, *The Nature of Legislative Intent* (OUP 2012) 215.

Philosophical hermeneutics 9

situations where they should be applied. For example, a law-maker legislating in the 1970s to regulate broadcast media would be unable to conceive of issues raised by the emergence of the internet, let alone decide whether his legislation could or should apply to it. For this reason, a judge in 2016 would be unable to determine how the 1970s legislation applies to the internet if her understanding was restricted to that intended by the law-maker.[10] To be sure, Hart makes it clear that such indeterminacy of fact and of aim also applies to seemingly straightforward rules such as banning vehicles from a park.[11]

It is the case, then, that a legislative provision – and, more generally, a text – always communicates more than was originally intended. As Gadamer states: 'Not just occasionally but always, the meaning of a text goes beyond its author'.[12] It is for this reason that to equate the meaning of a text with authorial intention would be to illegitimately restrict its meaning. Indeed, as noted earlier, an author's viewpoint when writing will be more parochial than those who read him in at least one sense: they will have read the work that he is creating. There is, therefore, no reason why his interpretation of his own work should be considered to be more valuable than that of the reader's:

> the artist who creates something is not the appointed interpreter of it. As an interpreter he has no automatic authority over the person who is simply receiving his work. Insofar as he reflects on his own work, he is his own reader. The meaning that he, as reader, gives his own work does not set the standard.[13]

For the same reason, we should eschew the idea that a legislator's intention when framing a statute – which we may attempt to reconstruct by reference to Hansard, White Papers, etc – should govern the meaning of that legislation for those who apply it.

The same is true, for similar reasons, with regard to historical events. To limit our understanding to what was intended by the actors in such events would be to fail to understand. To understand the Merchant Shipping Act 1988 simply by reference to the intention of those Parliamentarians that enacted it would be insufficient. It would fail to appreciate the significance of this Act of Parliament as the first to be prevented from taking effect by the UK courts because of a potential conflict with European Community law.[14] The meaning of a historical event – and, indeed, whether we understand events to have historical meaning – can only be judged through subsequent events and in its relation to the present, not by what was intended by the historical actors. As Habermas writes:

---

10 Waldron makes a similar point with regard to the framers of the US Constitution: Jeremy Waldron, *Law and Disagreement* (OUP 1999) 123. See, also, Paul P Craig, *Public Law and Democracy in the United Kingdom and the United States of America* (OUP 1990) 8.
11 *The Concept of Law* (n 9) 126.
12 *Truth and Method* (n 2) 296.
13 ibid 193.
14 *R v Secretary of State for Transport, ex p Factortame and Others (No 2)* [1991] 1 AC 603 (HL).

10 *Intention, Supremacy and Judicial Review*

> The sentence, "The Thirty Years War began in 1618," presupposes that at least those events have elapsed which are relevant for the history of the war up to the Peace of Westphalia, events that could not have been narrated by any observer at the outbreak of the war.[15]

In addition, the intention of the actors may not be reflected in what has actually happened. There may be a losing side in a battle but that is unlikely to have been the intention of the commander of that side. Using the events of the battle to identify the intention of any of its participants – including the victorious commander – would be to ignore the military adage that no battle plan survives the first encounter with the enemy intact. Because our plans – what we intend to happen – do not usually survive unaltered when confronted with the world, we cannot make events the key to understanding intentions.

This hermeneutical insight may again be applied to the understanding of legislation. For example, to understand a government-sponsored Act of Parliament by reference to what Ministers intended would be to ignore the compromises and alterations forced on them by the legislative process. Often, Bills will not survive this process to emerge in their original form. Furthermore, to talk of the 'intention of Parliament' when construing legislation ignores the fact that Parliament consists of a number of fluctuating and unstable political groupings existing in both Houses and that the legislation will, in most cases, represent a compromise among those groupings and between the Houses, rather than the intention of them as a whole.[16]

The rejection of intention described in this section, whether of an author or historical actor, has significant implications for the current work. This is because the *ultra vires* theory asks us to assume that Parliament intends the courts to develop and apply the standards of good administration, breach of which may found a claim in judicial review. The supporters of this theory argue that, without such a presumption, the courts would be breaching the doctrine of legislative sovereignty when applying those standards to discretionary public power derived from Parliament. This argument, and arguments concerning its validity, will be explored in Chapters Three and Four.

Application and interpretation

If understanding does not mean divining originally intended meaning, the question arises as to what it does mean. For Gadamer, when attempting to understand a text or artwork, we are trying to understand its claim to truth. That is, what we may take from it. Similarly, when understanding historical events, we wish to

---

15 Jürgen Habermas, 'A Review of Gadamer's *Truth and Method*' (F R Dallmayr and T McCarthy trs) in Gayle L Ormiston and Alan D Schrift (eds), *The Hermeneutic Tradition: From Ast to Ricoeur* (State University of New York Press 1990) 225.

16 See, also, Waldron, *Law and Disagreement* (n 10) 125, 145. I return to this point in Chapter Four pp 50–52.

know the significance they have. In all these things we understand how the text, the artwork or the historical event relates to us in our situation. That is, the claim to truth is determined by, and is relevant for us in, the here and now. This is the case, *a fortiori*, when understanding a legal rule or principle: we want to know how it applies to the instant case and so we must place it in the context of that case. Indeed, this is the only way we can understand. Understanding is therefore situational and a person who wishes to understand 'must not seek to disregard himself and his particular hermeneutical situation. He must relate the text to this situation, if he wants to understand at all'.[17]

Thus, application, relating the text to one's situation and circumstances, is an integral component of understanding. Indeed, Gadamer views understanding, application and interpretation as 'comprising one unified process'.[18] Within this process, the three elements of understanding are each a necessary constituent part of the others: understanding involves interpretation and application; interpretation involves understanding and application; and application involves understanding and interpretation.

That understanding is a unified process can be seen with a simple example. Let us imagine that a lecturer is explaining to a class of students that a claimant in judicial review must have sufficient interest in the matter to which the claim relates.[19] Let us also imagine that, to illustrate the meaning of sufficient interest, the lecturer creates a fictional scenario whereby one student will have sufficient interest to bring a claim by way of judicial review but his fellow students will not. Here, the lecturer is aiding the students' understanding in two ways. First, through interpretation in that the students are encouraged to transpose the strange and abstract into the familiar and concrete by using an example to which they can relate. Second, through application: the test of sufficient interest is addressed to that specific example.

Of course (one would hope), the lecturer already understands the concept of sufficient interest. Therefore, because understanding already exists, no understanding would take place; there would be no occasion of understanding on the part of the lecturer. By already understanding, the lecturer does not need to understand afresh. Understanding, then, means coming to an understanding; it is an event arising out of a process.[20] This should not be taken to mean that it happens suddenly so that in one instant there is understanding where previously there had been none. As will be shown, understanding progressively unfolds in an incremental way through one's continued engagement with, say, a text or a

---

17 *Truth and Method* (n 2) 324.

18 ibid 308.

19 As required by the Senior Court Act 1981 s 31(3).

20 Indeed, as Habermas notes, *Understanding and Event* was a suggested title for Gadamer's *magnum opus* before *Truth and Method* was decided upon: Jürgen Habermas, 'After Historicism, Is Metaphysics Still Possible? On Hans-George Gadamer's 100th Birthday' (P Malone tr) in Bruce Krajewski (ed), *Gadamer's Repercussions: Reconsidering Philosophical Hermeneutics* (University of California Press 2003) 15.

12 Intention, Supremacy and Judicial Review

conversation partner. Rather, 'event' is used here in contrast with the situation where understanding is not needed because it is already present.

For Gadamer, because application, along with interpretation, is always an integral part of understanding, it is not subsequent to understanding. We do not understand in the abstract, and then decide whether to apply this to the situation at hand. Rather, application, along with understanding and interpretation, determines meaning from the start.[21]

A judge, then, does not understand a legal rule or principle in the abstract and before applying it to the case with which he is dealing. In fact, while laws may exist in the abstract, they take on a concrete existence only in being applied. In understanding a law, a judge must understand it – or, at least, understand it in a new way – as it applies to the case before him. The meaning, scope and relevance of a rule or principle is therefore constantly determined and re-determined afresh in the ongoing process of being applied and re-applied and is continuously understood, 'in a new and different way'.[22] This, in turn, means that understanding is not a passive reception of an already completely formed meaning but is a generative process: 'Motivated by the particular questions of the moment, understanding is not just reproductive but, because it involves application, always also a productive activity'.[23]

Understanding is, therefore, necessarily open-ended, with each new application leading to a new understanding. Because of this, there can be no final, complete and absolute understanding. There is no final word from an ultimate perspective but only a contingent participation in an ongoing conversation.

It should perhaps be noted here that it is not Gadamer's position that there is no true understanding. On the contrary, throughout his work, Gadamer discusses how one can differentiate a true from a false understanding, or a true from a false prejudice.[24] His position is that there is no final, complete understanding because application from a different, not yet formulated, perspective will always reveal a new aspect of the object to be understood.

That a law is constantly re-determined anew in the course of its concrete application means that application is not simply the subsumption of a particular case under a universal rule or principle. Rather, the relationship is one between a particular – a constituent element – and a 'not-yet-given whole'.[25] The particular case is not merely an example of the universal, the whole, but also itself determines

---

21 *Truth and Method* (n 2) 324.

22 ibid 309.

23 Grondin, *Introduction to Philosophical Hermeneutics* (n 1) 116 (citation omitted).

24 For instance, Gadamer argues that distorted understanding may be revealed in the encounter with other traditions (*Truth and Method* (n 2) 546) or through the 'productivity of temporal distance' (ibid 298) and Hans-Georg Gadamer, 'Reply to my Critics' (G H Leiner tr) in Gayle L Ormiston and Alan D Schrift (eds), *The Hermeneutic Tradition: From Ast to Ricoeur* (State University of New York Press 1990) 285.

25 Joel Weinsheimer, *Gadamer's Hermeneutics: A Reading of Truth and Method* (Yale University Press 1985) 78.

Philosophical hermeneutics 13

the meaning of that universal.[26] This demonstrates, again, that understanding is 'always a productive activity'.[27] This may be illustrated by reference to Gadamer's description of the difference between practical and technical knowledge.

For Gadamer, technical knowledge is exemplified by the craftswoman making an object. In such a case, it is possible for her to fully visualise the object in the abstract before she has produced it. In contrast, practical knowledge is the ability to know what is required in a particular situation and can therefore only be completely realised in that situation. So, while someone may be able to envisage particular examples of, say, courage, it is only in the concrete situation that one can decide what is required for a course of action to be recognised as truly courageous. Gadamer writes:

> The image that man has of what he ought to be – i.e., his ideas of right and wrong, of decency, courage, dignity, loyalty, and so forth (all concepts that have their equivalents in Aristotle's catalogue of virtues) – are certainly in some sense images that he uses to guide his conduct. But there is still a basic difference between this and the guiding image the craftsman uses: the plan of the object he is going to make. What is right, for example, cannot be fully determined independently of the situation that requires a right action from me, whereas the eidos of what a craftsman wants to make is fully determined by the use for which it is intended.[28]

So, while a person might have examples of courage to guide her in deciding how to act courageously, it is only in the contingences of the particular situation that she can decide what courage requires. In some cases, courage would require her to fight while in others to refuse to fight.[29]

The difference between technical and practical knowledge may also be illustrated using the example that public law decisions must be fairly reached. A lawyer advising a disparate group of decision-makers may be able to draft a general set of rules to attempt to ensure that their decisions are reached using a fair procedure. This drafting will be akin to an exercise of technical knowledge because it can largely be done apart from the particular situations in which the rules are to be applied. However, Lord Mustill has stated:

> What does fairness require in [any particular] case? My Lords, I think it unnecessary to refer by name or to quote from, any of the often-cited authorities in which the courts have explained what is essentially an intuitive judgment. . . . The standards of fairness are not immutable. They may change with the passage of time, both in the general and in their application

---

26 Gadamer, *Truth and Method* (n 2) 557, 570.
27 Text to n 23; also, Gadamer, *Truth and Method* (ibid) 296.
28 *Truth and Method* (ibid) 317.
29 Warnke uses the example of courage to illustrate the operation of practical knowledge: Georgia Warnke, *Gadamer: Hermeneutics, Tradition and Reason* (Stanford University Press 1987) 93.

14   *Intention, Supremacy and Judicial Review*

to decisions of a particular type. . . . The principles of fairness are not to be applied by rote identically in every situation. What fairness demands is dependent on the context of the decision, and this is to be taken into account in all its aspects.[30]

That is, what is fair in any individual case is an intuitive judgement that can only be made in the context of the facts and circumstances of that case. Because of this, the determination of whether any particular decision was fair is an exercise of practical knowledge and judgement. Moreover, each particular case will further determine the meaning of fairness.

If, during the process of legal interpretation, each new application of a rule or principle re-determines its meaning, how are we to know what is required in the instant case? How are we to bridge the gap between the instant case and the whole which that case determines anew? The answer, it would seem, lies with 'experience'. For Gadamer, the experienced person is, 'radically undogmatic; who, because of the many experiences he has had and the knowledge he has drawn from them, is particularly well equipped to have new experiences and to learn from them'.[31] Such a person will be acquainted with different ways of coping with the world. Because of this, she will have acquired the practical knowledge of taste, tact and judgement.

One has tact when one knows what to say and how to act in a particular situation.[32] One has taste when one knows what is right for a situation.[33] Similarly, one has judgement when one can discern the correct course of action required by the circumstances.[34] These three qualities are pragmatic ways of knowing. The person with such knowledge will know, 'how to discriminate between good and bad, right and wrong, important and unimportant and so on'.[35] That is, they will know what is required in the concrete situation. So, for instance, experiences of, say, fairness – acquired either directly or vicariously – will endow one with a seasoned or mature sense of tact, sense of taste and sense of judgement for what fairness requires in any particular case. Indeed, as Douzinas *et al* note with regard to deciding how an ethical or legal rule should apply: 'It takes experience, intuition

---

30 *R v Secretary of State for the Home Department, ex p Doody and Others* [1994] 1 AC 531 (HL), 560. Similarly, Geoffrey Lane LJ has stated: 'What is fair cannot be decided in a vacuum: it has to be determined against the whole background of any particular case', *R v Secretary of State for the Home Department, ex p Hosenball* [1977] 1 WLR 766 (CA) 786. See, also, Lord Bridge: 'what the requirements of fairness demand when any body . . . has to make a decision which will affect the rights of individuals depends on the character of the decision-making body, the kind of decision it has to make and the statutory or other framework in which it operates', *Lloyd v McMahon* [1987] AC 625 (HL) 702.
31 *Truth and Method* (n 2) 355.
32 ibid 16.
33 ibid 35–42, 159.
34 ibid 30–34.
35 Warnke, *Gadamer: Hermeneutics, Tradition and Reason* (n 29) 159.

Philosophical hermeneutics 15

and practical acumen to carry out this non-determinant dialectic between general and particular'.[36]

I should be clear what is being said here. First, for Gadamer, experience is not a characteristic that one acquires simply through the passage of time or by being exposed to a variety of situations. It is, rather, an openness to the world and a willingness to learn from each situation in which we find ourselves. There is, then, a qualitative, as well as a quantitative, dimension to experience.

Second, by describing the pragmatic ways of knowing in the manner that he does, Gadamer is not suggesting that there is room for differences of opinion – for different tastes or judgements to dictate what should be done. Rather, the person who possesses the qualities of tact, taste and judgement will know precisely what a particular situation requires and this will be an assessment with which all persons in that tradition should agree. Gadamer writes, for instance, that taste has 'special normative power, peculiar to it alone: the knowledge that it is certain of the agreement of an ideal community'.[37]

Acquired experiences may guide in another way. Gadamer argues that, in attempting to understand a text, we should, 'assume its completeness'.[38] When trying to understand a part of the text we should suppose the text to be a coherent whole and understand the part as it best fits with this whole. That is, we understand the individual case in terms of the rule, the rule in terms of the general principle and the principle in terms of the legal system or doctrine. Using the same approach, we can understand what would amount to a fair procedure in the instant case by choosing that which best fits with our experience of fairness.

So, understanding always involves application and interpretation and is therefore situational. It is also a 'productive activity'. This is particularly the case with rules or principles with the consequence that they will be re-determined and understood in a different way with each application.[39] The significance of this will be apparent in Chapter Four, where it will be shown that, because the application of the standards of good administration inevitably involves interpretation, the courts will draw on principles derived from the common law when developing and applying them. Indeed, it will be seen that this is the way in which the development of these standards is explicated in both the *ultra vires* and common law theories. However, I also assess whether this corresponds with the requirements of parliamentary sovereignty as it is understood in each of these theories. In Chapter Six, I argue that Acts of Parliament are balanced against these common

---

36 Costas Douzinas, Ronnie Warrington and Shaun McVeigh, *Postmodern Jurisprudence: The Law of Text in the Text of Law* (Routledge 1991) 38.

37 *Truth and Method* (n 2) 37–38. A similar reliance on such practical wisdom can be found in Gadamer's description of the study of law as 'a kind of intelligence or wisdom in judging' and in his characterisation of Plato's ideal statesman as someone who can 'strike the "right measure," [and find] what is appropriate', Hans-Georg Gadamer, 'From Word to Concept: The Task of Hermeneutics as Philosophy' (R E Palmer tr) in Bruce Krajewski (ed), *Gadamer's Repercussions: Reconsidering Philosophical Hermeneutics* (University of California Press 2003) 4, 5.

38 *Truth and Method* (ibid) 294.

39 I qualify this assertion below, pp 21–22.

16 *Intention, Supremacy and Judicial Review*

law principles. In Chapter Seven, I contend that judges will be guided by their experience when balancing principles against each other.

Tradition and prejudice

Understanding is situational in a sense other than with regard to application. Our understanding is always conditioned by the tradition we inhabit. Tradition is the medium through which we exist. It gives our understanding direction. Our initial assumptions, beliefs and values are derived from those of the tradition to which we belong. Our understanding is facilitated and restricted by our tradition. Gadamer refers to the influence of tradition as its 'history of effect'.[40] Its conditioning power may be explicit or implicit; it need not be fully recognised by those it affects in order to be effective. Indeed, its influence will often be through taken-for-granted assumptions which remain at least partly hidden: 'in all understanding, *whether we are expressly aware of it or not*, the efficacy of history is at work' (emphasis added).[41]

Tradition, then, provides the interpretative framework and resources in which the process of understanding takes place. This means that it not only confines but also allows and facilitates that understanding. The assumptions, beliefs, prejudices, etc that we derive from the tradition we inhabit provide the necessary platform from which understanding can proceed. Without them there can be no understanding. It follows, therefore, that, 'To be situated within a tradition does not limit the freedom of knowledge but makes it possible'.[42]

We can see the efficacy of history at work in the operation of law. A judge will be conditioned by the tradition in which she works when understanding a legal rule or principle. So, when deciding a case in new circumstances, she will be bound by the operative force of tradition. Indeed, in one sense, this happens explicitly: a judge's decision in the instant case will be influenced and may be bound by a chain of precedents. Moreover, the tradition will also contain other assumptions, prejudices and beliefs – both explicit and implicit – which are not part of the doctrine of precedent but which condition the judge's understanding. In this way, history of effect ensures that the operation of law is not simply arbitrary but is confined by tradition.

It should be clear, at this point, that Gadamer rejects the objective/subjective dichotomy. Our understanding is not objective in the positivist sense of being free from all prejudice and guiding beliefs. This is because, as we have seen, it will change with each new perspective and each new situation. Similarly, it cannot be wholly subjective because it will be conditioned by the tradition we inhabit – our effective-history – and, again, the particular situation in which we find ourselves.

We understand, then, not only how a text has meaning for us in our situation, but also from a particular vantage point which will be derived from our tradition.

---

40 *Truth and Method* (n 2) 299–300.
41 ibid 301.
42 ibid 361.

Philosophical hermeneutics 17

Each vantage point will provide a particular view of the phenomenon under study. The phenomenon is never understood independently of our situation. A person viewing the same phenomenon from a different tradition, and thus from a different perspective, will have a different understanding of it.

It was noted earlier that, because application is necessarily a part of understanding, all understanding determines a phenomenon 'in a new and different way'[43] and that, therefore, understanding is continuous and open-ended. We can now see that this is the case for another reason. Each act of understanding is historically effected. It will always proceed from, and be influenced by, an ongoing system of different assumptions and prejudices, many of which will be implicit and unnoticed but which will, nonetheless, be reiterated and perpetuated. For this reason, and because of the continuous need to apply and re-apply, understanding is never complete; it is always provisional. Absolute knowledge – in the sense of being final, complete and perfect – is not possible. There is always more to learn and a new understanding to be reached from a different perspective which is applied to a different situation.

Just as we are located in a particular tradition, so too will be the object of our enquiry, the thing we are trying to understand. For instance, any text that we attempt to understand will be situated in a particular genre. This genre will have its own assumptions and prejudices which govern how works of that kind are to be read and understood. One will, for instance, read law reports with certain expectations: that they will contain a description of the relevant facts of the case and an account of the legal rationale for the court's decision. Similarly, a legal rule may be viewed as a type which should be construed, or has habitually been interpreted, in a particular way by the courts. For example, legislation which has the potential to infringe a fundamental right will be interpreted in a narrow, restrictive way by the courts in order to protect that fundamental.[44] So, just like the person attempting to understand, the object of inquiry will itself be hermeneutically situated. Giddens refers to the situatedness of *both* the interpreter and the object of inquiry as the 'double hermeneutic'.[45]

That there may be a traditional way of approaching an object, or a particular genre, allows us to see again how all understanding is, from the start and throughout, prejudiced. It is worth repeating here that Gadamer uses this term in a particular way. It simply means that we make certain pre-judgements about any object that we attempt to understand. That is, a prejudice is simply 'a judgment that is rendered before all the elements that determine a situation have been finally examined'.[46] As with tradition, these pre-judgements are necessary and unavoidable.[47] Gadamer's recognition of the unavoidability of pre-judgement is

---

43 Text to n 22.
44 See Chapter Six pp 116–118.
45 Anthony Giddens, *New Rules of Sociological Method* (Hutchinson & Co 1976) 158.
46 *Truth and Method* (n 2) 270.
47 ibid.

18 *Intention, Supremacy and Judicial Review*

an attempt to rehabilitate prejudice or to reverse the 'prejudice against prejudice' engendered by the Enlightenment.[48]

Prejudices, in this sense, are not necessarily false judgements.[49] Not only do our prejudices give us a starting point from which to understand, they may also be true. Moreover, we may say that one cannot help, at least initially, judging a book by its cover, or by what we know of the author, or of books of that type. For instance, we may assume that a legal text published under a particular series title will, for that reason, have a more critical edge than, say, one aimed at law undergraduates and, in turn, assume that this latter text has more substance than a small 'exam cribber' type book.

We therefore project an initial meaning onto a text or object when we first encounter it. Further, this pre-judgement will be constantly modified as we encounter more of the text or object to be understood. As Gadamer writes:

> A person who is trying to understand a text is always projecting. He projects a meaning for the text as a whole as soon as some initial meaning emerges in the text. Again, the initial meaning emerges only because he is reading the text with particular expectations in regard to a certain meaning. Working out this fore-projection, which is constantly revised in terms of what emerges as he penetrates into the meaning, is understanding what is there.[50]

So, for example, when reading a law report, we may understand a case to be a claim for judicial review because of the way the parties to the case are listed in the citation. We will gain a better understanding of the issues in the case by reading the headnote. This understanding will, itself, be refined by reading and re-reading the judgments in full.

The conditioning effects of tradition will be referred to at a number of points in the following chapters. In Chapter Four, I note the similarity between Gadamer's account of the operative force of tradition and Dicey's suggestion that, when interpreting legislation, judges are guided by 'the spirit of the common law' rather than by reference to legislative intent.[51] In Chapter Seven, I argue that the development and application of the standards of good administration, as well as the way legislation is interpreted, will be conditioned by tradition and that the tradition itself will be shaped by legislation.[52]

---

48 ibid 270, 272; Hans-Georg Gadamer, 'The Universality of the Hermeneutical Problem' (David E Linge tr) in David E Linge (ed), *Philosophical Hermeneutics* (University of California Press 1976) 9.

49 Habermas questions Gadamer's assumptions on this point, 'But does it follow from the unavoidability of hermeneutic anticipation eo ipso that there are legitimate prejudices?', 'A Review of Gadamer's *Truth and Method*' (n 15) 236.

50 *Truth and Method* (n 2) 267.

51 Chapter Four p 48.

52 Chapter Seven pp 137–140.

Gadamer and Dworkin

It is appropriate to note here the close coincidence between the work of Gadamer and that of Dworkin. Though there are numerous examples, it will be sufficient for present purposes simply to state four of the more obvious and tangible.

First, Dworkin, like Gadamer, is critical of the notion that the meaning of a text – or of a law – is simply that which was intended by its author or enactor.[53] In fact, he relies on Gadamer to argue that any attempt to recreate intended meaning will itself be an act of interpretation that will be conditioned by the situatedness of the interpreter.[54] Second, in his so-called 'rights thesis', Dworkin argues – against the positivist view – that judges do not have a large degree of discretion in deciding those hard cases for which the existing legal rules do not seem to provide an answer. Rather, the judge will refer to past cases and the values and goals of her society to identify the legal principles inherent within it. This will allow her to determine the rights of the parties to the case and, in turn, the correct outcome.[55] This resonates strongly with Gadamer's explication of history of effect whereby our understanding is conditioned by the tradition that we inhabit.[56] Third, in his adjudicative principle of integrity, Dworkin contends that the law should be seen as a coherent whole and that a judge should decide each case in the way that best fits the existing norms and principles.[57] This is consistent with Gadamer's assertion that we should assume the completeness of a text and understand its constituent parts in the way that best fits and integrates with this complete whole.[58] Fourth, Dworkin echoes Gadamer when he argues that interpretation is creative and will be influenced by history including the traditional way of interpreting works of art or social practices of that genre or form.[59] Other commentators have also noted similarities in the work of Dworkin and Gadamer.[60]

These similarities indicate that the work of Dworkin sits within the general framework of philosophical hermeneutics and, consequently, within the present research. Dworkin's work is relevant in two ways. First, Dworkin is of particular interest because of Craig and his position as the leading advocate of the common

---

53 See, for example, Ronald Dworkin, 'How Law is like Literature' in Ronald Dworkin, *A Matter of Principle* (OUP 1985) 154–158, 162–164.

54 Ronald Dworkin, *Law's Empire* (Hart Publishing 1998) 55–56, 61–62.

55 Ronald Dworkin, *Taking Rights Seriously* (Duckworth & Co 1977) 101–123. Cf Hart, *The Concept of Law* (n 9) 127, 132, 272.

56 Above p 16.

57 A concise account of this is given in *Law's Empire* (n 54) 225. See, also, *Taking Rights Seriously* (n 55) 115–118; 'How Law is like Literature' (n 53) 151–152, 158–162.

58 Above p 15.

59 *Law's Empire* (n 54) 52.

60 Henley, 'Protestant Hermeneutics and the Rule of Law: Gadamer and Dworkin' (n 4) 14, 16, 18, 21, 22, 24. Warnke uses Dworkin in defence of Gadamer's work: *Gadamer: Hermeneutics, Tradition and Reason* (n 29) 54–55. Henley also notes some differences between Gadamer and Dworkin: ibid 21, 25.

20 Intention, Supremacy and Judicial Review

law theory.[61] Craig has declared himself to be a supporter of Dworkin's theory of adjudication[62] and, what is more, states that the common law theory 'naturally lends itself to [a Dworkinian] approach'.[63] This point will be returned to in Chapter Four where an evaluation will be made of the use of the doctrine of the rule of law in both the common law theory and the *ultra vires* theory.[64]

Second, and of greater significance, is the distinction Dworkin draws among 'rules', 'principles' and 'policies'. Rules function in an 'all-or-nothing' fashion.[65] A legal standard that states that a particular result should follow when certain conditions are present is a rule.[66] To use Dworkin's own example, if the law requires a will to be signed by three witnesses in order to be valid, then it will not be valid if it is signed by only two.[67] It might be that there are some exceptions to the rule but it is characteristic of rules that, at least in theory, all the exceptions might be given so as to create a more accurate statement of it.[68] Also, if two rules conflict, then one of them cannot remain as a valid rule.[69] Thus, if one rule states that two witnesses are required for a will to be valid, while another rule requires three, a court deciding a case would have to alter or discard at least one of the rules. In doing this, the court might appeal 'to considerations beyond the rules themselves'.[70] If, for instance, one rule was derived from case law and the other from an Act of Parliament then the courts would refer to the doctrine of legislative supremacy when deciding that the latter should prevail over the former.

Principles and policies differ from rules. A policy is a standard that furthers some community goal.[71] In contrast, principles do not attempt to secure community goals but protect individual or group rights and are 'a requirement of justice or fairness or some other dimension of morality'.[72] A decision which aimed to reduce the number of teenage births would be an attempt to achieve a societal goal and so would be a policy. The standard that everyone has a right to a family life protects individual or group rights and is – like justice or fairness – an aspect of morality: it is therefore a principle. Though nothing turns on it for the present work, Dworkin argues that legislation may be engendered by arguments of both

---

61 Briefly, the contention of this theory is that the courts develop and apply the standards of good administration pursuant to an inherent jurisdiction and guided by values derived from the rule of law and justice.

62 Paul P Craig, *Administrative Law* (7th edn, Sweet & Maxwell 2012) 18–20; Paul P Craig, 'Constitutional Foundations, the Rule of Law and Supremacy' [2003] *PL* 92, 97; Paul P Craig, 'Legislative Intent and Legislative Supremacy: A Reply to Professor Allan' (2004) 24 *OJLS* 585, 589.

63 Paul P Craig, 'The Common Law, Shared Power and Judicial Review' (2004) 24 *OJLS* 237, 241 (citation omitted).

64 Chapter Four pp 58–60.

65 Dworkin, *Taking Rights Seriously* (n 55) 24.

66 ibid.

67 ibid 25.

68 ibid.

69 ibid 27.

70 ibid.

71 ibid 22, 82.

72 ibid 22; see, also, 82.

Philosophical hermeneutics 21

policy and principle whereas only the latter should generate common law judicial decisions.[73] Dworkin often uses the term 'principle' in a generic sense to refer to both principles and policies.[74] This is the way in which I will use the term for the remainder of the text.

Principles do not operate in the all-or-nothing fashion that is characteristic of rules. Like rules, they indicate the direction to be taken in a case. However, where they are relevant, principles simply demand consideration rather than a particular result. Also, principles possess a characteristic that is absent in rules: 'the dimension of weight or importance'.[75] Where there is a conflict between two principles in a particular dispute, the court will resolve it by taking into account the relevant weight of each as it applies in the case to be decided.[76] Yet, unlike rules, both may both survive the conflict intact. A person's right to privacy might outweigh another's freedom of expression in one instance, but this will not mean that the latter principle has been altered or amended. Consequently, again in contrast to rules, we could not, even in theory, list all the possible 'counter-instances' and thereby produce a more comprehensive account of a principle: 'Listing some of [the counter-instances] might sharpen our sense of the principle's weight . . . but it would not make for a more accurate statement of the principle'.[77]

The idea that counter-instances will hone one's sense of how a principle operates has echoes of Gadamer's view that experience will sharpen one's understanding of what is required in a particular situation. As noted above, experience of what has been found to be fair will guide one's judgement when determining what fairness requires in any particular case.[78]

I can, at this point, qualify an earlier assertion. I stated above that the application of a law *always* determines its meaning anew.[79] This, it is suggested, is true of principles. For example, as noted in the preceding two paragraphs, the application of the principle of fairness will sharpen one's sense of it. This means that our understanding of 'fairness' *is* re-determined in its application. Indeed, it will be

---

73 ibid 82–86; *Law's Empire* (n 54) 244. There are two main reasons for this. First, issues of policy involve the balancing of competing societal goals when deciding what is best for the community as a whole. Elected legislators are suited to this task because they are exposed to arguments posited by different interest groups whereas judges, being unelected and insulated from such pressures, are not. Second, adjudicating by reference to policy considerations amounts to imposing retrospective duties on the parties to a case, and is thus illegitimate, whereas drawing on existing principles means that a case is decided according to pre-existing rights. However, when interpreting a statute, a judge should have recourse to the policy of the statute as constructed from the words used: 'Any competent justification of the Endangered Species Act . . . must appeal to a policy of protecting endangered species' (*Law's Empire* (ibid) 339).

74 *Taking Rights Seriously* (n 55) 22

75 ibid 26.

76 ibid.

77 ibid 25–26.

78 Above pp 14–15. Allan writes: 'The appropriate weight of principles is something learned by experience: it cannot be decreed in the manner of enacting a rule, but must be correctly understood', TRS Allan, *Law, Liberty and Justice: The Legal Foundations of British Constitutionalism* (Clarendon Press 1993) 151.

79 Above p 15.

22 *Intention, Supremacy and Judicial Review*

seen that the application of principles is a form of practical knowledge because what is required can only be realised in the concrete situation – that is, in the context of the particular case.[80]

In contrast, the application of a rule – defined as a legal standard that operates in an all-or-nothing fashion – will not *always* re-determine it anew. It may be that a dispute *does* reveal a new exception to an existing rule.[81] This, though, will not always be the case. A rule that there should be two signatures in order for a will to be valid may be applied to disqualify a will which does not meet this requirement without qualifying the rule or leading to a new understanding of it. In fact, the application of rules will often be akin to technical knowledge in that their meaning is not inevitably dependent on the contingencies of the particular case. In summary, Gadamer's contention that a law will 'always be understood in a new and different way'[82] is not necessarily true of rules.

It is worth noting here that the sharp distinction Dworkin draws between rules and principles has been questioned. Hart, for instance, states that rules do not necessarily apply in an all-or-nothing fashion. Rather, one rule might be displaced in a particular case by another, more important rule. Yet, when this happens, the defeated rule may, like a principle, survive to be applied in other cases.[83] Indeed, R-Toubes Muñiz notes that Dworkin's own example of *Riggs v Palmer* demonstrates that the operation of a rule may be precluded by a principle but that this does not necessarily eradicate the rule. This suggests that rules have characteristics that Dworkin claims are possessed only by principles.[84]

Raz challenges the way in which Dworkin distinguishes between rules and principles. He claims that rules, like principles, may have weight, that they may conflict with other rules, and that in some types of conflict rules will behave like principles.[85] He also argues that not all rules and principles fit the definitions provided by Dworkin.[86] For Raz, the difference between rules and principles lies with how specific they are: 'Rules prescribe relatively specific acts; principles prescribe highly unspecific actions.'[87] On this account, principles and rules do not exist as distinctly separate standards in the way Dworkin describes. Rather, they exist on a spectrum of standards of varying degrees of specificity.

I should also note a criticism made by Altman. He argues that there is 'no discoverable metaprinciple' by which the weight to be attributed to competing

---

80 This is recognised by Allan: 'Each application of a principle in a previous decision will necessarily be unique – a judgment of value dependent on the facts of that case, which will never be exactly repeated', *Law, Liberty and Justice* (n 78) 116.

81 This seems to occur in Dworkin's own example of *Riggs v Palmer* 115 N.Y. 506; 22 N.E. 188 (1889), cited in *Taking Rights Seriously* (n 55) 23, where the operation of a legal rule was qualified by a principle.

82 Text to n 22.

83 *The Concept of Law* (n 9) 261–262.

84 Joaquín R-Toubes Muñiz, 'Legal Principles and Legal Theory' (1997) 10 *Ratio Juris* 267, 271.

85 Joseph Raz, 'Legal Principles and the Limits of Law' (1972) 81 *Yale LJ* 823, 829–834.

86 ibid 834–839.

87 ibid 838.

principles may be ascertained.[88] He claims that such a metaprinciple is necessary because Dworkin's professed commitment to the rule of law requires that the evaluation of competing principles does not rely on 'intuitionism' but on standards that can be determined and conveyed.

These criticisms aside, Dworkin's distinction between rules and principles is particularly useful for the present work and will be drawn on in Chapters Four, Six and Seven to analyse the way in which the doctrine of parliamentary sovereignty is understood. In Chapter Four, I argue that parliamentary sovereignty is assumed to function as a Dworkinian rule in both the *ultra vires* and common law theories. However, in Chapter Six, I contend that in practice the doctrine operates in the manner of a Dworkinian principle and, in Chapter Seven, I examine the implications of this for the way in which the exercise of judicial review may be justified.

Language

In this section, I detail Gadamer's account of a genuine conversation, and the pre-eminence he ascribes to language in the process of understanding. First, though, I provide a brief explication of his concept of the fusion of horizons.

I have observed that we approach any object we wish to understand from a particular standpoint and with particular assumptions. Viewing from a particular perspective places things within and things outside of our view. This delineation between things we can and cannot see forms our 'horizon'. Our situatedness and our assumptions, together, form the horizon of our understanding. Because the object itself will, like us, be hermeneutically situated, it will have its own horizon. As we come to an understanding of the object, we will gain an enlarged horizon which encompasses our old one. A lawyer's horizon of understanding of, say, judicial review, will be shaped by the cases with which she deals. Each new case may provide a different perspective and a different horizon which will encompass her previous understanding. This is referred to by Gadamer as a fusion of horizons: '*understanding is always the fusion of these horizons supposedly existing by themselves*' (emphasis in original).[89]

Such a fusion occurs in an authentic conversation as described by Gadamer. He suggests that, in a true conversation, one should approach one's conversation partner with a view that one has something to learn from her. There are, here, similarities between a genuine dialogue and an experienced person.[90] Both are, for Gadamer, characterised by an openness, receptiveness and non-dogmatic willingness to learn. In such a conversation, one is not attempting to get the better of the other participants.[91] Rather, one is endeavouring to work with one's

---

88 Andrew Altman, 'Legal Realism, Critical Legal Studies and Dworkin' (1986) 15 *Phil Pub Aff* 205, 217–218.
89 *Truth and Method* (n 2) 306.
90 See above p 14.
91 *Truth and Method* (n 2) 367.

24 *Intention, Supremacy and Judicial Review*

conversation partner, to learn from her, and to achieve a joint understanding of the subject matter of the conversation.[92] Similarly, in trying to understand a text one enters into a conversation with it and attempts to understand what one can learn from it. Again, we see here that all understanding is coming to an understanding. In this way, in a genuine conversation, each participant will come to a more sophisticated, fuller, nuanced and balanced understanding of the subject of the discussion. Each participant's original position will have been changed. That is, each of their original horizons of understanding will have fused with aspects of that of the other's to form a new horizon of understanding of the object.[93]

The fusion of horizons that occurs in dialogue can be illustrated in another way. Gadamer argues that, during a conversation, the participants work towards an understanding by developing a common language and terms of reference that are not one conversation partner's or the other's but are the result of their joint efforts: 'Arriving at a common understanding of a common object is a linguistic process that requires achieving a common language'.[94] Their aim is to ensure that they are not talking at cross-purposes and so they will attempt to find a form of language – words, phrases, etc – that each understands as pertinent to the object. This common language represents the fusion of horizons.

The contention that conversation partners should find a common language in order to understand illustrates the primacy, for Gadamer, of language. Language is the medium in and through which we exist. As such, understanding necessarily takes place in language: 'All understanding is interpretation, and all interpretation takes place in the medium of language that allows the object to come into words and yet is at the same time the interpreter's own language'.[95] Again, we can see that understanding means finding a common language which is both mine and my conversation partner's or, as the case may be, the text's. We can also see, again, that understanding means coming to an understanding. Furthermore, finding the words that allow, say, a text to speak to me – transposing the initially strange into the familiar – is an interpretive act. In fact, it is often an indicator of a more complete understanding if one is able to rephrase what one has read or been told and yet retain the same meaning.

That is not to say that language can always adequately communicate meaning. The experience of being unable to find the right words to express one's full meaning – for example, in response to exceptional events or grief – is a common one. Yet even here, where language fails us, we still search for the right words in order to try to reach an understanding. It is this searching, even when the words cannot be found, that demonstrates the linguistic nature of understanding: 'The essential linguisticality of understanding expresses itself less in our statements than in our search for the language to say what we have on our minds and hearts'.[96] In fact,

---

92 ibid 387.

93 ibid 388.

94 Weinsheimer, *Gadamer's Hermeneutics: A Reading of Truth and Method* (n 25) 219. See, also, Habermas, 'A Review of Gadamer's *Truth and Method*' (n 15) 216.

95 *Truth and Method* (n 2) 389.

96 Grondin, *Introduction to Philosophical Hermeneutics* (n 1) 120.

Philosophical hermeneutics 25

our failure to find the words is only apparent in our feeling that there is a way to say what we mean that escapes us: 'The unsayable is only unsayable in light of what one would like to say, but cannot'.[97] To be sure, when we recall the right words for the object, we feel we have grasped it better. In addition, language is constantly developing so that we can describe what was previously indescribable. Understanding, then, presupposes language in that we assume that language can always develop to communicate meaning.

The question arises, however, whether an inability to find the right words is, for Gadamer, indicative of a lack of understanding. This would seem to be the inference that we can take from his statement that, 'All understanding is interpretation, and all interpretation takes place in the medium of language'.[98] Yet Gadamer also asserts that understanding always exceeds language:

> Indeed, language often seems ill suited to express what we feel. In the face of the overwhelming presence of works of art, the task of expressing in words what they say to us seems like an infinite and hopeless undertaking . . . *our desire and capacity to understand always go beyond any statement that we can make* (emphasis added).[99]

Furthermore, practical understanding – understanding that can only be realised in the concrete situation – seems to envisage an understanding that cannot be communicated in a wholly linguistic way. We cannot, for instance, describe the nature of courage in a way that is true for all circumstances. On the contrary, as noted above, an understanding of courage – like all practical knowledge – is achieved through acquired experiences.[100]

However, while understanding can occur in a non-verbal way, it would seem that, for Gadamer, language is paradigmatic of all understanding so that, even when understanding is non-lingual, we still search for the words to express meaning.

The concepts of a fusion of horizons and a genuine conversation, as elucidated in this section, will be used in Chapter Five where I draw on them to indicate the limits of the requirement that statutes should be interpreted so as to maintain access to the courts which, I argue, is inherent in both the *ultra vires* and common law theories.[101]

97 Jean Grondin, 'Gadamer's Basic Understanding of Understanding' in Robert J Dostal (ed), *The Cambridge Companion to Gadamer* (CUP 2002) 42.
98 Text to n 95.
99 *Truth and Method* (n 2) 401.
100 Above p 13.
101 Chapter Five p 83.

26 *Intention, Supremacy and Judicial Review*

Bibliography

Allan TRS, *Law, Liberty and Justice: The Legal Foundations of British Constitutionalism* (Clarendon Press 1993)

Altman A, 'Legal Realism, Critical Legal Studies and Dworkin' (1986) 15 *Philosophy and Public Affairs* 205

Craig P P, *Public Law and Democracy in the United Kingdom and the United States of America* (OUP 1990)

— 'Constitutional Foundations, the Rule of Law and Supremacy' (2003) *Public Law* 92

— 'Legislative Intent and Legislative Supremacy: A Reply to Professor Allan' (2004) 24 *Oxford Journal of Legal Studies* 585

— 'The Common Law, Shared Power and Judicial Review' (2004) 24 *Oxford Journal of Legal Studies* 237

— *Administrative Law* (7th edn, Sweet & Maxwell 2012)

Douzinas C, Warrington R and McVeigh S, *Postmodern Jurisprudence: The Law of Text in the Text of Law* (Routledge 1991)

Dworkin R, *Taking Rights Seriously* (Duckworth & Co 1977)

— 'How Law is like Literature' in Ronald Dworkin, *A Matter of Principle* (OUP 1985)

— *Law's Empire* (Hart Publishing 1998)

Ekins R, *The Nature of Legislative Intent* (OUP 2012)

Gadamer H-G, 'On the Scope and Function of Hermeneutical Reflection' (G B Hess and R E Palmer trs) in David E Linge (ed), *Philosophical Hermeneutics* (University of California Press 1976)

— 'The Universality of the Hermeneutical Problem' (David E Linge tr) in David E Linge (ed), *Philosophical Hermeneutics* (University of California Press 1976)

— *Truth and Method* (D G Marshall and Joel Weinsheimer trs, 2nd edn, Sheed and Ward 1989)

— 'Reply to my Critics' (G H Leiner tr) in Gayle L Ormiston and Alan D Schrift (eds), *The Hermeneutic Tradition: From Ast to Ricoeur* (State University of New York Press 1990)

— 'From Word to Concept: The Task of Hermeneutics as Philosophy' (R E Palmer tr) in Bruce Krajewski (ed), *Gadamer's Repercussions: Reconsidering Philosophical Hermeneutics* (University of California Press 2003)

Giddens A, *New Rules of Sociological Method* (Hutchinson & Co 1976)

Grondin J, *Introduction to Philosophical Hermeneutics* (Joel Weinshiemer tr, Yale University Press 1994)

— 'Gadamer's Basic Understanding of Understanding' in Robert J Dostal (ed), *The Cambridge Companion to Gadamer* (CUP 2002)

Habermas J, 'A Review of Gadamer's *Truth and Method*' (F R Dallmayr and T McCarthy trs) in Gayle L Ormiston and Alan D Schrift (eds), *The Hermeneutic Tradition: From Ast to Ricoeur* (State University of New York Press 1990)

— 'After Historicism, Is Metaphysics Still Possible? On Hans-George Gadamer's 100th Birthday' (P Malone tr) in Bruce Krajewski (ed), *Gadamer's Repercussions: Reconsidering Philosophical Hermeneutics* (University of California Press 2003)

Hart HLA, *The Concept of Law* (3rd edn, OUP 2012)

Henley K, 'Protestant Hermeneutics and the Rule of Law: Gadamer and Dworkin' (1990) 3 *Ratio Juris* 14

Raz J, 'Legal Principles and the Limits of Law' (1972) 81 *Yale Law Journal* 823

R-Toubes Muñiz J, 'Legal Principles and Legal Theory' (1997) 10 *Ratio Juris* 267

Waldron J, *Law and Disagreement* (OUP 1999)

Warnke G, *Gadamer: Hermeneutics, Tradition and Reason* (Stanford University Press 1987)

Weinsheimer J, *Gadamer's Hermeneutics: A Reading of Truth and Method* (Yale University Press 1985)

3 The *ultra vires* theory and the common law theory of judicial review

This chapter will describe the two alternative theories that are commonly posited as providing the constitutional legitimacy of judicial review: the *ultra vires* theory and the common law theory. I begin with a brief account of the judicial review jurisdiction, and of why it is considered necessary to provide a constitutional justification for this jurisdiction, before examining the two theories in detail.

Judicial review, which is also known as the courts' supervisory jurisdiction,[1] is the procedure by which the courts in England and Wales ensure that those exercising discretionary public power do so lawfully. Such power may be derived from an Act of Parliament (often known as the enabling Act), from the Royal prerogative, or it may simply exist *de facto*. Judicial review may also be used to claim that UK law conflicts with European Union law[2] or to bring a challenge under the Human Rights Act 1998 that a 'public authority' has not acted in conformity, or that a statute is not compatible, with the Convention rights.[3]

In judicial review the courts assess whether any limits on, or requirements of, the exercise of public power have been complied with. In the case of power derived from statute or the Royal prerogative, this may simply entail an inquiry into the boundary of that power, or, indeed, into whether it exists at all.[4] Other limits or requirements may be imposed on the exercise of public power by statute. For example, a failure by a Minister to engage in a process of consultation

---

1 'Supervisory jurisdiction' is used throughout this text as a synonymous term for 'judicial review'. However, the term is sometimes used elsewhere to refer to any supervision over the exercise of power, whether public or private, undertaken by the courts: see, Dawn Oliver, 'Common Values in Public and Private Law and the Public/Private Divide' [1997] *PL* 630, 630–632, 635–636, 638; Dawn Oliver, 'Review of (Non-Statutory) Discretions' in Christopher F Forsyth (ed), *Judicial Review and the Constitution* (Hart Publishing 2000) 307.

2 *R v Secretary of State for Transport, ex p Factortame and Others (No 2)* [1991] 1 AC 603 (HL).

3 Section 7. The Human Rights Act 1998 s 6(1) imposes on public authorities an obligation not to act incompatibly with the Convention rights. Section 4(2) and (3) empowers the courts to make a declaration that a provision of primary or secondary legislation is incompatible with the Convention rights. It is questionable, however, whether a claim that a statutory provision does not comply with the Convention rights can be used as the sole, stand alone ground of challenge in a claim for judicial review: Rabinder Singh, 'The Declaration of Incompatibility' [2002] *JR* 237, paras 13–15.

4 *Entick v Carrington* (1765) 19 St. Tr. 1030.

The *ultra vires and common law theories* 29

with certain parties before making a particular decision may form the basis of a successful claim if such consultation was a mandatory requirement imposed by legislation.[5] A number of other requirements, not concerned with delineating the prerogative and not explicitly contained in statute, also compose the grounds of judicial review. I refer to these as the standards of good administration; they include, among others, requirements that those exercising public power must not unlawfully fetter[6] or delegate their discretion;[7] that a decision-maker must take into account all relevant considerations and discount all those that are irrelevant;[8] and that such power must be exercised fairly[9] and reasonably.[10] In *Council of Civil Service Unions v Minister for the Civil Service*, Lord Diplock categorised the various grounds on which a claim for judicial review may be made under three heads: illegality, irrationality and procedural impropriety.[11]

Where a claim for judicial review is successful, the courts may award one or more of a number of remedies. These include: a quashing order; a prohibiting order; a mandatory order; an injunction or simply a declaration that the action complained of was unlawful.[12]

The imposition of these standards on public power not derived from statute is seen by the supporters of both the *ultra vires* theory and the common law theory as relatively uncontroversial.[13] The primary difference between the two theories is the way in which they attempt to legitimise the imposition of the standards of good administration on the exercise of power derived from Acts of Parliament. The supporters of the *ultra vires* theory contend that we must assume that Parliament intends the courts to develop and apply these standards to such power. The supporters of the common law theory argue that they are

---

5 *Agriculture, Horticultural and Forestry Industry Training Board v Aylesbury Mushrooms Ltd* [1972] 1 WLR 190 (QBD) 195 (Donaldson J).

6 *British Oxygen Co Ltd v Minister of Technology* [1971] AC 610 (HL) 625 (Lord Reid).

7 *Vine v National Dock Labour Board* [1957] AC 488 (HL) 499 (Viscount Kilmuir), 502 (Lord Morton), 510 (Lord Somervell).

8 *R v Somerset County Council, ex p Fewings and others* [1995] 1 WLR 1037 (CA).

9 *Council of Civil Service Unions v Minister for the Civil Service* [1985] AC 374 (HL) 414–415 (Lord Roskill).

10 *Associated Provincial Picture Houses Ltd v Wednesbury Corporation* [1948] 1 KB 223 (CA) 230 (Lord Greene).

11 *Council of Civil Service Unions v Minister for the Civil Service* (n 9) 410.

12 CPR 54.2 and 54.3(1). By virtue of CPR 54.3(2), damages may be awarded if these would have been available in a private claim.

13 As will be shown, under the common law theory judicial review is seen as an inherent jurisdiction of the courts to supervise the exercise of discretionary public power; it therefore applies to all public power whatever its source, statutory or non-statutory. Supporters of the *ultra vires* theory argue that judicial review of non-statutory power may be explained as the courts ensuring obedience to the rule of law – see Mark C Elliott, 'The Ultra Vires Doctrine in a Constitutional Setting: Still the Central Principle of Administrative Law' [1999] *CLJ* 129, 154–156; Mark C Elliott, *The Constitutional Foundations of Judicial Review* (Hart Publishing 2001) Chapter Five. Forsyth has suggested that review of non-statutory power may be based on a common law duty imposed on those exercising monopoly power: Christopher F Forsyth, 'Of Fig Leaves and Fairy Tales: The Ultra Vires Doctrine, the Sovereignty of Parliament and Judicial Review' [1996] *CLJ* 122, 125.

30 Intention, Supremacy and Judicial Review

wholly judicial creations and that the courts impose them as part of their inherent common law jurisdiction, rather than pursuant to a presumed intention of the legislature.

The question arises as to why it is thought necessary to justify the supervisory jurisdiction at all. A comparison with a familiar example might prove instructive here. The written constitution of the United States of America establishes and limits the powers of the three branches of government: the executive, the legislature and the judiciary. In *Marbury v Madison*, the US Supreme Court concluded that it was implicit in such a constitution that legislative acts which transcend these limits are unlawful. It further stated that the constitution confers a power of adjudication on the Court over such issues.[14] Thus, the Supreme Court was able to base its review jurisdiction upon the power of adjudication given to it, and the limits on legislative – and, indeed, executive – power imposed, by the constitution.[15]

In contrast, in the United Kingdom, there is no written constitution. Furthermore, the doctrine of parliamentary sovereignty, as it is traditionally understood, dictates that there are no limits to the legislative competence of Parliament. Wade and Forsyth use the first of these as part of the reason why the *ultra vires* theory is needed:

> Having no written constitution on which he can fall back, the judge must in every case be able to demonstrate that he is carrying out the will of Parliament as expressed in the statute conferring the power. He is on safe ground only where he can show that the offending act is outside the power. The only way in which he can do this, in the absence of an express provision, is by finding an implied term or condition in the Act, violation of which then entails the condemnation of ultra vires.[16]

We shall see, though, that it is primarily the fact that the supervisory jurisdiction involves governing the exercise of power derived from an apparently unlimited legislature that leads to the conclusion that some form of constitutional justification is necessary. The following sections of this chapter describe in greater detail the two competing theories offered as justification, and the rationales on which they are based.

The *ultra vires* theory

The purpose of the *ultra vires* theory is to provide a constitutional justification for judicial review which also accommodates the doctrine of legislative supremacy.[17]

---

14 *Marbury v Madison* 1 Cranch 137 (1803) 173–180.

15 Of course, the review jurisdiction of the US Supreme Court is wider than that of the UK courts in that US primary legislation may be struck down as unconstitutional.

16 HWR Wade and Christopher F Forsyth, *Administrative Law* (11th edn, OUP 2014) 28. It is worth noting that this quotation is taken from a section in Wade and Forsyth's text entitled 'Necessary Artificialities'.

17 Forsyth and Elliott write: 'The purpose of the . . . *ultra vires* doctrine is to provide a conceptual

The *ultra* vires *and common law theories* 31

Under the theory, we are asked to assume that the imposition of the standards of good administration on public power derived from primary legislation is required by Parliament. That is, when the courts supervise the exercise of such power they are simply carrying out the presumed will of the legislature. This assumption is said to provide judicial review with its constitutional legitimacy. The proponents of this theory argue that the assumption is necessary because, otherwise, the imposition of these standards on such statutory power would be an infringement of parliamentary sovereignty.

An example employed by Forsyth will illustrate the reasoning here.[18] If an Act of Parliament gives a Minister power to enact secondary legislation which she uses to produce regulations that are vague then, in a claim for judicial review, she would be found to have acted unlawfully. This prohibition on the enactment of vague regulations may not be explicitly stated in the enabling legislation. Nevertheless, the supporters of the *ultra vires* theory maintain that Parliament must either intend such regulations to be prohibited or intend that they be permitted. There is, they claim, no neutral position in which the legislature can be taken to have no opinion on whether the making of vague regulations should or should not be allowable.[19] They then argue that, if it is Parliament's intention that the Minister should be free to make such regulations, their prohibition by the courts would be contrary to that intention and would, for that reason, be an infringement of parliamentary sovereignty. This conclusion may only be avoided if we assume that the prohibition of vague regulations – and, indeed, the application of all the standards of good administration to public power derived from statute – is required by Parliament.

In short, the supporters of this theory argue that, because legislative supremacy means that Parliament may enact any law whatsoever, including one enabling the donee of statutory power to breach the standards of good administration, the application of these standards to such power must be assumed to be intended by Parliament.[20] This, in turn, means that the standards are implicit in the enabling Act and, in exercising their supervisory jurisdiction, the courts are merely keeping

---

framework within which judicial review and parliamentary sovereignty may co-exist', Christopher F Forsyth and Mark C Elliott, 'The Legitimacy of Judicial Review' [2003] *PL* 286, 296. See, also, 287; Elliott, *The Constitutional Foundations of Judicial Review* (n 13) 3, 9, 23, 26, 65, 117. Elliott also writes: 'This logic [of the *ultra vires* theory] is particularly compelling in a legal system, like that of the United Kingdom, which embraces the principle of parliamentary sovereignty, for if judicial review can be characterised simply as the implementation of the legislature's unimpeachable intention, the courts find themselves on solid ground', Mark C Elliott, *Beatson, Matthews and Elliott's Administrative Law: Text and Materials* (4th edn, OUP 2011) 11.

18 Forsyth, 'Of Fig Leaves and Fairy Tales' (n 13) 133–134.

19 ibid 133; Elliott, 'The Ultra Vires Doctrine in a Constitutional Setting' (n 13) 145–146; Mark C Elliott, 'Legislative Intention Versus Judicial Creativity? Administrative Law as a Co-operative Endeavour' in Christopher F Forsyth (ed), *Judicial Review and the Constitution* (Hart Publishing 2000) 358; Elliott, *The Constitutional Foundations of Judicial Review* (n 13) 132.

20 Elliott, 'Legislative Intention Versus Judicial Creativity?' (ibid); Elliott, *The Constitutional Foundations of Judicial Review* (ibid) 74–75, 83–84; Forsyth and Elliott, 'The Legitimacy of Judicial Review' (n 17) 297.

32   Intention, Supremacy and Judicial Review

the Minister, or any other body exercising powers derived from statute, within the four corners of the power granted.

We can see, then, that the theory is posited as a logical corollary of the fact that limits are placed on the exercise of power derived from a sovereign Parliament.[21] Furthermore, Forsyth states that, 'by adhering to the doctrine of ultra vires the judiciary shows that it adheres to its proper constitutional position and that it recognises that Parliament is free to dispense with the judicially developed grounds of judicial review'.[22]

An analogy with the *Marbury v Madison* case referred to above might again be useful to understand the reasoning here. In that case, as we have seen, the US Supreme Court held that the US Constitution imposed limits on legislative power. It then held that it was inherent in these limits that they should be enforced by the Court.[23] The supporters of the *ultra vires* theory operate the same reasoning in reverse, so to speak. They start from the fact that in judicial review cases the courts impose limits, in the form of the standards of good administration, on the exercise of statutory public power. They then conclude that a warrant for the imposition of these limits must be found and that it can be found to be implicit in the enabling legislation granting the power in question.

Critics of this theory assert that it is unrealistic to suppose that Parliament makes a positive decision, each time that it grants a discretionary public power, that the standards of good administration should govern its exercise.[24] This scepticism is based on a number of arguments. In the first place, 'because legislative intent can be used to legitimate almost all types of judicial control . . . it loses its potency to legitimate any particular one'.[25] Moreover, appeals to parliamentary intent cannot explain how the standards of good administration have developed and changed over time when this has occurred according to a pattern that is seemingly unrelated to any identified intent.[26] Indeed, in some cases, under the *ultra vires* theory, we may be asked to assume that when Parliament enacted legislation it intended the courts to apply standards that were not developed until

---

21 Elliott, *The Constitutional Foundations of Judicial Review* (ibid) 89, 94, 96; Forsyth and Elliott, 'The Legitimacy of Judicial Review' (ibid) 306; TRS Allan, 'Legislative Supremacy and Legislative Intent: A Reply to Professor Craig' (2004) 24 *OJLS* 563, 565–566.

22 'Of Fig Leaves and Fairy Tales' (n 13) 136. See, also, Christopher F Forsyth and Linda Whittle, 'Judicial Creativity and Judicial Legitimacy in Administrative Law' (2002) 8 *Canta LR* 453, 462: 'through continued deference to the will of Parliament, via ultra vires, a challenge to sovereignty is averted, and constitutional orthodoxy remains intact'.

23 Above p 30.

24 Paul P Craig, 'Ultra Vires and the Foundations of Judicial Review' [1998] *CLJ* 63, 67.

25 ibid 66–67. As Allan writes, the argument is that the *ultra vires* theory 'is consistent with anything and therefore legitimates nothing', TRS Allan, *Constitutional Justice: A Liberal Theory of the Rule of Law* (OUP 2001) 208.

26 Ivan Hare, 'The Separation of Powers and Judicial Review for Error of Law' in Christopher F Forsyth and Ivan Hare (eds), *The Golden Metwand and the Crooked Cord: Essays on Public Law in Honour of Sir William Wade QC* (Clarendon Press 1998) 121; Craig, 'Ultra Vires and the Foundations of Judicial Review' (ibid) 68.

The *ultra* vires *and common law theories* 33

decades later.[27] Second, the standards of good administration are, or have now become, 'too rich to be attributed to the intention of a legislature when passing a statute on a possibly mundane matter'.[28]

The supporters of the *ultra vires* theory have amended it in response to such criticisms.[29] They concede that the standards of good administration are judicial creations.[30] Nevertheless, they state that this creativity often takes place against, and is therefore conditioned by, a statutory framework.[31] Moreover, they also note that Parliament has not legislated to prevent or reverse the development of the supervisory jurisdiction. They claim that this should be taken to mean it has granted the courts an 'imprimatur' to develop the law in this area.[32] This is part of a wider assumption that Parliament intends to legislate in accordance with the rule of law which, the advocates of this theory contend, includes the standards of good administration.[33]

Thus, under this modified version of the *ultra vires* theory, the assumed intention of Parliament is not that a specific public power be exercised in a particular way; it is now a general intention that such power should be exercised in accordance with the rule of law, which includes the standards of good administration.[34] For example, when the courts require that discretionary power should be exercised rationally, this is because the rational exercise of such power is necessitated by the rule of law. There is no breach of sovereignty because the courts are simply fulfilling the will of Parliament.[35]

The proponents of this theory also claim that it is the law, citing four House of Lords decisions in which the 'leading speeches clearly favour the . . . ultra vires

27 Paul P Craig, 'Legislative Intent and Legislative Supremacy: A Reply to Professor Allan' (2004) 24 *OJLS* 585, 588.

28 Jeffrey L Jowell, 'Of Vires and Vacuums: The Constitutional Context of Judicial Review' [1999] *PL* 448, 452.

29 For the remainder of the book, references to the *ultra vires* theory should be taken to mean this amended, modified version.

30 Forsyth, 'Of Fig Leaves and Fairy Tales' (n 13) 134.

31 Forsyth and Elliott, 'The Legitimacy of Judicial Review' (n 17) 299–300.

32 'since the legislature took no steps to overturn the extension and development of judicial review by the judges, it may reasonably be taken to have accepted the judicial role . . . [and] may reasonably be taken to have given tacit approval to the development by the judiciary of the principles of judicial review. . . . [T]he legislature is taken to have granted an *imprimatur* to the judges to develop the law in [this] area' (emphasis in original), Forsyth, 'Of Fig Leaves and Fairy Tales' (n 13) 135. The assumption that we may take Parliament's inaction as approval of the *status quo* will be critically assessed in the next chapter.

33 Elliott, 'The Ultra Vires Doctrine in a Constitutional Setting' (n 13) 143; Elliott, 'Legislative Intention Versus Judicial Creativity?' (n 19) 360, 362; Elliott, *The Constitutional Foundations of Judicial Review* (n 13) 110. It is worth noting that Wade and Forsyth appear to express the opposite sentiment elsewhere: '[The courts] preserve the rule of law, of which *Parliament often appears surprisingly heedless*' (emphasis added), *Administrative Law* (n 16) 287.

34 Forsyth and Elliott, 'The Legitimacy of Judicial Review' (n 17) 287. See, also, TRS Allan, *The Sovereignty of Law: Freedom, Constitution, and Common Law* (OUP 2013) 208 ff.

35 Allan questions whether the modified version of the *ultra vires* theory 'truly differs from [the] . . . original', *The Sovereignty of Law* (ibid) 226.

34 Intention, Supremacy and Judicial Review

doctrine (or something very similar)'.[36] However, Jowell writes of such curial support: 'These dicta may well . . . have been guided by shrewd judicial politics based upon a desire in the courts not to provoke the other arms of government at a sensitive moment'.[37] That is, a bald assertion that the courts are able to control public power, without a corresponding claim that this is expressly or impliedly required by the legislature, might lead to criticism of the judiciary. As Wade writes,

> If [judges] are seen to be building a yet greater empire and claiming to be independent of Parliament, they will only encourage the familiar charge of being unelected and unaccountable and undemocratic. It behoves them, surely, to be circumspect in their claims.[38]

In fact, Forsyth and Elliott note that there has recently been a greater tendency by government figures to claim that the judiciary have moved beyond their constitutional boundaries.[39] Such criticism could, in turn, lead to calls that judicial power should be limited. It may be, then, that judicial support for the *ultra vires* theory is little more than an attempt to avoid such damaging criticism of non-elected judges engaged in *de facto* law-making activities.

The common law theory

The common law theory is proposed as an alternative to the *ultra vires* theory.[40] Its supporters assert that the courts' power of judicial review is based on an inherent

---

36 Christopher F Forsyth, 'Heat and Light: A Plea for Reconciliation' in Christopher F Forsyth (ed), *Judicial Review and the Constitution* (Hart Publishing 2000) 397 (citation omitted). The cases to which he refers are: *R v Lord President of the Privy Council, ex p Page* [1993] AC 682 (HL); *R v Secretary of State for the Home Department, ex p Abdi* [1996] 1 WLR 298 (HL); *R v Secretary of State for the Home Department, ex p Pierson* [1998] AC 539 (HL); and *Boddington v British Transport Police* [1999] 2 AC 143 (HL). See, also, Forsyth, 'Of Fig Leaves and Fairy Tales' (n 13) 123; Mark C Elliott, 'Fundamental Rights as Interpretative Constructs: The Constitutional Logic of the Human Rights Act 1998' in Christopher F Forsyth (ed), *Judicial Review and the Constitution* (Hart Publishing 2000) 271, fn 14.

37 'Of Vires and Vacuums: The Constitutional Context of Judicial Review' (n 28) 457. Sir John Laws makes a related point, that judicial claims to be applying the will of Parliament 'does not make it so', Sir John Laws, *The Hamlyn Lectures: The Common Law Constitution* (CUP 2014) 17. Incidentally, elsewhere, Jowell suggests that the same might be true with regard to the perceived deference shown by the courts to Parliament when deciding whether a statute is compatible with the Convention rights: Jeffrey L Jowell, 'Judicial Deference: Servility, Civility or Institutional Capacity' [2003] *PL* 592, 596–597.

38 HWR Wade 'Constitutional Realities and Judicial Prudence' in Christopher F Forsyth (ed), *Judicial Review and the Constitution* (Hart Publishing 2000) 431.

39 Forsyth and Elliott, 'The Legitimacy of Judicial Review' (n 17) 286–287. For criticism of such governmental claims see, HWR Wade, *The Hamlyn Lectures: Constitutional Fundamentals* (Stevens 1980) 70.

40 When describing the common law theory, I will – in the main – rely on the work of Paul Craig. The work of other commentators will, of course, be relied on where appropriate. It should be noted, however, that the various common law theorists disagree on some points. Nevertheless, I

The ultra vires *and common law theories* 35

jurisdiction of the superior courts not on statute.[41] The development and application of the standards of good administration to discretionary public power is 'normatively justified' by reference to 'justice, the rule of law, etc'.[42] In deciding what is required in a particular case, the courts will choose the interpretation of, say, fairness, 'that [provides] the best constructive interpretation of the community's legal practice judged in the light of previous case law'.[43] This, they argue, reflects the reality that the standards are developed by the courts.[44] They therefore eschew the idea, on which the *ultra vires* theory is based, that the supervisory jurisdiction must be legitimated by reference to a presumed legislative intent. Rather, the standards are judge made and are therefore 'the creation of the common law'.[45]

Ironically, this 'common law' view may also be found in the work of the supporters of the *ultra vires* theory. Wade and Forsyth, two of the leading advocates of the theory, write, with regard to limited time ouster clauses: 'The whole basis of judicial review is therefore *changed*. Instead of depending, *as it normally does, upon the inherent powers of the court at common law*, it depends upon the terms of the Act' (emphasis added).[46] This is a curious sentence to be found in the writings of those who otherwise claim that we must assume that review is founded on an assumed intention of Parliament, rather than 'the inherent powers of the court at common law'.[47] Likewise, the common law view may also be detected

---

concur with Thomas Poole's assessment here that the 'surface dissonances' among these common law theorists 'mask a more fundamental harmony', Thomas Poole, 'Legitimacy, Rights and Judicial Review' (2005) 25 *OJLS* 697, 700.

41 Allan, *The Sovereignty of Law* (n 34) 208.

42 Paul P Craig, 'Competing Models of Judicial Review' [1999] *PL* 428, 429, 431. See also Philip A Joseph, 'The Demise of *Ultra Vires* – Judicial Review in the New Zealand Courts' [2001] *PL* 354, 355; Paul P Craig and Nicholas Bamforth, 'Constitutional Analysis, Constitutional Principle and Judicial Review' [2001] *PL* 763, 767; Paul P Craig, 'Constitutional Foundations, the Rule of Law and Supremacy' [2003] *PL* 92, 93; Paul P Craig, 'The Common Law, Shared Power and Judicial Review' (2004) 24 *OJLS* 237, 238; Paul P Craig, *Administrative Law* (7th edn, Sweet & Maxwell 2012) 15, 18; Allan, *The Sovereignty of Law* (ibid) 208.

43 Craig, 'Legislative Intent and Legislative Supremacy: A Reply to Professor Allan' (n 27) 590. In making this claim, Craig explicitly draws on Dworkin's 'law as integrity' thesis: Ronald Dworkin, *Law's Empire* (Hart Publishing 1998) 225.

44 Craig, 'Ultra Vires and the Foundations of Judicial Review' (n 24) 67; Craig and Bamforth, 'Constitutional Analysis, Constitutional Principle and Judicial Review' (n 42) 767.

45 Craig, 'Competing Models of Judicial Review' (n 42) 429; Michael Fordham, 'Judicial Review: The Future' [2008] *JR* 66, para 15.

46 *Administrative Law* (n 16) 620.

47 It is possible that this apparent coincidence with the common law theory owes more to Wade than it does to Forsyth. This supposition is founded on two observations. First, Wade seems less absolute than some others in his support for the *ultra vires* theory. For instance, Elliott suggests that, particularly with regard to his explanation of the courts' treatment of ouster clauses, Wade's support for the *ultra vires* theory does not seem to possess the logical coherence that is to be found in the work of other advocates of this theory (*The Constitutional Foundations of Judicial Review* (n 13) 32). Second, and in addition, the text in which Wade and Forsyth seem to support the common law approach was, for the first six editions, solely authored by Wade. It is possible, then, that – even in the eleventh edition, published after Wade's death – it is imbued with Wade's approach more than it is Forsyth's.

36 Intention, Supremacy and Judicial Review

in the work of Elliott, another leading supporter of the *ultra vires* theory. He writes that those exercising power derived from statute must do so according to common law constitutional principles, unless Parliament explicitly provides to the contrary[48] and that such principles are not dependent for their existence on any legislative will.[49]

The rejection of parliamentary intent which is inherent in the common law theory is founded on a number of arguments. First, adherents of the theory note that no problem of infringing the sovereignty of Parliament has ever been identified by the courts who developed judicial review without reference to the need to give effect to the intention of the legislature.[50]

Second, the common law theorists note that the common law rules of civil liability such as contract and tort are not justified by reference to legislative intent even when they are applied to bodies created by primary legislation.[51] We would not, for instance, argue that the creation and cultivation of the law of negligence was intended by Parliament simply because we wish to sue a public body created by statute. Yet, the *ultra vires* theorists would argue that, in a claim for judicial review against the same body, we must assume that the standards of good administration were developed as intended by the legislature simply because it exercises powers derived from Parliament. The point is simply this: if we can accept that there is no requirement to identify a legislative warrant for the development and application of the rules of civil liability, then we should surely accept the same with regard to the standards of good administration. To put it another way, if the application of these standards to public bodies deriving their power from Parliament is an infringement of sovereignty unless justified by reference to legislative intent, the same must be true when the rules of civil liability are applied to such bodies. There is, though, no corresponding argument that these rules must be justified in the same way.

Furthermore, in judicial review cases, 'the courts . . . pay little attention to questions of jurisdiction or the *ultra vires* rule'.[52] The supporters of the common law theory argue that this is because the relevant factor in deciding whether the exercise of a power will be susceptible to judicial review is not its *source* but its *subject matter*.[53] That is, power will be subject to the standards of good

---

48 Mark C Elliott, 'The Principle of Parliamentary Sovereignty in Legal, Constitutional, and Political Perspective' in Jeffrey L Jowell, Dawn Oliver and Colm O'Cinneide (eds), *The Changing Constitution* (8th edn, OUP 2015) 56.

49 Mark C Elliott, 'Constitutional Legislation, European Union Law and the Nature of the United Kingdom's Contemporary Constitution' (2014) 10(3) *ECLR* 379, 391; also 'The Principle of Parliamentary Sovereignty in Legal, Constitutional, and Political Perspective' (ibid) 57.

50 Craig, 'Ultra Vires and the Foundations of Judicial Review' (n 24) 73–74. The view that it is possible to ascertain the intention of Parliament will be critically discussed in the next chapter.

51 Craig, 'Competing Models of Judicial Review' (n 42) 433–434, 438–439.

52 Dawn Oliver, 'Is the *Ultra Vires* Rule the Basis of Judicial Review?' [1987] PL 543, 543. See, also, Lord Steyn, 'Democracy Through Law' (2002 Robin Cooke Lecture, Victoria University of Wellington, 18 September 2002), 15.

53 Oliver, 'Is the *Ultra Vires* Rule the Basis of Judicial Review?' (ibid) 546; Lord Woolf of Barnes, '*Droit Public* – English Style' [1995] *PL* 57, 63–64; Sir Stephen Sedley, 'Public Power and Private

administration on the basis of whether it is deemed to be 'public' in nature, not on the basis of whether it has been derived from the legislature.[54] Thus, the argument goes, if the source of the power is not the controlling factor, then the standards of good administration should not be seen as being derived from that source.[55] As support for this proposition, Oliver claims that, in *Council of Civil Service Unions v Minister for the Civil Service*,[56] Lord Diplock, in listing the grounds of review,[57] had in mind that power, whatever its source, would be subject to the same grounds.[58] She therefore concludes that: 'judicial review is not based solely on principles of statutory (or other) interpretation, but on the application of some general principles of good administration to the exercise of power'.[59] She submits that these are imposed by virtue of the common law.[60]

It is worth noting as a supplementary point here that Oliver contends that the courts have a general common law jurisdiction to control the exercise of both public and private power. She argues that similar obligations are imposed on both and that, in private law cases, the courts impose duties similar to the public law duties of fairness and rationality.[61] She writes:

> [There is a] common law right of those seriously affected by decisions taken by powerful bodies to have the effects of a decision upon them considered and taken into account fairly and rationally before that decision is made. In short, there exists a broad common law duty of considerate decision making, the exact content of which will depend upon the circumstances but which spans the public/private divide.[62]

A claim for judicial review under Part 54 of the Civil Procedure Rules is part of this jurisdiction.[63] For Oliver, then, judicial review is not an example of statutory

---

Power' in Christopher F Forsyth (ed), *Judicial Review and the Constitution* (Hart Publishing 2000) 298; Oliver, 'Review of (Non-Statutory) Discretions' (n 1) 323.

54 Oliver, 'Is the *Ultra Vires* Rule the Basis of Judicial Review?' (ibid) 551.

55 ibid 545–547.

56 *Council of Civil Service Unions v Minister for the Civil Service* (n 9).

57 As noted above (p 29), Lord Diplock listed the heads under which administrative action may be controlled by way of judicial review as being illegality, irrationality and procedural impropriety. He also stated that other grounds of review may be developed in the future, citing proportionality as an example, ibid 410.

58 Oliver, 'Is the *Ultra Vires* Rule the Basis of Judicial Review?' (n 52) 547.

59 ibid.

60 ibid 567. See, also, Oliver, 'Review of (Non-Statutory) Discretions' (n 1) 307, 311–312, 321, 322, 324.

61 'Common Values in Public and Private Law and the Public/Private Divide' (n 1) 633–634. Oliver draws on cases regarding common callings (eg: innkeepers, ferrymen, and common carriers) *de jure* or *de facto* monopolies and cases concerning 'prime necessities' as support for this contention. Michael Taggart describes common callings as those callings in which labour, goods and services were made available to the public, Michael Taggart, 'The Province of Administrative Law Determined?' in Michael Taggart, (ed) *The Province of Administrative Law* (Hart Publishing 1997) 6.

62 ibid 638.

63 Incidentally, Oliver argues that the privileges that the CPR 54 procedure affords defendants

38 *Intention, Supremacy and Judicial Review*

interpretation but is, rather, an instance of the application of a general duty of good decision-making required as a matter of policy by the common law.

So, the advocates of the common law theory reject the contention that there is a need to legitimise judicial review by reference to legislative intent. They claim, however, that, under the theory, the courts will have reference to the context created by, and apply any limits expressly stated in, an Act of Parliament.[64] Furthermore, like the *ultra vires* theorists, they are keen to emphasise that the common law theory involves no infringement of parliamentary sovereignty.[65] They do this by arguing that the exercise of the supervisory jurisdiction would amount to an infringement of sovereignty *only* if Parliament was to enact legislation explicitly stating that it was not to be applied in a particular case: '[An attack on sovereignty] entails the proposition that the courts will continue to apply their judicially developed tools even where there is an express or unequivocal Parliamentary intention to the contrary'.[66] If Parliament did legislate in this way, the supporters of this theory contend that the courts would adhere to the statute and that the standards of good administration would not be applied.[67]

Summary

The proponents of both the *ultra vires* and common law theories claim that the standards of good administration are developed and applied according to the

> should be restricted to those bodies that are directly or indirectly democratically accountable, ibid 633.

64 Oliver, 'Review of (Non-Statutory) Discretions' (n 1) 324; Craig and Bamforth, 'Constitutional Analysis, Constitutional Principle and Judicial Review' (n 42) 767, 772, 773–774, 777; Craig, 'Constitutional Foundations, the Rule of Law and Supremacy' (n 42) 95; Craig, 'The Common Law, Shared Power and Judicial Review' (n 42) 238, 245, 253; Craig, 'Legislative Intent and Legislative Supremacy: A Reply to Professor Allan' (n 27) 587, 589–590, 592–593.

65 Ringhand writes: 'all of the critics [of the *ultra vires* doctrine] reject the assertion that their position requires a foundational change in British constitutional doctrine. In other words, these writers deny that they are revolutionaries; each attempts to ground his approach in accepted British norms and legal traditions', Lori A Ringhand, 'Fig Leaves, Fairy Tales, and Constitutional Foundations: Debating Judicial Review in Britain' (2005) 43(3) *Columbia Journal of Transnational Law* 865, 880.

66 Craig, 'Competing Models of Judicial Review' (n 42) 438. See, also, Craig, 'Ultra Vires and the Foundations of Judicial review' (n 24) 74; Jowell, 'Of Vires and Vacuums: The Constitutional Context of Judicial Review' (n 28) 458; Craig, *Administrative Law* (n 42) 15, 18; Craig and Bamforth, 'Constitutional Analysis, Constitutional Principle and Judicial Review' (n 42) 767, 773–774; Craig, 'Constitutional Foundations, the Rule of Law and Supremacy' (n 42) 93.

67 Craig writes: 'if Parliament *were* to state explicitly in the enabling legislation that the minister should be thus empowered [to breach the standards of good administration] then judicial review would be correspondingly curtailed' (emphasis in original), 'Ultra Vires and the Foundations of Judicial review' (ibid) 74. Also, Craig, 'Competing Models of Judicial Review' (ibid) 429, 437–438, 443, 444; Craig and Bamforth, 'Constitutional Analysis, Constitutional Principle and Judicial Review' (ibid) 767, 773–774, 777; Craig, 'Constitutional Foundations, the Rule of Law and Supremacy' (ibid) 93; Craig, 'The Common Law, Shared Power and Judicial Review' (n 42) 238, 251, 253.

The ultra vires *and common law theories* 39

requirements of the rule of law. It is their opinions of the requirements of parliamentary sovereignty that both unite and differentiate the two theories. In both theories, judicial obedience to the legislature is guaranteed by an assertion that the courts will adhere to an Act of Parliament which explicitly prohibits or limits the exercise of the supervisory jurisdiction.[68] The theories differ, however, on the question of whether judicial review must be legitimised by reference to legislative intent. The supporters of the *ultra vires* theory argue that we must assume that the development and application of the standards of good administration to discretionary public power derived from primary legislation is intended by Parliament. This, they contend, is necessary in order to avoid an infringement of parliamentary sovereignty. In contrast, the supporters of the common law theory argue that the supervisory jurisdiction is an inherent one of the courts. It is not granted by Parliament and its exercise does not infringe legislative sovereignty.

---

68 Bradley and Ewing question why the issue of parliamentary sovereignty has become a central part of this debate: 'it is difficult to see why a debate about the foundations of judicial review should become a debate about the supremacy of Parliament. It is not contended by either side that Parliament has no authority to legislate on the scope of judicial review', A W Bradley and K D Ewing, *Constitutional and Administrative Law* (14th edn, Longman 2007) 696.

40 *Intention, Supremacy and Judicial Review*

Bibliography

Allan TRS, *Constitutional Justice: A Liberal Theory of the Rule of Law* (OUP 2001)
— 'Legislative Supremacy and Legislative Intent: A Reply to Professor Craig' (2004) 24 *Oxford Journal of Legal Studies* 563
— *The Sovereignty of Law: Freedom, Constitution, and Common Law* (OUP 2013)
Bradley A W and Ewing K D, *Constitutional and Administrative Law* (14th edn, Longman 2007)
Craig P P, 'Ultra Vires and the Foundations of Judicial Review' [1998] *Cambridge Law Journal* 63
— 'Competing Models of Judicial Review' [1999] *Public Law* 428
— 'Constitutional Foundations, the Rule of Law and Supremacy' [2003] *Public Law* 92
— 'Legislative Intent and Legislative Supremacy: A Reply to Professor Allan' (2004) 24 *Oxford Journal of Legal Studies* 585
— 'The Common Law, Shared Power and Judicial Review' (2004) 24 *Oxford Journal of Legal Studies* 237
— *Administrative Law* (7th edn, Sweet & Maxwell 2012)
— and Bamforth N, 'Constitutional Analysis, Constitutional Principle and Judicial Review' [2001] *Public Law* 763
Dworkin R, *Law's Empire* (Hart Publishing 1998)
Elliott M C, 'The Ultra Vires Doctrine in a Constitutional Setting: Still the Central Principle of Administrative Law' [1999] *Cambridge Law Journal* 129
— 'Fundamental Rights as Interpretative Constructs: The Constitutional Logic of the Human Rights Act 1998' in Christopher F Forsyth (ed), *Judicial Review and the Constitution* (Hart Publishing 2000)
— 'Legislative Intention Versus Judicial Creativity? Administrative Law as a Co-operative Endeavour' in Christopher F Forsyth (ed), *Judicial Review and the Constitution* (Hart Publishing 2000)
— *The Constitutional Foundations of Judicial Review* (Hart Publishing 2001)
— *Beatson, Matthews and Elliott's Administrative Law: Text and Materials* (4th edn, OUP 2011)
— 'Constitutional Legislation, European Union Law and the Nature of the United Kingdom's Contemporary Constitution' (2014) 10(3) *European Constitutional Law Review* 379
— 'The Principle of Parliamentary Sovereignty in Legal, Constitutional, and Political Perspective' in Jeffrey L Jowell, Dawn Oliver and Colm O'Cinneide (eds), *The Changing Constitution* (8th edn, OUP 2015)
Fordham M, 'Judicial Review: The Future' [2008] *Judicial Review* 66
Forsyth C F, 'Of Fig Leaves and Fairy Tales: The Ultra Vires Doctrine, the Sovereignty of Parliament and Judicial Review' [1996] *Cambridge Law Journal* 122
— 'Heat and Light: A Plea for Reconciliation' in Christopher F Forsyth (ed), *Judicial Review and the Constitution* (Hart Publishing 2000)
— and Elliott M C, 'The Legitimacy of Judicial Review' [2003] *Public Law* 286
— and Whittle L, 'Judicial Creativity and Judicial Legitimacy in Administrative Law' (2002) 8 *Canterbury Law Review* 453
Hare I, 'The Separation of Powers and Judicial Review for Error of Law' in Christopher F Forsyth and Ivan Hare (eds), *The Golden Metwand and the Crooked Cord: Essays on Public Law in Honour of Sir William Wade QC* (Clarendon Press 1998)

The ultra vires *and common law theories* 41

Joseph P A, 'The Demise of *Ultra Vires* – Judicial Review in the New Zealand Courts' [2001] *Public Law* 354

Jowell J L, 'Of Vires and Vacuums: The Constitutional Context of Judicial Review' [1999] *Public Law* 448

— 'Judicial Deference: Servility, Civility or Institutional Capacity' [2003] *Public Law* 592

Laws Sir John, *The Hamlyn Lectures: The Common Law Constitution* (CUP 2014)

Oliver D, 'Is the *Ultra Vires* Rule the Basis of Judicial Review?' [1987] *Public Law* 543

— 'Common Values in Public and Private Law and the Public/Private Divide' [1997] *Public Law* 630

— 'Review of (Non-Statutory) Discretions' in Christopher F Forsyth (ed), *Judicial Review and the Constitution* (Hart Publishing 2000)

Poole T, 'Legitimacy, Rights and Judicial Review' (2005) 25 *Oxford Journal of Legal Studies* 697

Ringhand L A, 'Fig Leaves, Fairy Tales, and Constitutional Foundations: Debating Judicial Review in Britain' (2005) 43(3) *Columbia Journal of Transnational Law* 865

Sedley Sir Stephen, 'Public Power and Private Power' in Christopher F Forsyth (ed), *Judicial Review and the Constitution* (Hart Publishing 2000)

Singh R, 'The Declaration of Incompatibility' [2002] *Judicial Review* 237

Steyn Lord, 'Democracy Through Law' (2002 Robin Cooke Lecture, Victoria University of Wellington, 18 September 2002)

Taggart M, 'The Province of Administrative Law Determined?' in Michael Taggart (ed) *The Province of Administrative Law* (Hart Publishing 1997)

Wade HWR, 'Constitutional Realities and Judicial Prudence' in Christopher F Forsyth (ed), *Judicial Review and the Constitution* (Hart Publishing 2000)

— *The Hamlyn Lectures: Constitutional Fundamentals* (Stevens 1980)

— and Forsyth C F, *Administrative Law* (11th edn, OUP 2014)

Woolf Lord, '*Droit Public* – English Style' [1995] *Public Law* 57

4 Themes of the debate

In this chapter, I critically review the main themes in the discussion about how the supervisory jurisdiction may be best justified in constitutional terms. The themes are: the sovereignty of Parliament; judicial review of bodies not deriving their power from statute; the doctrine of the rule of law; ouster clauses; and the argument that the *ultra vires* theory is structurally coherent.

Conceptions of parliamentary sovereignty

This section will examine parliamentary sovereignty as it is conceived in the *ultra vires* and common law theories. I first argue that in both theories parliamentary sovereignty is assumed to function in the manner of a Dworkinian rule. I further argue that, despite this shared assumption, in other respects, the two theories rely on different conceptions of sovereignty. Next, I compare the view of sovereignty inherent in both theories with traditional conceptions of the doctrine, particularly that of Dicey. This section also evaluates the validity of relying on the intention of Parliament and examines some of the drawbacks that such reliance might cause. Finally, I examine the implications for the present work of claims that Parliament is no longer sovereign.

As discussed in Chapter Three, both the *ultra vires* theory and the common law theory attempt to provide an account of judicial review that accommodates the doctrine of parliamentary sovereignty. Here, it will be argued that there is an assumption implicit in both theories that parliamentary sovereignty functions as a Dworkinian rule.

I noted in Chapter Two that Dworkin distinguishes between the operation of rules and the operation of principles. The former are applicable in an 'all-or-nothing' fashion.[1] A rule demands that a particular result should occur if the conditions which are stipulated within it are present. So, to use Dworkin's own example, an assertion that, 'A will is invalid unless signed by three witnesses' is a

---

1 Chapter Two p 20. See, also, Ronald Dworkin, *Taking Rights Seriously* (Duckworth & Co 1977) 24.

Themes of the debate 43

rule because, unless signed by the requisite number of witnesses, the will would be invalid.[2]

In contrast, principles do not work in this conclusive, all-or-nothing way. They do not demand a particular result but simply incline in one direction or another.[3] Moreover, principles possess a quality that is absent in rules: 'the dimension of weight or importance'.[4] In any particular case where they are operative, principles will be balanced against each other, according to their relative weights, in order to reach a decision.

It is clear that the advocates of the common law theory assume that legislative supremacy operates as a rule. As shown in Chapter Three, they contend that, if Parliament were to enact legislation explicitly excluding the supervisory jurisdiction, then this would be adhered to by the courts. They claim that a failure to do this would amount to an infringement of sovereignty.[5] It is therefore assumed that legislative supremacy does not function like a principle, merely indicating the direction to be taken. Rather, it necessitates a particular decision – that, ultimately, the courts must adhere to an Act of Parliament and that a failure to do so would amount to a breach of parliamentary sovereignty. For this reason, it has the conclusive nature that is characteristic of rules.

The same can be said for the *ultra vires* theory. I noted in Chapter Three that the supporters of this theory insist that we must assume Parliament intends the courts to impose the standards of good administration on discretionary public power, at least where that power is derived from an Act of Parliament. They argue that this presumption is necessary to prevent a breach of parliamentary sovereignty.[6] Forsyth makes the point in the following way:

> The analytical difficulty is this: what an all powerful Parliament does not prohibit, it must authorise either expressly or impliedly. Likewise if Parliament grants a power to a minister, that minister either acts within those powers or outside those powers. *There is no grey area between authorisation and prohibition or between empowerment and denial of power.* Thus, if the making of . . . vague regulations is within the powers granted by a sovereign Parliament, on what basis may the courts challenge Parliament's will and hold that the regulations are invalid? If Parliament has authorised vague regulations, those regulations cannot be challenged without challenging Parliament's authority to authorise such regulations (emphasis added).[7]

In short, because Parliament is free to enable the minister to make vague regulations, we must assume that the courts' prohibition of such regulations

---

2 Dworkin, *Taking Rights Seriously* (ibid).
3 ibid 26.
4 ibid.
5 Chapter Three p 38.
6 Chapter Three pp 31–32.
7 Christopher F Forsyth, 'Of Fig Leaves and Fairy Tales: The Ultra Vires Doctrine, the Sovereignty of Parliament and Judicial Review' [1996] *CLJ* 122, 133–134.

44 *Intention, Supremacy and Judicial Review*

– and, indeed, the imposition of the other standards of good administration – is intended by Parliament.

So, sovereignty under the *ultra vires* theory is perceived as operating in terms of binary opposites. There is no 'grey area' or indication that competing interests should be balanced against each other. The application of the standards of good administration in a manner contrary to the intention of Parliament is simply seen as a breach of sovereignty. Accordingly, legislative supremacy, as understood under the *ultra vires* theory, does not merely indicate a direction to be taken; rather, it necessitates a particular decision: that the courts must comply with the will of Parliament. As with the common law theory, this suggests that it is considered to be a Dworkinian rule.

The assumption, implicit in both theories, that parliamentary sovereignty functions as a rule will be challenged in Chapter Six where it will be argued that it operates as a Dworkinian principle.

While it may be a shared assumption of both theories that parliamentary sovereignty functions as a rule, it seems that the supporters of each theory rely on different conceptions of the doctrine. This may be inferred from the rationalisation that takes place in each. As detailed in Chapter Three, the supporters of the *ultra vires* theory maintain that we must assume that Parliament intends the courts to apply the standards of good administration to discretionary public power that it grants. Without such an assumption, they contend, the courts would be acting contrary to the intention of Parliament which would amount to an infringement of sovereignty.[8] It is therefore inherent in the *ultra vires* theory that parliamentary sovereignty requires the courts not to act against the *assumed intention* of Parliament.

A contrasting view of legislative supremacy is implicit in the common law theory. Jowell writes:

> Another feature of [the common law] approach is its acceptance of Parliament's supremacy; if Parliament goes so far as to exclude a constitutional principle . . . the courts . . . will have to accept that. *But, in order to command that acceptance, Parliament will have to make itself clear.* Even ambiguity may not be enough to coax the courts into agreeing to displace democracy's foundational features (emphasis added).[9]

Here, sovereignty obliges the courts to adhere to the will of Parliament made unequivocally clear. We may assume that such clarity may only be achieved

---

8 Chapter Three pp 31–32.

9 Jeffrey L Jowell, 'Of Vires and Vacuums: The Constitutional Context of Judicial Review' [1999] *PL* 448, 458. See, also, Paul P Craig, 'Competing Models of Judicial Review' [1999] *PL* 428, 438; Paul P Craig, 'Ultra Vires and the Foundations of Judicial Review' [1998] *CLJ* 63, 74; Paul P Craig, *Administrative Law* (7th edn, Sweet & Maxwell 2012) 15, 18; Paul P Craig and Nicholas Bamforth, 'Constitutional Analysis, Constitutional Principle and Judicial Review' [2001] *PL* 763, 767, 773–774; Paul P Craig, 'Constitutional Foundations, the Rule of Law and Supremacy' [2003] *PL* 92, 93.

Themes of the debate 45

through the use of express statutory language. Indeed, Craig suggests that it is only by using express words that Parliament may limit the supervisory jurisdiction:

> if Parliament *were* to state explicitly in the enabling legislation that the minister should be thus empowered [to breach the standards of good administration] then judicial review would be correspondingly curtailed (emphasis in original).[10]

If so, this suggests that, under the common law theory, the doctrine of sovereignty would be breached only if the courts acted contrary to the words contained in an Act of Parliament. This means that sovereignty is not defined, as in the *ultra vires* theory, by reference to the assumed intention of Parliament. Rather, sovereignty requires adherence to the *language* used in primary legislation.

The reliance on legislative intent in the *ultra vires* theory conflicts with the long-established assumption that Parliament has legislative supremacy only in, and through, Acts of Parliament. As Lord Templeman has stated: 'Parliamentary supremacy over the judiciary is only exercisable by statute'.[11] Lord Diplock agrees: 'Parliament, under our constitution, is sovereign only in respect of what it expresses by the words used in the legislation it has passed'.[12] Moreover, Wade and Forsyth, two leading supporters of the *ultra vires* theory, have written that Parliament is sovereign only through legislation: 'This legal paramountcy [parliamentary sovereignty] can be exercised *only* by an Act of the sovereign Parliament' (emphasis added).[13] Given this acknowledgement by Wade and Forsyth, it is curious that, when making arguments in favour of the *ultra vires* theory, they assume that the courts are bound, not only by statute, but also by legislative intent.

This assumption is all the more questionable because, as we have seen in Chapter Three, the legislative intent inherent in the *ultra vires* theory is not an actual, particular intent which arose during the enactment, and relates to the meaning and application, of particular Acts of Parliament; rather, it is a presumed, continuing and general intent that, when Parliament grants a discretionary public power, it intends that power to be exercised in accordance with the rule of law which includes the standards of good administration.[14] That is, if it is correct to claim that parliamentary sovereignty inheres only in the words used in Acts of Parliament, as Wade and Forsyth appear to suggest, it is surely the case that it does not extend to the general presumed intent claimed by the *ultra vires* theory as modified.

---

10 'Ultra Vires and the Foundations of Judicial Review' (ibid).

11 *M v Home Office* [1994] 1 AC 377, 395.

12 *Black-Clawson International Ltd v Papierwerke Waldhof-Aschaffenburg AG* [1975] AC 591 (HL) 638. Similarly, Allan writes: 'legislative sovereignty inheres in the words enacted – interpreted correctly in accordance with the constitutional premises of the rule of law – and not in the aspirations of government or even parliamentary majority', TRS Allan, *Law, Liberty and Justice: The Legal Foundations of British Constitutionalism* (Clarendon Press 1993) 68 (citation omitted); also, 82.

13 HWR Wade and Christopher F Forsyth, *Administrative Law* (11th edn, OUP 2014) 20.

14 Chapter Three p 43.

46 *Intention, Supremacy and Judicial Review*

In addition, it is significant that between the supporters of the two theories – the *ultra vires* theory and the common law theory – not only is there no agreement about what parliamentary sovereignty requires, there does not seem to be any *explicit* recognition that there are two versions of the doctrine being relied upon: one which requires adherence to the presumed intention of Parliament and one that merely requires adherence to the words used in statute.

It is interesting to compare the two versions of parliamentary sovereignty with the traditional view given by Dicey. He states:

> The principle of Parliamentary sovereignty means neither more nor less than this, namely, that Parliament thus defined has, under the English constitution, the right to make or unmake any law whatever; and, further, that no person or body is recognised by the law of England as having a right to override or set aside the legislation of Parliament.[15]

This contrasts with the assumptions of the supporters of the *ultra vires* theory which seem to require more. For them, as we have seen, legislative supremacy obliges the courts not to act contrary to the implied *intention* of Parliament whereas, for Dicey, it merely requires the courts not to 'override or set aside' an Act of Parliament. The version of sovereignty that is implicit in the common law theory is, perhaps, easier to reconcile with Dicey's view. This is because both seem to require fidelity to the legislation, rather than the intention, of Parliament.

Dicey's view of parliamentary sovereignty also appears to envisage an interpretative role for the courts which conflicts with the conception inherent in the *ultra vires* theory. He writes:

> Parliament is supreme legislator, but from the moment Parliament has uttered its will as lawgiver, that will becomes subject to the interpretation put upon it by the judges of the land, and the judges, who are influenced by the feelings of magistrates no less than by the general spirit of the common law, are disposed to construe statutory exceptions to common law principles in a mode which would not commend itself either to a body of officials, or to the Houses of Parliament, if the Houses were called upon to interpret their own enactments.[16]

Lord Simmonds makes a similar point:

> the general proposition that it is the duty of the court to find out the intention of Parliament – and not only of Parliament but of Ministers also –

---

15 A V Dicey, *Introduction to the Study of the Law of the Constitution* (8th edn, Macmillan 1915) 3–4.

16 ibid 273. Laws expresses similar sentiments: 'it is long established law that the interpretation of statutes is within the judges' province', Sir John Laws, 'Judicial Review and the Meaning of Law' in Christopher F Forsyth (ed), *Judicial Review and the Constitution* (Hart Publishing 2000) 187.

cannot by any means be supported. The duty of the court is to interpret the words that the legislature has used.[17]

The contention that the courts are obliged to interpret the words used in legislation, 'in a mode which would not commend itself ... to the Houses of Parliament', cannot be easily reconciled with the assumption that underlies the *ultra vires* theory: that parliamentary sovereignty requires adherence to the assumed intention of the legislature.

On the other hand, as will be shown below, the *ultra vires* theorists sometimes acknowledge that the courts draw on principles inherent in the legal system when developing the standards of good administration.[18] In other words, they accept that the courts do indeed rely on the spirit and principles of the common law and that this conditions their judgments. In addition, they write that the courts' treatment of ouster clauses, 'envisages an interaction between ... "common law" rights and the words of a statute and that the outcome of that interaction is the actual meaning given to statute'.[19] They argue that this approach is consistent with the *ultra vires* theory.[20] Yet, as will be demonstrated, the *ultra vires* theorists concede that the courts' interpretation of ouster clauses amounts to a disobedience of Parliament.[21] If so, this interpretation must conflict with the intention of Parliament and, consequently, with the conception of legislative sovereignty inherent in the *ultra vires* theory.

Legitimating review of statutory power by reference to the common law rather than legislative intent is, of course, the principle on which the common law theory is founded. This is one of the reasons – its similarity to the views of Dicey – why its supporters maintain that it most closely resembles academic opinion.[22] They also claim that it best portrays the historical development of judicial review: 'The common law model of illegality best captures what the courts have done for the last three hundred and fifty years, and it continues to do so'.[23] They argue that, historically, the law of judicial review has not been founded on giving effect

---

17 *Magnor and St Melens Rural District Council v Newport Corporation* [1952] AC 189 (HL) 191. Also, Lord Reid has stated: 'We often say that we are looking for the intention of Parliament, but that is not quite accurate. We are seeking the meaning of the words which Parliament used. We are seeking not what Parliament meant but the true meaning of what they said', *Black-Clawson International Ltd* (n 12) 613.

18 Below p 59.

19 Christopher F Forsyth and Mark C Elliott, 'The Legitimacy of Judicial Review' [2003] *PL* 286, 304

20 ibid.

21 Below p 65.

22 Craig, 'Competing Models of Judicial Review' (n 9) 444–446. Craig also claims that the common law theory coincides with Jowell's work 'which can be taken as representative of modern mainstream thinking about the rule of law [and sovereignty]', ibid 445–446.

23 ibid 446; see, also, Paul P Craig, 'The Common Law, Shared Power and Judicial Review' (2004) 24 *OJLS* 237, 250. Similar sentiments are expressed by Sir Stephen Sedley, 'Public Power and Private Power' in Christopher F Forsyth (ed), *Judicial Review and the Constitution* (Hart Publishing 2000) 302–303.

48 Intention, Supremacy and Judicial Review

to the intention of Parliament but has, rather, developed from the prerogative writs which evolved to correct governmental errors.[24] Furthermore, even after Parliament came to be seen as omnipotent and sovereign, the courts would, more often than not, develop and apply the standards of good administration without reference to legislative intent. In contrast, it is argued that the *ultra vires* theory 'represents a uniquely modern view of judicial review' that is 'profoundly ahistorical'.[25] This appeal to history by the common law theorists has, however, been criticised on the basis that much of judicial review, as it exists today, has been developed since the latter half of the twentieth century and it is this modern supervisory jurisdiction that needs to be justified, not its historical antecedents.[26]

It is worth observing the symmetry between Dicey's and, particularly, Lord Simmonds' descriptions of the courts' role when interpreting legislation[27] and the account in philosophical hermeneutics of a reader interpreting a text. I noted in Chapter Two that, in philosophical hermeneutics as advanced by Gadamer, the aim of the reader should not be to discover the meaning intended by the author in writing the text.[28] Similarly, it is implicit in Dicey's account of the judicial interpretation of legislation – 'which would not commend itself . . . to the Houses of Parliament' – that the aim is not to discover the intention of the legislature. Furthermore, in both Gadamer's and Dicey's account of interpretation, the reader or judge is not guided by divined intention but is, rather, guided by tradition. For the reader, it may be, among other things, a traditional way of interpreting works of that genre or by that author.[29] For the judge it is, 'the general spirit of the common law' and 'common law principles'.

In addition, Gadamer's dictum that an author's interpretation of her own work has no priority over the interpretation of any other reader is relevant here. In Chapter Two, it was argued that, among other things, an author's view of her own work is more parochial than any would-be reader and that the meaning of a

---

24 Craig notes that the modern law of judicial review developed from the writs of certiorari and mandamus: 'Ultra Vires and the Foundations of Judicial Review' (n 9) 79–86. Lord Woolf also states that the 'history [of public law] is intertwined with that of the prerogative writs', Lord Woolf of Barnes, '*Droit Public* – English Style' [1995] *PL* 57, 60. Similarly, Galligan writes: 'the primary source of principles of good administration lies beyond Parliament, and their justification depends on values in the constitutional order that precede the doctrine of sovereignty', D J Galligan, 'Judicial Review and the Textbook Writers' (1982) 2 *OJLS* 257, 262.

25 Philip A Joseph, 'The Demise of *Ultra Vires* – Judicial Review in the New Zealand Courts' [2001] *PL* 354, 367; also, 363–365 and Philip A Joseph, 'The Demise of Ultra Vires – A Reply to Christopher Forsyth and Linda Whittle' (2002) 8 *Canta LR* 463, 463–466.

26 Stephen H Bailey, 'Judicial Review in a Modern Context' in Christopher F Forsyth (ed), *Judicial Review and the Constitution* (Hart Publishing 2000) 421–422. See, also, Christopher F Forsyth, 'Heat and Light: a Plea for Reconciliation' in Christopher F Forsyth (ed), *Judicial Review and the Constitution* (Hart Publishing 2000) 399.

27 Text to nn 16 and 17.

28 Chapter One p 7.

29 ibid p 17.

Themes of the debate 49

text always goes beyond its author.[30] I argued that, for the same reason, we should reject any reliance on the intention of Parliament when construing legislation.[31]

However, Gadamer does not merely assert that it is not desirable to attempt to recreate the intention of the author of a text. As was shown in Chapter Two, he rejects the very possibility of discovering such intention at all. This is because the reader will inevitably be differently situated, and conditioned by different influences, than the author.[32] This has obvious implications for the reliance on parliamentary intent which is implicit in the *ultra vires* theory. When hearing a particular case, a court will inevitably be differently situated than the Parliament that enacted the legislation which is being considered or applied. This is certainly the case in at least one sense: the courts will be interpreting the legislation in the light of facts of which the legislature was unaware and, often, did not even imagine. So, just as Gadamer's reader cannot recreate the intention of the author, it is not possible for the courts to recreate the intention of Parliament. This, in turn, brings into question the validity of the *ultra vires* theory under which we are asked to assume a particular intention of Parliament.

We may also criticise the view, noted in Chapter Three, that, because Parliament has not legislated to curtail the courts' judicial review jurisdiction, it must intend that jurisdiction to be exercised over discretionary public power.[33] In the first place, as will be argued below, the plain meaning of ouster clauses is that the courts' supervisory jurisdiction should be limited or excluded.[34] While, as will also be shown, this is not the interpretation given to such clauses by the courts, it does at least bring into question the assertion that Parliament has not attempted to restrict the judicial review jurisdiction.

However, even if the contention were accurate, the view that it is possible to recreate the intentions of actors in historical events by reference to those events was rejected in Chapter Two.[35] This is because their intention may not be reflected in what actually happened. Similarly, legislative inaction on a particular issue may not be indicative of any intention. It may, for example, simply be the result of a lack of parliamentary time.[36] It may be that members of Parliament have not considered legislating in a particular way so that this should not consequently be taken as evidence of a positive intention.[37] It is, therefore, not valid

30 ibid p 9.
31 ibid.
32 ibid pp 7–8.
33 Chapter Three p 33.
34 Below p 64–65.
35 Chapter Two pp 9–10.
36 Indeed, Dworkin writes on this point: 'Legislative time is a scarce resource, to be allocated with some sense of political priorities, and it may well be that a judicial decision would be overruled if Parliament had time to pass every law it would like to pass, but will not be overruled because Parliament does not', Ronald Dworkin, 'Political Judges and the Rule of Law' in Ronald Dworkin, *A Matter of Principle* (OUP 1985) 18.
37 Craig writes: 'Reasoning which derives its authority from general statements concerning legislative intent or parliamentary omission should be viewed with caution. A concealed premiss underlying the argument is that the parliamentary process operates in such a way that, on each occasion on

50 Intention, Supremacy and Judicial Review

to conclude that the absence of legislation modifying the supervisory jurisdiction means that Parliament intends it to be exercised just as it is. Chu agrees: 'Inaction or silence plainly can never be construed or understood as explicit expression'.[38]

Moreover, as was also argued in Chapter Two, one may question whether we can accurately talk of the intention of the legislature at all.[39] Parliament is a body made up of two Houses – the Commons and the Lords – these, in turn, comprising individual Members of Parliament and Peers.[40] These individuals do not form a homogeneous whole. Rather, Parliament consists of a number of formal and informal, stable and changing political groupings representing a variety of ideas and political ideals. To assume that a legislature has a single intent is, Shelpse claims, to commit the fallacy of a 'false personification of a collectivity'.[41] Moreover, enacted legislation will – in most, if not all, cases – be passed by a simple majority which may itself be the result of a number of compromises.[42] Radin writes:

> A legislature certainly has no intention whatever in connection with words which some two or three men drafted, which a considerable number rejected, and in regard to which many of the approving majority might have had, and often demonstrably did have, different ideas and beliefs.[43]

Indeed, as Waldron notes: 'It is perfectly possible . . . that [legislation], taken as a whole does not reflect the purposes or intentions of *any* of the legislators who together enacted it' (emphasis added).[44] Moreover, Gardner argues that it is possible that, when voting for a particular legislative provision, some legislators 'had no intentions at all', acting simply as 'lobby fodder who voted when they were told to by their political masters'.[45]

Goldsworthy rejects such arguments. He writes: 'Despite occasional sugges-

---

which legislation is enacted, the question as to whether [the standards of good administration] should be required will be carefully considered; that the advantages and disadvantages of the inclusion of such an obligation will be carefully weighed and the appropriate conclusion will be reached', Paul P Craig, *Public Law and Democracy in the United Kingdom and the United States of America* (OUP 1990) 163.

38 John Chu, 'One Controversy, Two Jurisdictions: A Comparative Evaluation of the Ultra Vires and Common Law Theories of Judicial Review' [2009] *JR* 347, para 12.

39 Chapter Two p 10.

40 'it makes little sense to talk of an institution such as Parliament, composed of hundreds of members, actually intending anything', TRS Allan, *The Sovereignty of Law: Freedom, Constitution, and Common Law* (OUP 2013) 219; see, also, 225.

41 Kenneth A Shelpse, 'Congress is a "They," Not an "It": Legislative Intent as Oxymoron' (1992) 12 *International Review of Law and Economics* 239, 239.

42 Craig draws on the work of Dworkin and Waldron to make similar points: 'The Common Law, Shared Power and Judicial Review' (n 23) 239–240.

43 Max Radin, 'Statutory Interpretation' (1930) 43 *Harv LR* 863, 870.

44 Jeremy Waldron, *Law and Disagreement* (OUP 1999) 125. See, also, Ronald Dworkin, 'The Forum of Principle' in Ronald Dworkin, *A Matter of Principle* (OUP 1985) 38.

45 John Gardner, 'Some Types of Law' in D E Edlin (ed), *Common Law Theory* (CUP 2007) 51–78, 56.

Themes of the debate 51

tions that collective intentions are mythical entities that cannot really exist, it is obvious that they can. We see them in action when we watch team sports, and hear them when we listen to orchestras'.[46] Ekins also disagrees. He argues that it is incorrect to assume that the intention of a legislature is an aggregate of the legislators' individual intentions.[47] Rather, the legislature should be considered to be a single entity such that each legislator understands the enactments of the legislature to represent their single joint intention even if, as individuals, they voted against a particular provision. This single intention arises from the interlocking intention of each legislator but does not reduce to the individual intention of any one or more of them. It comprises a standing intention to adopt appropriate procedures to enable the legislature to alter the law for the common good and that the enactments of the legislature shall be those of all of the legislators.[48] It also consists of a particular intention to enact particular legislative proposals and so to alter the law by making reasoned choices.[49]

Despite these arguments, the supporters of the *ultra vires* theory seem to acknowledge that it is not possible to recreate the intention of Parliament, conceding that it 'is inevitably an artificial construct'.[50] Nevertheless, they also attempt to shore up claims for its validity by maintaining that the assumption that Parliament intends the standards of good administration to be imposed on public power derived from statute is plausible and reasonable.[51] Indeed, they state that this is the *only* 'logical and plausible' assumption which can be made given that we have a sovereign legislature.[52] That is, while reference to the intention of Parliament is artificial, assuming that Parliament intends the courts to operate the supervisory jurisdiction is a logical corollary of exercising review over power derived from a sovereign Parliament and is also reasonable and plausible.

The argument that the *ultra vires* theory is logically necessary is part of a wider claim that the theory is structurally coherent; I deal with this claim later in this chapter. Here, I evaluate the contention that a specific intention may plausibly be ascribed to Parliament. In the first place, as already noted, a number of disparate

---

46 Jeffrey Goldsworthy, *The Sovereignty of Parliament: History and Philosophy* (OUP 1999) 251 (citation omitted). See, also, Aileen Kavanagh, 'The Role of Parliamentary Intention in Adjudication under the Human Rights Act 1998' (2006) 26 *OJLS* 179, 182.

47 Richard Ekins, *The Nature of Legislative Intent* (OUP 2012) 25 and throughout.

48 ibid 219–224.

49 ibid 230–236.

50 Forsyth, 'Heat and Light' (n 26) 408, fn 47. See, also, Christopher F Forsyth and Linda Whittle, 'Judicial Creativity and Judicial Legitimacy in Administrative Law' (2002) 8 *Canta LR* 453, 456 and Allan who argues that legislative intent here is 'constructive' rather than literal: TRS Allan, 'Constitutional Dialogue and the Justification of Judicial Review' (2003) 23 *OJLS* 563, 565–566, 567, 568–569, 570, 573.

51 'it is not unreasonable or implausible to impute to Parliament the intention that decision-makers should comply with the principles of good administration', Forsyth, 'Heat and Light' (ibid). Also, Mark C Elliott, *The Constitutional Foundations of Judicial Review* (Hart Publishing 2001) 110, 133.

52 Mark C Elliott, 'The Ultra Vires Doctrine in a Constitutional Setting: Still the Central Principle of Administrative Law' [1999] *CLJ* 129, 140–146.

52 *Intention, Supremacy and Judicial Review*

individuals and groups compose Parliament. It is, therefore, questionable whether one can assert that Parliament has any intention at all, let alone any *particular* intention. Second, even if Parliament had one joint intention, as Goldsworthy and Ekins argue, it would not be possible to determine what would or would not be the *only* plausible intention for it to possess at a particular point in time. Our different situatedness to Parliament, which prevents us from divining its intention, also prevents us from determining whether it is credible to assume it had any one particular intention over another. It is, therefore, not plausible to ascribe any particular intention to the legislature.

We may also ask whether we can confidently ascribe the same general intention to Parliament over a number of years, as the *ultra vires* theorists suggest, regardless of the changing composition of that body. The political configuration of the legislature may radically change at a general election. So, what may have been thought a safe assumption to make about Parliament at one time – with regard to the rule of law, standards of good administration or anything else – may not be such a safe assumption at another point in time.

In addition, as argued above, it is implicit in the work of both Dicey and Gadamer that it should not be the aim of the courts to attempt to recreate the intention of Parliament. Jowell goes further, asserting: 'For the courts to decide these questions on the basis of an assessment of how the legislature would have decided the matter had it been a judge in its own cause . . . is ultimately an abdication of judicial responsibility'.[53] We may go further still and argue that it is illegitimate to attempt, as the *ultra vires* theorists do, to rationalise judicial review by reference to an intention which they concede is artificial and which we have seen is not possible to accurately recreate, nor necessarily plausible to assume.

Craig makes a related criticism of the *ultra vires* theory: that justifying the supervisory jurisdiction by reference to parliamentary intent means that no further enquiry is made about how desirable it is to develop and apply a particular aspect of the standards of good administration. On this point, he has written: 'An important cost of using the ultra vires doctrine based on legislative intent is to conceal the true policy considerations which affect the law in this area'.[54] That is, the courts develop a particular aspect of the standards of good administration in pursuit of a particular policy consideration but the appeal to the intention of Parliament to justify the imposition of these standards may mean that there is no discussion of the true reasons for their development and application in any particular case. Craig argues that if the common law was considered to be the basis of review – as in the common law theory – then constraints on power, and any developments of such constraints, would be subject to considered discussion and expressly justified in normative terms: 'Thus, for example, rather than "justify-

---

53 'Of Vires and Vacuums: The Constitutional Context of Judicial Review' (n 9) 459. Cotterell makes a similar point, arguing that the *ultra vires* theory reduces the courts to 'modest underworkers', Roger Cotterell, 'Judicial Review and Legal Theory' in Genevra Richardson and Hazel Genn (eds), *Administrative Law and Government Action: The Courts and Alternative Mechanisms of Review* (Clarendon Press 1994) 16.
54 'Ultra Vires and the Foundations of Judicial Review' (n 9) 76.

Themes of the debate 53

ing" a particular reading of jurisdictional error by reference to legislative intent, there should instead be a reasoned argument as to why this view of jurisdictional error was felt to be correct'.[55]

We may question Craig's reasoning here. I noted in Chapter Three that the *ultra vires* theorists accept that the standards of good administration are judicial creations.[56] There is, therefore, no reason why there cannot be reasoned argument about whether a particular aspect of judicial review can be justified in policy terms. In fact, Craig himself suggests that the courts currently justify the imposition of these standards by reference to justice and the rule of law.[57] Furthermore, the courts do this while explicitly claiming, for the most part, that the *ultra vires* theory provides the constitutional justification for the supervisory jurisdiction.[58] In short, the courts currently justify the standards of good administration by reference to justice and rule of law values and do so while considering the *ultra vires* theory to be the justification for review. Given this, it may overstate the matter to suggest that the theory prevents discussion about whether the application of these values to a particular case is appropriate.

We may, however, make a criticism that is similar to Craig's: that the assumption demanded by the *ultra vires* theory – that the control of statutorily derived public power is commensurate with the doctrine of parliamentary sovereignty – makes it difficult to find a position from which we may criticise any particular decision for being contrary to the doctrine. Because of this, the *ultra vires* theory encourages its supporters to assume that the decisions made by the courts when supervising the exercise of discretionary public power derived from statute are intended by Parliament and to attempt to justify them as such.

A clear example of this is the courts' treatment of ouster clauses. As will be argued below, the courts interpret such clauses in a way which is contrary to their plain meaning.[59] However, Elliott suggests that this interpretation is consistent with Parliament's intention.[60] No doubt he adopts this rationalisation because, otherwise, the interpretation given to such clauses would bring the *ultra vires* theory into question. This is the difficulty. There is, in principle, nothing to prevent the *ultra vires* theorists from criticising a court's interpretation of legislation as being mistaken. Yet, the theory encourages its advocates to find that all interpretations are compatible with the intention of the legislature. As Joseph writes, the supporters of the *ultra vires* theory 'indulge in Procrustean scholarship – [they] find a convenient legal categorisation and force conformity with it'.[61]

This means that the *ultra vires* theory is, to some extent at least, self-justifying.

---

55 ibid 89.

56 Chapter Three p 33.

57 ibid p 35.

58 See, for example, *Boddington v British Transport Police* [1999] 2 AC 143 (HL) 171 (Lord Steyn).

59 Below pp 64–65.

60 ibid.

61 Joseph, 'The Demise of Ultra Vires – A Reply to Christopher Forsyth and Linda Whittle' (n 25) 468 – Joseph's comment relates to the *ultra vires* theorists' explanation of review of non-statutory power but it applies equally well here.

54 Intention, Supremacy and Judicial Review

It compels its supporters to assume that in judicial review cases all interpretations of legislation are intended by Parliament. Consequently, this appears to prove the very assumption on which theory rests: that when controlling statutorily derived public power, the courts are simply acting as the legislature intends them to do.

Finally in this section, there have been some suggestions that Parliament should no longer be considered to be sovereign and that this has implications for theories which attempt to justify the judicial review jurisdiction in a way which respects legislative supremacy.

Of course, the traditional conception of legislative supremacy has been amended by membership of the European Union. For instance, and most famously, in *R v Secretary of State for Transport, ex p Factortame and Others (No 2)*, the House of Lords granted an interim injunction to prevent the Merchant Shipping Act 1988 from being applied because of its potential conflict with Community law.[62] In doing so, their Lordships breached the prohibition, contained in the traditional view of sovereignty, on overriding or setting aside an Act of Parliament.[63]

Yet, even where there is no issue of European Union law in play, some suggest that Parliament's legislative competence may be limited in order to protect constitutional fundamentals. Lord Steyn, for instance, has stated:

> In exceptional circumstances involving an attempt to abolish judicial review or the ordinary role of the courts, the Appellate Committee of the House of Lords or a new Supreme Court may have to consider whether this is a constitutional fundamental which even a sovereign Parliament acting at the behest of a complaisant House of Commons cannot abolish.[64]

Other senior judges have also asserted, extra-judicially, that there are, or should be, limits on the legislative competence of Parliament.[65] Such claims, if true, would call into question the necessity of the *ultra vires* and common law theories. This is because the *raison d'être* of both theories is to provide a constitutional justification for judicial review which also accommodates the doctrine of legislative

---

62 *R v Secretary of State for Transport, ex p Factortame and Others (No 2)* [1991] 1 AC 603 (HL); see, also, *R v Secretary of State for Employment, ex p Equal Opportunities Commission and Another* [1995] 1 AC 1 where the House of Lords granted a declaration that primary legislation was incompatible with European Community law and *Benkharbouche v Embassy of the Republic of Sudan* [2015] EWCA Civ 33, [2015] 3 WLR 301 where the Court of Appeal upheld the decision of the Employment Appeal Tribunal to disapply provisions of the State Immunity Act 1978 to the extent that they conflicted with the Charter of Fundamental Rights of the European Union Art 47 protecting their right to an effective remedy for a breach of rights protected by EU law.

63 As articulated by Dicey, *Introduction to the Study of the Law of the Constitution* (n 15) 3–4.

64 *R (Jackson) v Attorney-General* [2005] UKHL 56, [2006] 1 AC 262 [102]. Similar sentiments were expressed by Lord Hope [107], and Baroness Hale [59].

65 For example: Lord Woolf, '*Droit Public* – English Style' (n 24) 69; Sir John Laws, 'Law and Democracy' [1995] *PL* 72, 75–76, 81–90; Sir John Laws, 'The Constitution: Morals and Rights' [1996] *PL* 622, 628, 635.

supremacy. If the doctrine does not exist, then it might seem that the theories are no longer necessary.

This issue would appear to be more acute with regard to the *ultra vires* theory because – as shown above – it is argued that this theory is a logical necessity of the supervisory jurisdiction governing the exercise of power derived from a sovereign legislature. That is, under the theory, because Parliament may make any law whatsoever – including one giving, say, a Minister the power to breach the standards of good administration – the application of those standards to discretionary power derived from statute must be assumed to be intended by Parliament.[66] If, however, Parliament is not free to legislate to enable a donee of power to breach these standards, then their application need not be assumed to be derived from Parliament.

The supporters of the *ultra vires* theory have attempted to address this issue. They argue that, even if the legislative competence of Parliament is limited, this would only prohibit extreme forms of legislation such as a statute completely denying access to the courts or attacking democratic fundamentals. Outside of such extremes, Parliament would still have full legislative capacity. They then claim that a statute amending the standards of good administration or permitting them to be transgressed would not amount to such extreme legislation and so would still be within Parliament's legislative competence. If Parliament retains this capacity, even if its legislative competence is attenuated in other ways, then the supporters of the *ultra vires* theory argue that we must still assume the application of the standards of good administration to statutorily derived public power to be intended by Parliament.[67] In short, the *ultra vires* theory would still be necessary to explain the exercise of the supervisory jurisdiction even with a legislature that has limited sovereignty.

Allan challenges this response. He rejects the distinction, on which the *ultra vires* theorists rely, between extreme legislation violating a constitutional fundamental and more modest provisions authorising one or more of the standards of good administration to be set aside. He accepts that some contraventions may be more serious than others. However, the standards of good administration help to preclude arbitrary treatment at the hands of the state and so go to the very heart of the rule of law. In any particular case, their infringement may be as objectionable as any other challenge to the constitutional order. For this reason, he contends, as with any constitutional fundamental, their abrogation should be considered to be outside the legislative competence of Parliament.[68]

---

66 Chapter Three pp 31–32.
67 Mark C Elliott, 'The Demise of Parliamentary Sovereignty? The Implications for Justifying Judicial Review' (1999) 115 *LQR* 119, 130–136; Elliott, *The Constitutional Foundations of Judicial Review* (n 51) 73–80; Forsyth and Elliott, 'The Legitimacy of Judicial Review' (n 19) 291–296.
68 TRS Allan, *Constitutional Justice: A Liberal Theory of the Rule of Law* (OUP 2001) 209–210.

Review of non-statutory power

I have argued above and in the preceding chapter that the *raison d'être* of both the *ultra vires* and common law theories is to provide a rationalisation of judicial review which accommodates the requirements of parliamentary sovereignty. For this reason, the focus of the dialogue that has taken place between the supporters of these two theories has been on the review of power derived from statute. However, the judicial review jurisdiction also extends to non-statutory power such as *de facto* power or power derived from the Royal prerogative. Because of this, the exponents of the two theories attempt to explain the review of such power.

Under the common law theory, judicial review is seen as an inherent jurisdiction of the courts to supervise the exercise of discretionary public power. It therefore applies to all public power whatever its source, statutory or non-statutory. Under the *ultra vires* theory, we are asked to assume that when Parliament grants a discretionary public power it intends it to be exercised in accordance with the rule of law including the standards of good administration.[69] Supporters of this latter theory also claim that judicial review of non-statutory power may be explained as the courts' ensuring obedience to the rule of law.[70] However, the advocates of this theory have been criticised as offering no good reason why this version of the rule of law should be preferred over any other, 'which is plainly problematic given the wide variety of possible definitions of the rule of law ranging from the purely procedural to the fully substantive'.[71]

Review of non-statutory power has also been justified by the *ultra vires* theorists as being the review of monopolistic power. Forsyth and Whittle write: 'there is a common law principle that prevents the abuse of monopoly power and that is the justification for judicial intervention in non-statutory cases'.[72] Forsyth notes that there is a common law duty imposed on the owners of monopolies to make only reasonable charges for the use of their properties, or for the provision of services. Building on this, he asks, 'why should the common law not impose on those who exercise monopoly power . . . a more general duty to act reasonably, for instance, to heed the rules of natural justice, not to act irrationally and not to abuse their powers?'[73] It is, therefore, Forsyth's suggestion that the ability of the common law to control the abuse of monopolies explains the power of the courts

---

69 Chapter Three p 33.

70 Elliott, 'The Ultra Vires Doctrine in a Constitutional Setting' (n 52) 154–156; Elliott, *The Constitutional Foundations of Judicial Review* (n 51) Chapter 5.

71 Nicholas Bamforth, 'Ultra Vires and Institutional Interdependence' in Christopher F Forsyth (ed), *Judicial Review and the Constitution* (Hart Publishing 2000) 124 (citation omitted). Elliott agrees that, 'The precise content of the rule of law is notoriously controversial', *The Constitutional Foundations of Judicial Review* (ibid) 100. Broadly speaking, procedural conceptions of the rule of law are prescriptive about how the law is made and applied but are silent on its content; substantive conceptions are prescriptive about both content and procedure.

72 'Judicial Creativity and Judicial Legitimacy in Administrative Law' (n 50) 453, fn 3.

73 'Of Fig Leaves and Fairy Tales' (n 7) 125.

to judicially review bodies such as the Panel on Take-Overs and Mergers.[74] Such bodies, he writes, 'clearly exercise monopoly powers'.[75] He also notes, though, that not all monopolies are susceptible to judicial review: the courts are reluctant to subject religious or sports governing bodies, which are non-governmental, to the supervisory jurisdiction. He goes on to argue that the common law does not draw a distinction between governmental monopolies and other monopolies. The implication would seem to be that judicial review should be expanded so that the exercise of all monopolistic power is susceptible to the supervisory jurisdiction.[76]

There are a number of problems with this explanation. As we have seen, when confronted with the fact that the courts do not review all monopolies, Forsyth implies that the courts are mistaken and should expand the power of review to all bodies exercising a monopolistic form of power. However, perhaps the more obvious explanation is not that the courts are mistaken, but that review of such power is not dependent upon whether it is monopolistic or not. Moreover, it is not clear what is meant by the word 'monopoly'. It is not apparent, for instance, over what size of geographical area one would need to be the sole provider of a good or service in order to be considered a monopoly.[77]

Jowell also criticises the attempt to explain the review of non-statutory power as the review of monopolistic power. He writes:

> To say, as Forsyth does, that such review is justified on the basis of the power of the courts to control monopoly power, begs a myriad of questions about the competence of the courts to pursue a policy about the appropriate role of competition in an economy.[78]

In addition to questioning whether the courts are competent to decide on, and pursue, a policy on the operation of competition, we may also challenge Forsyth's rationalisation on a related point. From Forsyth's own examples it is clear that the 'almost forgotten' jurisdiction to control monopoly power was a jurisdiction to prevent such monopolies from exploiting their position to charge unreasonable prices for goods or services. Thus, when viewed in terms of policy and social function, it would seem to be a jurisdiction to prevent economic exploitation. I

---

74 *R v Panel on Take-Overs and Mergers, ex p Datafin and Another* [1987] QB 815 (CA); *R v Panel on Take-Overs and Mergers, ex p Guinness* [1990] 1 QB 146 (CA). As the name suggests, the Panel performs a regulative function in the London Stock Exchange policing, among other things, takeover bids to secure the fair treatment of all shareholders.

75 'Of Fig Leaves and Fairy Tales' (n 7) 125.

76 ibid 126. Lord Woolf also supports this argument, see '*Droit Public* – English Style' (n 24) 63–64.

77 A possible definition of 'monopolistic' is given by Pannick. He writes that a body should be susceptible to judicial review if it has 'such a de facto monopoly over an important area of public life that an individual has no effective choice but to comply with [its] rules, regulations and decisions in order to operate in that area', David Pannick, 'Who is Subject to Judicial Review and in Respect of What?' [1992] *PL* 1, 3. However, he also notes the cases where this approach has not been followed, ibid 3–4.

78 'Of Vires and Vacuums: The Constitutional Context of Judicial Review' (n 9) 459 (citation omitted).

58 *Intention, Supremacy and Judicial Review*

noted that Forsyth asks, 'why should the common law not impose on those who exercise monopoly power . . . a more general duty to act reasonably, for instance, to heed the rules of natural justice, not to act irrationally and not to abuse their powers?'[79] We may now answer that we should not necessarily assume that a power to prevent economic exploitation should be extended to control the abuse of power generally.

The rule of law

The rule of law is central to both the *ultra vires* theory and the common law theory.[80] In both, the doctrine is used – at least in part – to legitimise the courts' development and application of the standards of good administration. In addition, it is implicit in both theories that the rule of law requires that the exercise of public power, but not private power, is subject to review. It therefore justifies the scope of review.

It will be argued in this section that, in both theories, the legitimation provided by the rule of law is Dworkinian in its approach. Yet, it will be argued that, for the *ultra vires* theory, this means that it conflicts with the positivism that is implicit in that theory. It will also be contended that this inherent positivism means that the *ultra vires* theory corresponds to a strong conception of the separation of powers doctrine.

The adherence to the rule of law – that there should be government according to law – is, of course, part of the rationale for the modern law of judicial review. Lord Hoffmann states: 'The principles of judicial review give effect to the rule of law. They ensure that administrative decisions will be taken rationally, in accordance with a fair procedure and within the powers conferred by Parliament'.[81]

The rule of law is not used in either theory to prescribe the content of the standards of good administration; indeed, Elliott makes it clear that it is too vague to be utilised in this way.[82] It is used, rather, to justify the courts' development and application of these standards. As we have seen, the *ultra vires* theorists contend that we must assume that Parliament intends the exercise of discretionary public power that it grants to correspond with the rule of law which includes the standards of good administration.[83] We have also seen that, under this theory,

79 Text to n 73.

80 Chapter Three pp 33, 35 and 38–39.

81 *R (Alconbury Developments Ltd and Others) v Secretary of State for the Environment, Transport and the Regions* [2001] UKHL 23, [2003] 2 AC 295 [73]. The importance of judicial review for keeping the government within its lawful bounds, and thereby maintaining the rule of law, is evident in the government's recent decision not to proceed with its suggestion to tighten the sufficient interest requirement; see Baroness Hale, 'Who Guards the Guardians?' [2014] *JR* 1 and John McGarry, 'The Importance of an Expansive Test of Standing' [2014] *JR* 60.

82 *The Constitutional Foundations of Judicial Review* (n 51) 104–106. Similarly, Craig writes: 'The detailed elaboration of the rule of law is a complex issue. It is wholly unrealistic to suggest that this can be explicated within the same debate as to the theoretical foundations of the subject', 'Constitutional Foundations, the Rule of Law and Supremacy' (n 9) 95.

83 Chapter Three p 33.

the legislature is assumed to have granted the courts an imprimatur to develop and apply these standards; the implication being that this should be undertaken in accordance with the rule of law.[84] Similarly, the advocates of the common law theory argue that the courts develop and apply the standards in conformity with the requirements of the rule of law and of justice.[85]

This explanation of the development and application of the standards of good administration echoes Dworkin. Simply put, Dworkin holds that a judge will interpret a legal rule, or decide a new case, in the way that best fits the legal norms and principles inherent in the society in which the case is heard.[86]

It is unsurprising that the arguments of Craig, the leading common law theorist, correspond with Dworkin. I noted in Chapter Two that he declares himself to be a supporter of Dworkin[87] and explicitly states that the common law theory 'naturally lends itself to [a Dworkinian] approach'.[88]

It is perhaps surprising, though, that the *ultra vires* theory also seems to correspond to the Dworkinian approach. The resonance with Dworkin can be clearly seen in Elliott's statement that, 'in effecting judicial review, the courts are seeking to *give effect to a body of norms which lies at the core of the British legal culture*' (emphasis added).[89] That is, like Dworkin, he suggests that the courts should draw on norms and principles inherent in the legal system when deciding cases.

In other respects, however, the *ultra vires* theory is similar to Austinian positivism by which it is claimed that

> Every positive law, or every law simply and strictly so called, is set, *directly or circuitously*, by a sovereign person or other body, to a member or members of the independent political society wherein that person or body is sovereign or supreme (emphasis added).[90]

It will be seen that there is a close coincidence between Austin's view that all law must emanate 'directly or circuitously' from a sovereign power and the view of the supporters of the *ultra vires* theory that control of all public power derived from statute must be authorised – directly or tacitly – by the sovereign Parliament.[91] Allan would appear to agree with this analysis. He, too, notes that

---

84 ibid.

85 ibid p 35.

86 Dworkin, *Taking Rights Seriously* (n 1) 225; Ronald Dworkin, 'How Law is like Literature' in Ronald Dworkin, *A Matter of Principle* (OUP 1985) 151–152, 158–162; Ronald Dworkin, *Law's Empire* (Hart Publishing 1998) 225.

87 Chapter Two p 20.

88 'The Common Law, Shared Power and Judicial Review' (n 23) 241 (citation omitted).

89 *The Constitutional Foundations of Judicial Review* (n 51) 104.

90 John Austin, *The Province of Jurisprudence Determined* (W E Rumble ed, 5th edn, CUP 1995) 285.

91 Indeed, this coincidence is perhaps even more apparent in Dworkin's description of Austin's positivism: 'people with political power have made the judges their lieutenants and tacitly adopt their commands as their own', *Law's Empire* (n 86) 34.

60 Intention, Supremacy and Judicial Review

the view of legislative supremacy which holds that the judicial review jurisdiction is founded on parliamentary intent is itself based on Austinian legal positivism.[92]

The interesting thing here is that Dworkin's approach was developed as a counter to positivism.[93] Indeed, the tension between positivism and Dworkin is reflected in the approach of the *ultra vires* theorists. On the one hand, they ask us to theoretically assume a positivist approach: that the development of judicial review, when used to control public power derived from statute, has a definite sovereign source – Parliament. However, they explain the reality in a Dworkinian way by arguing that the standards of good administration are developed by the courts in accordance with norms that are inherent within our legal system.

The positivism inherent in the *ultra vires* theory also means that it corresponds to a strong conception of the separation of powers doctrine. The rationale of the doctrine is to prevent a concentration of power in one person or group leading to tyranny[94] and this is achieved, in part, by there being a system of checks and balances among the different arms of the state to act as a brake on power.[95] In the United Kingdom, the operation of judicial review is one of the ways in which this aspect of the separation of powers doctrine is fulfilled: 'In seeking to ensure that the executive does not exceed the scope of its legal powers, judicial review of administrative action is an important mechanism by which the separation of powers is upheld in the UK'.[96]

Of course, the doctrine also requires that there should be separation: that the three functions of government – legislative, executive and judicial – should be performed by three different arms of the state.[97] Lord Mustill has expressed it as existing in the United Kingdom in the following way: 'It is a feature of the peculiarly British conception of the separation of powers that Parliament, the executive and the courts have each their distinct and *largely exclusive* domain' (emphasis added).[98]

---

92 Allan, *Law, Liberty and Justice* (n 12) 16–19. See, also, Allan, *The Sovereignty of Law* (n 40) 229 where Allan states that the focus on sources of law is 'characteristic of legal positivism'.

93 This is clear throughout Dworkin's work and is explicitly stated in *Taking Rights Seriously* (n 1) vii, 22.

94 One of the best known expressions of this sentiment can be found in Montesquieu's work: Baron de Montesquieu, *The Spirit of the Laws* (T Nugent tr, Hafner Publishing Company 1949) 151–152. The doctrine may also augment the efficiency of government by ensuring that government bodies perform the tasks to which they are best suited.

95 Montesquieu writes: 'To prevent ... abuse, it is necessary from the very nature of things that power should be a check on power', ibid 150. However, Saunders writes: 'There is an open question whether this qualifies a system of separation of powers or completes it by "giving each department the necessary constitutional means ... to resist encroachment by the others"', Cheryl Saunders, 'Separation of Powers and the Judicial Branch' [2006] *JR* 337 [6].

96 Elliott, *The Constitutional Foundations of Judicial Review* (n 51) 226.

97 However, it is questionable whether it is possible to clearly demarcate these three functions. Also, it is worth noting that Tomkins argues that the position in the United Kingdom, when viewed from a historical perspective, is that there is not so much a separation of powers – ie: a separation of these three functions – but, rather, a separation of power between the Crown and Parliament: Adam Tomkins, *Public Law* (OUP 2003) 33–60.

98 *R v Secretary of State for the Home Department, ex p Fire Brigades Union and Others* [1995] 2 AC 513 (HL) 567.

Themes of the debate 61

This exclusivity may be taken to mean a number of things. It may simply be an acknowledgement of the rule that the courts 'should not encroach upon the exclusive province of proceedings in the Houses of Parliament'.[99] It might also mean that, for some decisions, the courts should be slow to substitute their judgment for that of the government or Parliament. This is simply an appreciation that 'Independence makes the courts more suited to deciding some kinds of questions and being elected makes the legislature or executive more suited to deciding others'.[100]

Exclusivity might additionally be taken to mean that there should be strict functional demarcation between the different arms of the state. For instance, Bradley and Ewing write: 'The concept of "separation" may mean ... that one organ of government should not exercise the functions of another, for example, that ministers should not have legislative powers'.[101] It may be thought that this functional separation precludes the courts from engaging in law making. Barendt, for instance, claims that both Lord Diplock and Lord Scarman used the doctrine of separation of powers to argue for judicial restraint on the basis that, 'the role of the courts is not to make law, but to interpret the words used by the legislature'.[102]

The assumption on which the *ultra vires* theory rests is commensurate with this latter view in that it seems to deny the courts an independent law-making power, at least as far as judicial review of public power derived from primary legislation is concerned. As adumbrated in Chapter Three, under the theory we *must* assume that any jurisdiction that the courts have to develop and apply the standards of good administration to such power is granted by Parliament, explicitly or implicitly.[103] Thus, for statutorily derived public power at least, the law creating function is Parliament's alone or must be seen to be authorised, implicitly or explicitly, by Parliament. It is for this reason that the theory seems to adhere to a strict, functionally exclusive, conception of the separation of powers doctrine.

99 Lord Woolf of Barnes, 'Judicial Review – The Tensions between the Executive and the Judiciary' (1998) 114 *LQR* 579, 581. A good example of the application of this rule can be found in *R v Parliamentary Commissioner for Standards, ex p Al Fayed* [1998] 1 WLR 669 (CA) 673 where the Court of Appeal upheld the first instance decision that decisions of the Commissioner are not suitable to scrutiny by the courts because they are concerned with activities inside Parliament.

100 *R (Prolife Alliance) v British Broadcasting Corporation* [2003] UKHL 23, [2004] 1 AC 185 [76] (Lord Hoffmann). Laws LJ has stated that the relative 'constitutional responsibility' of the executive, legislature and the courts may be relevant in deciding whether the courts should intervene: *International Transport Roth GmbH and Others v Secretary of State for the Home Department* [2002] EWCA Civ 158, [2003] QB 728 [85]–[87].

101 A W Bradley and K D Ewing, *Constitutional and Administrative Law* (14th edn, Longman 2007) 84. In the latest edition of their work, Bradley, Ewing and Knight use a slightly different example: 'the concept of "separation" [means] ... one branch should not exercise the functions of another (so, for example, ministers should not have power to create criminal offences or to commit offenders to prison)', A W Bradley, K D Ewing and CJS Knight, *Constitutional and Administrative Law* (16th edn, Pearson Education, 2014) 92.

102 Eric Barendt, 'Separation of Powers and Constitutional Government' [1995] *PL* 599, 616. Their Lordships' comments may be found in *Duport Steel v Sirs* [1980] 1 WLR 142 (HL) 157, 169.

103 Chapter Three pp 31–34.

62 Intention, Supremacy and Judicial Review

Moreover, this denial of the courts' independent law-making function does not appear to recognise that the adjudicative function necessarily involves the creation of law and that, as Gadamer argues, the application of legal rules is 'always a productive activity'.[104] Indeed, it is over forty years since Lord Reid famously dismissed as a 'fairy tale' the contention that judges do not make law but simply declare it[105] yet the supporters of the *ultra vires* theory wish to maintain the fairy tale that the development and application of the standards of good administration to statutorily derived public power is intended by Parliament. As Laws states: 'We do not need the fig-leaf any more'.[106]

There are, then, a number of tensions within the *ultra vires* theory. Its proponents explain the reality of the courts' development of the standards of good administration in a Dworkinian way. However, the theory also seems to correlate to Austinian positivism. This positivist approach, itself, corresponds to a strict, functionally exclusive conception of the separation of powers doctrine. Yet, this, in turn, conflicts with the view that the adjudicative function necessarily involves law making. The same tensions are not, of course, to be found within the common law theory. This is because the common law theorists recognise an independent law-making role for the courts.

Ouster clauses

While both the *ultra vires* theory and the common law theory attempt to provide an explanation of judicial review which accommodates the requirements of parliamentary sovereignty, the courts' treatment of ouster clauses places that rationalisation in doubt. It is little wonder, then, that such clauses are one of the main themes in the debate that has taken place between the adherents of these theories.

An ouster clause is a provision in an Act of Parliament which appears to limit or exclude the courts' supervisory or appellate jurisdiction on a particular matter. There are essentially two types: limited time and total ouster clauses. The former commonly allow a challenge to be made within a prescribed period of time – often six weeks. The courts' jurisdiction is excluded after this. The latter excludes the courts' jurisdiction over a particular issue altogether. The former are interpreted faithfully, to give effect to their plain meaning; this is not the case with the latter.

The approach commonly taken with total ouster clauses is typified in *Anisminic Ltd v Foreign Compensation Commission*.[107] In that case, an application was made to review a decision by the Foreign Compensation Commission. Section 4(4) of the Foreign Compensation Act 1950 reads: 'The determination by the Commission of any application made to them under this Act *shall not be called in*

---

104 Chapter Two pp 12–13.
105 Lord Reid, 'The Judge as Law-Maker' (1972) 12 *JSPTL* 22, 22.
106 'Law and Democracy' (n 65) 79.
107 [1969] 2 AC 147 (HL).

question in any court of law' (emphasis added). While this would seem to preclude the supervisory jurisdiction, the majority of the House of Lords held that the clause did not prevent the courts reviewing *ultra vires* decisions. They held that such decisions are outside of the powers granted by the legislation. This led to the conclusion that these decisions are not *actual* determinations but are merely *purported* determinations and so are not protected by the ouster clause. They further held that, if Parliament had intended to oust the jurisdiction of the courts, there would be 'something much more specific than the bald statement that a determination shall not be called in question in any court of law'.[108] In recent times, several judges have gone further than this and indicated – both curially and extra-curially – that if a statute explicitly stated that the courts' supervisory jurisdiction was not to apply to certain cases, then the courts would overrule it.[109]

While the courts do not appear to give effect to the clear meaning of total ouster clauses, they seem to take a different approach with limited time clauses. With regard to these, Mann LJ has stated:

> When [such clauses] . . . are used, then the legislative intention is that questions as to invalidity may be raised on the specified grounds in the prescribed time and in the prescribed manner, but that otherwise the jurisdiction of the court is excluded in the interest of certainty.[110]

That is, the courts hold that such clauses prohibit review outside of the prescribed time period. Thus, in contrast to total ouster clauses, the courts will allow limited time clauses to restrict their supervisory jurisdiction in precisely the way that the provision seems to require.

It would appear, then, that where legislation allows some – albeit limited – time within which the supervisory jurisdiction may operate, the courts will give effect to it. However, where an Act of Parliament seems to wholly preclude the jurisdiction, the courts are unwilling to adhere to it. This treatment of total ouster clauses brings into question the courts' compliance with the doctrine of parliamentary sovereignty and, in turn, the *ultra vires* theory and the common law theory, both of which attempt to reconcile the exercise of the supervisory jurisdiction with that doctrine. Elliott, writing with regard to the *ultra vires* theory, accurately identifies the dilemma:

> if the courts are entitled, by ignoring an ouster clause, to effect review contrary to Parliament's will, it makes no sense to say that the vindication

---

108 ibid 170 (Lord Reid). See, also, 200 (Lord Pearce).

109 *R (Jackson) v Attorney-General* (n 64) [103] (Lord Steyn); Lord Woolf, '*Droit Public* – English Style' (n 24) 69; Laws, 'Law and Democracy' (n 65) 90; see, also, Joshua Rozenburg, 'Law Lords Raise Stakes on Asylum', *The Daily Telegraph* (London, 5 March 2004) <http://www.telegraph.co.uk/news/main.jhtml?xml=/news/2004/03/05/nasy05.xml> accessed 25 September 2006; John McGarry, 'Parliamentary Sovereignty, Judges and the Asylum and Immigration (Treatment of Claimants, etc) Bill' (2005) 26 *Liv LR* 1.

110 *R v Cornwall County Council, ex p Huntington and Another* [1992] 3 All ER 566 (QBD) 575.

64 Intention, Supremacy and Judicial Review

of legislative intention forms any part of the constitutional justification for review.[111]

This issue will be explored more fully in Chapters Five and Six. Here, the way in which the treatment of ouster clauses is explained in, and even used to support, both theories will be detailed and critiqued. I begin with the *ultra vires* theory.

It will be remembered that under the *ultra vires* theory we are asked to assume that Parliament intends the courts to exercise the supervisory jurisdiction in accordance with the rule of law.[112] Elliott builds on this claiming that the rule of law is strongly in favour of access to the courts. If a statutory provision – such as an ouster clause – tries to exclude access, then tension ensues:

> Two countervailing forces are therefore at work. The courts must attempt to find the right constitutional balance between the prima facie meaning of the provision and the strong preference for access to justice which the rule of law embodies.[113]

That is, the interpretation of ouster clauses, in a way which maintains access to the courts, can be rationalised as the courts attempting to resolve the tension between the plain meaning of the legislation and the rule of law. The same argument may also be used to explain the courts' attitude to limited time clauses. Because these allow review for a period of time – and so do not wholly exclude the jurisdiction – there is less tension between the statute and the rule of law. It is for this reason, Elliott claims, that the courts are able to give effect to the plain meaning of such clauses.[114]

Elliott attempts to retain deference to legislative supremacy in this explanation of the courts' treatment of ouster clauses by stating: 'any *irreconcilable* conflict between the intention of Parliament and the rule of law must be resolved in favour of the former' (emphasis in original).[115] It must surely be the case, however, that total ouster clauses represent such an irreconcilable conflict. The supporters of the *ultra vires* theory, including Elliott, concede that the plain meaning of such

---

111 *The Constitutional Foundations of Judicial Review* (n 51) 32.

112 Chapter Three p 33.

113 'The Ultra Vires Doctrine in a Constitutional Setting' (n 52) 151. See, also, Elliott, *The Constitutional Foundations of Judicial Review* (n 51) 121–125.

114 'the courts give effect to the literal meaning of clauses which preclude review only after a certain period of time: in this area, there is less tension between the plain meaning of the provision and the dictates of the rule of law, because judicial review is not precluded altogether by the clause', Elliott, 'The Ultra Vires Doctrine in a Constitutional Setting' (ibid) 152 (citation omitted).

115 ibid 153 (citation omitted). See, also, Elliott, *The Constitutional Foundations of Judicial Review* (n 51) 124. Allan agrees to some extent, stating that in ordinary cases, and in ordinary circumstances, any apparent conflict between an Act of Parliament and, say, the rule of law can be resolved interpretively: 'Constitutional Dialogue and the Justification of Judicial Review' (n 50) 569–573; 'The Constitutional Foundations of Judicial Review: Conceptual Conundrum or Interpretative Inquiry?' [2002] *CLJ* 87, 102–105.

Themes of the debate 65

clauses is that the supervisory jurisdiction should be excluded.[116] An interpretation, therefore, that such clauses do not exclude the jurisdiction is not so much a reconciliation between the requirements of parliamentary sovereignty and the rule of law but the overriding of the former to accommodate the latter. Indeed, Wade and Forsyth, two leading proponents of the *ultra vires* theory, write of the treatment of ouster clauses: 'The policy of the courts thus becomes one of total disobedience to Parliament'.[117]

This non-reconciliation is also puzzling because, as we have seen, the rationale of the *ultra vires* theory is that parliamentary sovereignty should not be infringed. The supporters of the theory appear to claim that the courts' interpretation of ouster clauses fulfils the intention of the legislature; Elliott writes that such clauses were '*never meant* to sanction interference with access to justice' (emphasis added).[118] Yet, if the interpretation of ouster clauses does amount to 'total disobedience to Parliament', it is difficult to see how this can be the case.[119] Indeed, Elliot's assertion is contradicted by Ringhand who states that the clear legislative command represented by the clause in *Anisminic* clearly prohibited the courts' from reviewing the decision in question and that this is supported by the clause's legislative history.[120] Furthermore, this interpretation also conflicts with the assertion that under the *ultra vires* theory the courts recognise 'that Parliament is free to dispense with the judicially developed grounds of judicial review'.[121]

Moreover, and significantly, the rationalisation of the courts' treatment of ouster clauses proffered by the supporters of the *ultra vires* theory prioritises an artificial, presumed intent that access to the courts should be maintained over explicit legislative language that the courts' jurisdiction should be excluded.[122] To be sure, the *ultra vires* theorists ask us to accept that the courts breach the requirements of parliamentary sovereignty when they act contrary to this

---

116 'In no sense can it be maintained that the House of Lords simply gave effect to the plain meaning of the preclusive provision in *Anisminic*', Elliott, *The Constitutional Foundations of Judicial Review* (ibid) 31, 121; also, Wade and Forsyth, *Administrative Law* (n 13) 713.

117 ibid 719. See, also, 720–721, 722; HRW Wade, 'Constitutional Realities and Judicial Prudence' in Christopher F Forsyth (ed), *Judicial Review and the Constitution* (Hart Publishing 2000) 431. It should be noted that Elliott distances himself from such assertions: *The Constitutional Foundations of Judicial Review* (ibid) 32. Allan suggests that 'Perhaps talk of disobedience is too histrionic', *Law, Liberty and Justice* (n 12) 65.

118 *The Constitutional Foundations of Judicial Review* (ibid) 144. He also writes that the courts interpret such legislation 'based on the presumption that Parliament does not intend to abrogate access to justice', ibid.

119 David Dyzenhaus, 'Form and Substance in the Rule of Law: A Democratic Justification for Judicial Review?' in Christopher F Forsyth (ed), *Judicial Review and the Constitution* (Hart Publishing 2000) 155; Michael Taggart, 'Ultra Vires as Distraction' in Christopher F Forsyth (ed), *Judicial Review and the Constitution* (Hart Publishing 2000) 429.

120 Lori A Ringhand, 'Fig Leaves, Fairy Tales, and Constitutional Foundations: Debating Judicial Review in Britain' (2005) 43(3) *Columbia Journal of Transnational Law* 865, 877.

121 Forsyth, 'Of Fig Leaves and Fairy Tales' (n 7) 136.

122 Ringhand and Chu make the same point: Ringhand, 'Fig Leaves, Fairy Tales, and Constitutional Foundations' (n 120) 877, 880; Chu, 'One Controversy, Two Jurisdictions' (n 38) para 13.

66 Intention, Supremacy and Judicial Review

presumed intent but not when they act contrary to the plain meaning of the legislation.

Adherents of the *ultra vires* theory also argue that its abandonment would lead to a weakening of judicial review where these clauses are concerned. It is worth noting as a preliminary point that, in making this argument, the *ultra vires* theorists are implicitly supporting the courts' interpretation of such clauses. They contend that if the theory was not considered to be the basis of judicial review, then ouster clauses would prevent challenges based on a breach of the standards of good administration. This is because they protect only determinations made within the powers granted by the enabling Act.[123]

An example might be useful here. Under the *ultra vires* theory, the rules of natural justice, say, are assumed to be derived from the enabling Act, or at least derived from a general intention of Parliament concerning the operation of the Act. Thus, any determination made in breach of these rules will have been made outside of the jurisdiction granted by the Act. This would make the determination a mere purported determination and it would therefore not be protected by the ouster clause. This means that, as with the *Anisminic* case, the courts would be able to review the decision. In contrast, the abandonment of the *ultra vires* theory would mean that the rules of natural justice derive from the common law and not from the intention of Parliament. Thus, a determination made in breach of the rules of natural justice would be unlawful at common law but would be within the jurisdiction granted by the enabling Act. It would, therefore, be an *actual*, rather than a purported, determination. This would, in consequence, mean that the decision would be protected by the ouster clause and so would not be reviewable by the courts.

In support of the argument that the abandonment of the *ultra vires* theory would result in a weakening of judicial review, Forsyth is able to point to similar consequences occurring in South Africa. He notes that in the South African case, *Straatspresident en andere v United Democratic Front en 'n ander*,[124] a rule against vague regulations was held to be derived from Roman-Dutch common law, rather than the intention of the legislature. This, in turn, resulted in a finding that an ouster clause was able to preclude the supervisory jurisdiction being exercised over such regulations.[125]

In response to this contention, we must question why Parliament would use legislative language which seems to preclude judicial review – indeed, why enact such provisions at all – if the supervisory jurisdiction is to continue unhindered?

---

123 Forsyth, 'Of Fig Leaves and Fairy Tales' (n 7) 129–131; Forsyth and Elliott, 'The Legitimacy of Judicial Review' (n 19) 288.

124 1988(4) S.A. 830(A).

125 Forsyth, 'Of Fig Leaves and Fairy Tales' (n 7) 129–131. Barber argues that the South African example to which Forsyth refers had more to do with the political sympathies of the judges than a result demanded by logic, Nicholas W Barber, 'The Academic Mythologians' (2001) 21 *OJLS* 369, 378. If so, one might similarly infer that the courts' current treatment of ouster clauses is similarly a political decision and is unlikely to be different whatever theoretical justification for judicial review is posited.

Themes of the debate   67

This question has become more imperative because of the development of the law in this area. At one time it was thought that a decision-maker might make an error of law but that this would not necessarily mean they had stepped outside of their jurisdiction. Because such a decision would be within jurisdiction it would be an actual – rather than a purported – determination and so would be protected from review by the clause. In short, such clauses would protect some decisions from review and so they would not be wholly otiose.

It is now clear, though, that all errors of law take the decision-maker out of jurisdiction.[126] The same would appear to be true for factual errors.[127] All decisions containing such errors will, therefore, be susceptible to review, even if there is an ouster clause in play. This means that there are no longer any areas on which such clauses may operate. This is a point accepted by the *ultra vires* supporters; Wade and Forsyth write: '"shall not be questioned" clauses must now be totally ineffective. Every error of law is jurisdictional; and error of fact, if material, is either jurisdictional or unreviewable anyway'.[128] This again indicates that the courts' treatment of ouster clauses amounts to a 'total disobedience to Parliament' which consequently suggests that such treatment is inconsistent with the intention of the legislature and, in turn, the *ultra vires* theory.

Advocates of the common law theory do not really attempt to reconcile the courts' treatment of ouster clauses with parliamentary sovereignty. They simply claim that, when confronted with them, the courts implicitly draw on a common law principle that legislation which seeks to limit access to the courts should be strictly construed.[129] However, this contention is not consistent with their asser-

---

126 *Re Racal Communications* [1981] AC 374 (HL) 383; *O'Reilly and Others v Mackman and Others* [1983] 2 AC 237 (HL) 278; *R v Lord President of the Privy Council, ex p Page* [1993] AC 682 (HL) 701, 706; *Boddington v British Transport Police* (n 58) 158 (Lord Irvine LC); *Regina (Lumba) v Secretary of State for the Home Department (JUSTICE and another intervening)* [2011] UKSC 12, [2012] 1 AC 245, [66] (Lord Dyson); *Cart v The Upper Tribunal* [2011] UKSC 28, [2012] 1 AC 663; Craig, 'Ultra Vires and the Foundations of Judicial Review' (n 9) 69–70; Wade and Forsyth, *Administrative Law* (n 13) 264–267, though the authors suggest that there may be some exceptions with regard to inferior courts and peculiar jurisdictions, eg ecclesiastic courts (267–268).

127 Error of precedent fact will take a decision-maker out of jurisdiction; Wade and Forsyth state that the 'earliest recognisable case appears to be *Terry v Huntington* (1668) Hardr. 480', ibid 208, fn 10. Misunderstanding of a material fact will be considered to be a ground of review: *R v Criminal Injuries Compensation Board, ex p A* [1999] 2 AC 330 (HL) 344–345 (Lord Slynn); *Alconbury Developments* (n 81) [53] (Lord Slynn); *E v Secretary of State for the Home Department* [2004] EWCA Civ 49, [2004] QB 1044 [66]–[67], [91]. Where a factual determination is one about which competent decision-makers may reasonably disagree – perhaps because it is not objectively ascertainable – the courts should only intervene if the determination is such that no reasonable decision-maker could have arrived at it: *R v Monopolies and Mergers Commission, ex p South Yorkshire Passenger Transport Authority* [1993] 1 WLR 23 (HL) 32 (Lord Mustill); Rebecca A Williams, 'When is an Error not an Error? Reform of Jurisidictional Error of Law and Fact' [2007] *PL* 793, 798–801.

128 ibid 719 (citation omitted). Also, HWR Wade, *The Hamlyn Lectures: Constitutional Fundamentals* (Stevens 1980) 65.

129 Craig, 'Ultra Vires and the Foundations of Judicial Review' (n 9) 72–73; TRS Allan, 'The Rule of Law as the Foundation of Judicial Review' in Christopher F Forsyth (ed), *Judicial Review and the*

68   Intention, Supremacy and Judicial Review

tion that if Parliament were to plainly legislate to exclude judicial review, the courts would not exercise the supervisory jurisdiction. Craig writes: 'if Parliament *were* to state explicitly in the enabling legislation that the minister should be thus empowered [to breach the standards of good administration] then judicial review would be correspondingly curtailed' (emphasis in original).[130] Ouster clauses must surely amount to such legislation and yet the courts clearly do not adhere to them.

The structural coherence of the *ultra vires* theory

I noted in Chapter Three that judicial review may be used to challenge a decision or secondary legislation that has been made unlawfully.[131] This is not the only route by which such decisions or legislation may be disputed. In the alternative, the citizen may simply engage in activity which, for example, secondary legislation has deemed illegal and, should any legal action be brought against her, use the unlawfulness of the provision in question as her defence. Proceeding in this way is known as collateral challenge. The supporters of the *ultra vires* theory argue that such challenges are possible only because of the assumptions on which the theory rests: that only an *ultra vires* exercise of power is void *ab initio*.

The reason for this is that, under the *ultra vires* theory, as shown above and in Chapter Three, we must assume that when Parliament grants a power to, say, enact secondary legislation, it intends that power to be exercised in accordance with the standards of good administration.[132] This assumption allows us to claim that secondary legislation enacted in breach of these standards has been made outside of the power conferred by the enabling statute and that, consequently, it has no, and never has had, lawful effect – it is void *ab initio*.[133] It is this void-ness that can be used as a defence in a court action which has been commenced because of a breach of such legislation.[134] That is, a defendant is able to claim that, because the legislation in question has never had lawful effect, it cannot be used as the basis for legal action against her.

The supporters of the *ultra vires* theory argue that such a defence would not

---

Constitution (Hart Publishing 2000) 417. Cf Elliott, *The Constitutional Foundations of Judicial Review* (n 51) 152–153.

130 'Ultra Vires and the Foundations of Judicial review' (ibid) 74. Also, Craig, 'Competing Models of Judicial Review' (n 9) 429, 437–438, 443, 444; Craig and Bamforth, 'Constitutional Analysis, Constitutional Principle and Judicial Review' (n 9) 767, 773–774, 777; Craig, 'Constitutional Foundations, the Rule of Law and Supremacy' (n 9) 93; Craig, 'The Common Law, Shared Power and Judicial Review' (n 23) 238, 251, 253.

131 Chapter Three pp 28–29.

132 Chapter Three p 33.

133 See, also, Allan, *The Sovereignty of Law* (n 40) 208, 214, 236.

134 Mark C Elliott, 'Fundamental Rights as Interpretative Constructs: The Constitutional Logic of the Human Rights Act 1998' in Christopher F Forsyth (ed), *Judicial Review and the Constitution* (Hart Publishing 2000) 283–285; Christopher F Forsyth, 'Showing the Fly the Way Out of the Flybottle: The Value of Formalism and Conceptual Reasoning in Administrative Law' [2007] *CLJ* 325, 338.

Themes of the debate 69

be available if we assume, as the common law theory asks us to, that the standards of good administration are derived from the common law rather than the assumed intention of Parliament. This is because, while the legislation in question may have been made in breach of these common law standards, it will not have been made in breach of the limits contained in the enabling Act. It follows from this that such legislation will be lawful until adjudged otherwise in judicial review proceedings. Consequently, a citizen would be unable to simply choose not to comply with its requirements and use its unlawfulness as a defence in any proceedings brought against her.[135]

This is the reason why it is claimed that the *ultra vires* theory is a logical corollary of allowing the citizen to collaterally challenge the use of public power. It will be recalled that its supporters also argue that the theory is a logical necessity of judicial review being used to control the exercise of public power derived from statute.[136] It would therefore seem that, for these supporters, parliamentary sovereignty, judicial review and collateral challenge must be rationalised in a way which is gapless and non-contradictory. Elliott refers to this as 'structural coherence' and writes that it is the 'principal claim which proponents of ultra vires make in favour of its retention as the justification for review of statutory power'.[137] Indeed, he goes further and contends that such coherence is '*essential* to a proper theory of the foundations of review' (emphasis added).[138] Yet, we have already seen that the courts interpret ouster clauses so that their supervisory jurisdiction is not excluded, an interpretation which is contrary to the plain meaning of these provisions. This must bring into question the supposition that it is possible to provide a seamless rationalisation of sovereignty and judicial review in the way in which the *ultra vires* theorists seem to attempt. In addition, the possibility of such a rationalisation may be challenged on the basis that remedies in judicial review are discretionary.

There are a number of remedies available in judicial review. Yet, even where a claim is successful, the courts have a discretion not to award a remedy.[139] Herein

---

135 Christopher F Forsyth, '"The Metaphysic of Nullity": Invalidity, Conceptual Reasoning and the Rule of Law' in Christopher F Forsyth and Ivan Hare (eds), *The Golden Metwand and the Crooked Cord: Essays on Public Law in Honour of Sir William Wade QC* (Clarendon Press 1998) 157; Elliott, 'Fundamental Rights as Interpretative Constructs' (ibid) 283–285; Mark C Elliott, 'Legislative Intention Versus Judicial Creativity? Administrative Law as a Co-operative Endeavour' in Christopher F Forsyth (ed), *Judicial Review and the Constitution* (Hart Publishing 2000) 364–368; Elliott, *The Constitutional Foundations of Judicial Review* (n 51) 157–161; Forsyth and Elliott, 'The Legitimacy of Judicial Review' (n 19) 288–289.

136 Chapter Three pp 31–32.

137 *The Constitutional Foundations of Judicial Review* (n 51) 24; see, also, 32.

138 ibid 35.

139 *R v Monopolies and Mergers Commission, ex p Argyll Group Plc* [1986] 1 WLR 763 (CA) 766; *R v Hillingdon LBC, ex p Pulhofer* [1986] AC 484 (HL) 518; Lord Justice Bingham, 'Should Public Law Remedies be Discretionary?' [1991] *PL* 64; Christopher F Forsyth, 'Collateral Challenge and the Foundations of Judicial Review: Orthodoxy Vindicated and Procedural Exclusivity Rejected' [1998] *PL* 364, 366; Wade and Forsyth, *Administrative Law* (n 13) 700–712. Christopher F Forsyth, 'The Rock and the Sand: Jurisdiction and Remedial Discretion' [2013] *JR* 360, para 1. Though it is not certain, it may be that if a body has acted in excess of jurisdiction on the face

70 *Intention, Supremacy and Judicial Review*

lies the problem. Let us imagine, for example, that secondary legislation has been enacted in breach of the standards of good administration. The *ultra vires* theorists' position would seem to be that such legislation is void *ab initio*. If so, by what right may the courts exercise their discretion to withhold a remedy, refuse to quash the legislation, and thereby leave it with lawful effect? That is, the logically gapless rationalisation of the supervisory jurisdiction that is seemingly used to argue that the *ultra vires* theory must be seen as the constitutional justification of judicial review would require the courts not to have a discretion over the granting of remedies. Lord Woolf makes a similar point:

> the doctrine of *ultra vires* does not for me sit comfortably with the ability of the court to refuse relief on discretionary grounds. If a decision was *ultra vires*, then it would normally follow that it was a nullity and that at any time it would be possible to challenge its validity and have it set aside.[140]

Forsyth has attempted to resolve the tension between the discretionary nature of remedies in judicial review and the rule of law.[141] He refers to the 2010 case of *HM Treasury v Ahmed and Others (No 2)*[142] where the Supreme Court refused an application by the Treasury to suspend the granting of remedies with regard to two Orders in Council which the Court had previously held to be unlawful. Lord Phillips stated:

> The problem with a suspension in this case is, however, that the court's order [granting the remedies], whenever it is made, will not alter the position in law. It will declare what that position is. It is true that it will also quash the [relevant orders], but these are provisions that are ultra vires and of no effect in law. The object of quashing them is to make it quite plain that this is the case.[143]

Forsyth argues that, if the granting of a remedy does 'not alter the position in law' – that is, that it does not make an act unlawful because it merely confirms the judgment of the court – then, by the same token, a discretionary refusal to grant a remedy cannot confer legality on an unlawful act: 'discretion cannot

---

of the record, a quashing order should be granted as of right: Bingham, 'Should Public Law Remedies be Discretionary?' 64, 75. Lord Reed suggests that the claimant's personal interest in the matter being challenged may be taken into account when considering whether the court should use its discretion to refuse a remedy and Lord Carnwath states that the discretionary nature of remedies is 'a necessary counterbalance to the widening of rules of standing', *AXA General Insurance Ltd and Others v HM Advocate and Others* [2011] UKSC 46, [2012] 1 AC 868 [95] and [103], respectively.

140 '*Droit Public* – English Style' (n 24) 65–66.
141 'The Rock and the Sand' (n 139).
142 [2010] UKSC 5, [2012] 2 AC 534.
143 ibid [4]. Lord Dyson MR concurs with the reasoning of Lord Phillips: *R (T) v Greater Manchester Chief Constable and others* [2013] EWCA Civ 25, [2013] 1 WLR 2515 [83].

Themes of the debate 71

deny invalidity'.[144] Forsyth does not disagree that the courts continue to have a discretion whether to grant remedies in judicial review[145] but he states that, where a court has ruled an act to be invalid, the refusal of a remedy cannot 'lend that act legal effect *de jure* or *de facto*'.[146] He concedes that his contentions are not explicitly found in the *Ahmed* judgment, but claims that they are a logical consequence of it.[147]

Forsyth's argument may support the structural coherence that is claimed for the *ultra vires* theory because, if correct, it confirms that unlawful decisions are, indeed, void *ab initio*. However, his argument also leaves the status of remedies in judicial review, particularly quashing orders, unclear. If a quashing order merely confirms a court's determination of illegality, such that their refusal does not confer lawful effect, *de jure* or *de facto*, onto a lawful act, then does it not also follow that the discretionary granting or withholding of a remedy is itself without lawful effect? Forsyth suggests this directly: 'the issue of a quashing order in fact quashes nothing'.[148] Yet, there is evidence that the courts continue to operate on the assumption that a finding of unlawfulness does not in itself quash a decision or act without the issuing of a remedy. This can be seen, for example, in the 2012 (ie two years after the judgment in *Ahmed* on which Forsyth relies) case of *R (Hurley and Moore) v Secretary of State for Business Innovation and Skills*[149] where the High Court held that, while there had been a breach of the requirements of the public sector equality duties, it would not be appropriate to, and the court would not, quash the regulations in question.

Moreover, Feldman convincingly argues that the case law does not support the proposition that a decision made in breach of the standards of good administration is necessarily void *ab initio*.[150] He suggests that the matter is governed by a number of factors including: legality, that no-one should be subject to coercion or penalty on the basis of a unlawful rule; legal certainty, that public bodies and others should be able to rely on the lawfulness of a rule or decision unless it is determined to be unlawful by a competent court; whether the breach complained of is substantial; the remedy being sought; and the desire to produce sensible and practical outcomes.

These questions about whether a breach of the standards of good administration inevitably result in a decision being considered void *ab initio*, along with questions about the discretionary nature of remedies and the courts' treatment of ouster clauses, surely leads to the conclusion that the *ultra vires* theory does not supply the 'structural coherence' which Elliott claims for it. This is problematic given that, as I have noted, he also maintains that such 'structural coherence' is

---

144 'The Rock and the Sand' (n 139) para 48.
145 ibid para 55.
146 ibid para 57.
147 ibid para 58.
148 ibid para 41.
149 [2012] EWHC 201 (Admin), [2012] HRLR 13.
150 David Feldman, 'Error of Law and Flawed Administrative Acts' [2014] *CLJ* 275

72 *Intention, Supremacy and Judicial Review*

'essential' and that it is the 'principal claim' which may be made in favour of the theory.

Conclusion

The purpose of this chapter has been to subject the two theories that are proposed as providing the constitutional justification of judicial review – the *ultra vires* theory and the common law theory – to critical analysis. In so doing, I have made a number of significant observations about the theories and the debate conducted in support of them.

I have argued that both theories share an inherent assumption that parliamentary sovereignty functions as a Dworkinian rule. Yet, I have also argued that the two theories are rationalised according to different conceptions of the doctrine of sovereignty. It is implicit in the *ultra vires* theory that the doctrine requires that the courts should not act contrary to the assumed intention of Parliament. In contrast, under the common law theory, the doctrine requires the courts to adhere to the language contained in an Act of Parliament.

I have also questioned the *ultra vires* theorists' reliance on the intention of Parliament. In the first place, it has been argued that rationalising judicial review as the courts' application of the will of the legislature diminishes the courts' role as interpreter. Second, it has been argued that it is neither desirable nor possible to divine the intention of Parliament. Indeed, it is not plausible to ascribe a particular intention to the legislature at all. Yet, those who support the *ultra vires* theory maintain that we must assume that Parliament intends the courts to develop and apply the standards of good administration in accordance with the rule of law and that this is the *only* plausible assumption to make. The impossibility of ascribing this, or any, specific intention to Parliament must therefore, once again, reduce the support on which the *ultra vires* theory rests.

Moreover, for both theories, we have seen that the way the courts deal with ouster clauses tests the claim that the exercise of judicial review can be reconciled with the requirements of sovereignty. This is because, while the plain meaning of such clauses is that the supervisory jurisdiction should be excluded, they are interpreted to ensure that access to the courts is maintained. Indeed, the assertion that the courts will adhere to explicit statutory language, as supporters of both theories claim, is especially questionable given that the interpretation of such clauses leaves them wholly without effect.

The treatment of ouster clauses – along with the discretionary nature of remedies – has also been used to claim that it is not possible to produce a logically seamless, non-contradictory account of judicial review, legislative supremacy and collateral challenge. The argument that such an account is necessary forms a significant part of the assertion that the *ultra vires* theory can provide the constitutional justification for judicial review. That it is unattainable must therefore reduce the foundation on which the theory rests.

It has also been shown that the advocates of the two theories make similar use of the normative effect of the rule of law. Both argue that in practice the courts

Themes of the debate 73

develop the standards of good administration drawing on rule of law values and other principles inherent within the legal system. It was submitted that this explication is Dworkinian in its approach. However, it was also submitted that, for the *ultra vires* theory, this approach conflicts with the positivism inherent within the theory. It was observed that this positivism itself means that the theory corresponds to a strong conception of the separation of powers doctrine.

Finally, the explanation of review of non-statutory power under both the *ultra vires* theory and the common law theory has been subject to criticism in this chapter. Supporters of both theories argue that review of such power is simply the application of the rule of law, which includes the standards of good administration, to the exercise of public power. Yet, they offer no reason why this version of the rule of law should be preferred over any other. Supporters of the *ultra vires* theory also claim that review of non-statutory power relies on an inherent jurisdiction of the courts to control monopoly power. However, as they concede, not all monopolies are susceptible to judicial review. Furthermore, there is no reason why a jurisdiction to control the supply of goods or services, thereby preventing economic exploitation, should be expanded to control the abuse of power generally.

Throughout this and the previous chapter we have seen evidence that protagonists on all sides of the debate believe that the proposed theories should match reality. For instance, critics of the *ultra vires* theory argue that it is unrealistic to suppose that Parliament specifically intends each of the standards of good administration to apply to the power that it grants and the supporters of that theory have amended it in response. Moreover, the proponents of the common law theory posit it as an alternative to the *ultra vires* theory because they believe that it better reflects the reality of review. Furthermore, though it is in a different context, Craig has explicitly recognised that theory and reality should coincide: 'If our theoretical constructs depart too much from reality, they risk becoming ... empty vessels'.[151] It is for these reasons that it is appropriate to systematically analyse how closely the theories match judicial review in practice. This is why the next chapter will be an immanent critique of both theories, evaluating them against the operation of judicial review.

---

151 *Public Law and Democracy in the United Kingdom and the United States of America* (n 37) 167.

74 Intention, Supremacy and Judicial Review

Bibliography

Allan TRS, *Law, Liberty and Justice: The Legal Foundations of British Constitutionalism* (Clarendon Press 1993)

— 'The Rule of Law as the Foundation of Judicial Review' in Christopher F Forsyth (ed), *Judicial Review and the Constitution* (Hart Publishing 2000)

— *Constitutional Justice: A Liberal Theory of the Rule of Law* (OUP 2001)

— 'The Constitutional Foundations of Judicial Review: Conceptual Conundrum or Interpretative Inquiry?' [2002] *Cambridge Law Journal* 87

— 'Constitutional Dialogue and the Justification of Judicial Review' (2003) 23 *Oxford Journal of Legal Studies* 563

— *The Sovereignty of Law: Freedom, Constitution, and Common Law* (OUP 2013)

Austin J, *The Province of Jurisprudence Determined* (W E Rumble ed, 5th edn, CUP 1995)

Bailey S H, 'Judicial Review in a Modern Context' in Christopher F Forsyth (ed), *Judicial Review and the Constitution* (Hart Publishing 2000)

Bamforth N, 'Ultra Vires and Institutional Interdependence' in Christopher F Forsyth (ed), *Judicial Review and the Constitution* (Hart Publishing 2000)

Barber N W, 'The Academic Mythologians' (2001) 21 *Oxford Journal of Legal Studies* 369

Barendt E, 'Separation of Powers and Constitutional Government' [1995] *Public Law* 599

Bingham Sir Thomas, 'Should Public Law Remedies be Discretionary?' [1991] *Public Law* 64

Bradley A W and Ewing K D, *Constitutional and Administrative Law* (14th edn, Longman 2007)

—, Ewing K D and Knight CJS, *Constitutional and Administrative Law* (16th edn, Pearson Education 2014)

Chu J, 'One Controversy, Two Jurisdictions: A Comparative Evaluation of the Ultra Vires and Common Law Theories of Judicial Review' [2009] *Judicial Review* 347

Cotterell R, 'Judicial Review and Legal Theory' in Genevra Richardson and Hazel Genn (eds), *Administrative Law and Government Action: The Courts and Alternative Mechanisms of Review* (Clarendon Press 1994)

Craig P P, *Public Law and Democracy in the United Kingdom and the United States of America* (OUP 1990)

— 'Ultra Vires and the Foundations of Judicial Review' [1998] *Cambridge Law Journal* 63

— 'Competing Models of Judicial Review' [1999] *Public Law* 428

— 'Constitutional Foundations, the Rule of Law and Supremacy' [2003] *Public Law* 92

— 'The Common Law, Shared Power and Judicial Review' (2004) 24 *Oxford Journal of Legal Studies* 237

— *Administrative Law* (7th edn, Sweet & Maxwell 2012)

— and Bamforth N, 'Constitutional Analysis, Constitutional Principle and Judicial Review' [2001] *Public Law* 763

Dicey A V, *Introduction to the Study of the Law of the Constitution* (8th edn, Macmillan 1915)

Dworkin R, *Taking Rights Seriously* (Duckworth & Co 1977)

— 'How Law is like Literature' in Ronald Dworkin, *A Matter of Principle* (OUP 1985)

— 'Political Judges and the Rule of Law' in Ronald Dworkin, *A Matter of Principle* (OUP 1985)

— 'The Forum of Principle' in Ronald Dworkin, *A Matter of Principle* (OUP 1985)

— *Law's Empire* (Hart Publishing 1998)

Dyzenhaus D, 'Form and Substance in the Rule of Law: A Democratic Justification for Judicial Review?' in Christopher F Forsyth (ed), *Judicial Review and the Constitution* (Hart Publishing 2000)

Ekins R, *The Nature of Legislative Intent* (OUP 2012)

Elliott M C, 'The Demise of Parliamentary Sovereignty? The Implications for Justifying Judicial Review' (1999) 115 *Law Quarterly Review* 119

— 'The Ultra Vires Doctrine in a Constitutional Setting: Still the Central Principle of Administrative Law' [1999] *Cambridge Law Journal* 129

— 'Fundamental Rights as Interpretative Constructs: The Constitutional Logic of the Human Rights Act 1998' in Christopher F Forsyth (ed), *Judicial Review and the Constitution* (Hart Publishing 2000)

— 'Legislative Intention Versus Judicial Creativity? Administrative Law as a Co-operative Endeavour' in Christopher F Forsyth (ed), *Judicial Review and the Constitution* (Hart Publishing 2000)

— *The Constitutional Foundations of Judicial Review* (Hart Publishing 2001)

Feldman D, 'Error of Law and Flawed Administrative Acts' [2014] *Cambridge Law Journal* 275

Forsyth C F, 'Of Fig Leaves and Fairy Tales: The Ultra Vires Doctrine, the Sovereignty of Parliament and Judicial Review' [1996] *Cambridge Law Journal* 122

— 'Collateral Challenge and the Foundations of Judicial Review: Orthodoxy Vindicated and Procedural Exclusivity Rejected' [1998] *Public Law* 364

— '"The Metaphysic of Nullity": Invalidity, Conceptual Reasoning and the Rule of Law' in Christopher F Forsyth and Ivan Hare (eds), *The Golden Metwand and the Crooked Cord: Essays on Public Law in Honour of Sir William Wade QC* (Clarendon Press 1998)

— 'Heat and Light: A Plea for Reconciliation' in Christopher F Forsyth (ed), *Judicial Review and the Constitution* (Hart Publishing 2000)

— 'Showing the Fly the Way Out of the Flybottle: The Value of Formalism and Conceptual Reasoning in Administrative Law' [2007] *Cambridge Law Journal* 325

— 'The Rock and the Sand: Jurisdiction and Remedial Discretion' [2013] *Judicial Review* 360

— and Elliott M C, 'The Legitimacy of Judicial Review' [2003] *Public Law* 286

— and Whittle L, 'Judicial Creativity and Judicial Legitimacy in Administrative Law' (2002) 8 *Canterbury Law Review* 453

Galligan D J, 'Judicial Review and the Textbook Writers' (1982) 2 *Oxford Journal of Legal Studies* 257

Gardner J, 'Some Types of Law' in D E Edlin (ed), *Common Law Theory* (CUP 2007)

Goldsworthy J, *The Sovereignty of Parliament: History and Philosophy* (OUP 1999)

Hale Baroness, 'Who Guards the Guardians?' [2014] *Judicial Review* 1

Joseph P A, 'The Demise of *Ultra Vires* – Judicial Review in the New Zealand Courts' [2001] *Public Law* 354

— 'The Demise of Ultra Vires – A Reply to Christopher Forsyth and Linda Whittle' (2002) 8 *Canterbury Law Review* 463

Jowell J L, 'Of Vires and Vacuums: The Constitutional Context of Judicial Review' [1999] *Public Law* 448

Kavanagh A, 'The Role of Parliamentary Intention in Adjudication under the Human Rights Act 1998' (2006) 26 *Oxford Journal of Legal Studies* 179

76 Intention, Supremacy and Judicial Review

Laws Sir John, 'Law and Democracy' [1995] *Public Law* 72

— 'The Constitution: Morals and Rights' [1996] *Public Law* 622

— 'Judicial Review and the Meaning of Law' in Christopher F Forsyth (ed), *Judicial Review and the Constitution* (Hart Publishing 2000)

McGarry J, 'Parliamentary Sovereignty, Judges and the Asylum and Immigration (Treatment of Claimants, etc) Bill' (2005) 26 *Liverpool Law Review* 1

— 'The Importance of an Expansive Test of Standing' [2014] *Judicial Review* 60

Montesquieu Baron de, *The Spirit of the Laws* (T Nugent tr, Hafner Publishing Company 1949)

Pannick D, 'Who is Subject to Judicial Review and in Respect of What?' [1992] *Public Law* 1

Radin M, 'Statutory Interpretation' (1930) 43 *Harvard Law Review* 863

Reid Lord, 'The Judge as Law-Maker' (1972) 12 *Journal of the Society of Public Teachers of Law* 22

Ringhand L A, 'Fig Leaves, Fairy Tales, and Constitutional Foundations: Debating Judicial Review in Britain' (2005) 43(3) *Columbia Journal of Transnational Law* 865

Rozenburg J, 'Law Lords Raise Stakes on Asylum', *The Daily Telegraph* (London, 5 March 2004)

Saunders C, 'Separation of Powers and the Judicial Branch' [2006] *Judicial Review* 337

Sedley Sir Stephen, 'Public Power and Private Power' in Christopher F Forsyth (ed), *Judicial Review and the Constitution* (Hart Publishing 2000)

Shelpse K A, 'Congress is a "They," Not an "It": Legislative Intent as Oxymoron' (1992) 12 *International Review of Law and Economics* 239

Taggart M, 'Ultra Vires as Distraction' in Christopher F Forsyth (ed), *Judicial Review and the Constitution* (Hart Publishing 2000)

Tomkins A, *Public Law* (OUP 2003)

Wade HWR, *The Hamlyn Lectures: Constitutional Fundamentals* (Stevens 1980)

— 'Constitutional Realities and Judicial Prudence' in Christopher F Forsyth (ed), *Judicial Review and the Constitution* (Hart Publishing 2000)

— and Forsyth CF, *Administrative Law* (11th edn, OUPs 2014)

Waldron J, *Law and Disagreement* (OUP 1999)

Williams R A, 'When is an Error not an Error? Reform of Jurisidictional Error of Law and Fact' [2007] *Public Law* 793

Woolf Lord, '*Droit Public* – English Style' [1995] *Public Law* 57

— 'Judicial Review – The Tensions between the Executive and the Judiciary' (1998) 114 *Law Quarterly Review* 579

5 Immanent critique and the theories of judicial review

In this chapter, I subject the *ultra vires* theory and the common law theory to additional analysis, this time by immanent critique. Immanent critique attempts to evaluate the degree to which theory matches practice. Subjecting the two theories to immanent critique will allow us to further evaluate the validity of claims that they provide the constitutional legitimacy for judicial review.

I begin by giving a brief account of immanent critique. I then identify the values underlying the *ultra vires* and common law theories. Next, I use the critique to examine six aspects of judicial review: the scope of judicial review; the permission stage; the time limits for bringing a claim; the sufficient interest requirement; the courts' treatment of ouster clauses; and the discretionary nature of remedies.

Immanent critique

Immanent critique is perhaps most closely associated with the critical theory of the Frankfurt School.[1] It can also be found in the work of the spiritual fathers of that School, Hegel and Marx,[2] though in its basic form it has a more ancient lineage.[3]

---

1 David Held, *Introduction to Critical Theory: Horkheimer to Habermas* (University of California Press 1980) 183.

2 Robert J Antonio, 'Immanent Critique as the Core of Critical Theory: Its Origins and Developments in Hegel, Marx and Contemporary Thought' (1981) 32(3) *The British Journal of Sociology* 330; Andrew Buchwalter, 'Hegel, Marx, and the Concept of Immanent Critique' (1991) 29(2) *Journal of the History of Philosophy* 253.

3 For instance, a simple form of the critique may be found in the discourses of Socrates. Gottlieb writes: 'Instead of proposing a thesis himself, Socrates lets the other man do so and then draws out the consequences', Anthony Gottlieb, 'Philosopher's Martyr: Socrates' in Ray Monk and Frederic Raphael', (eds), *The Great Philosophers: From Socrates to Turing* (Pheonix 2001) 11. An example of this can be seen in *The Republic* where Socrates identifies the values which he takes to be inherent in Cephalus' conception of justice: to pay one's debts and speak the truth. He then asks whether it would be just to return weapons to a friend who was not in his right mind. Cephalus answers that this would not be just and so implicitly concedes that his conception of justice is inadequate by reference to its own standards, Plato, *The Republic* (D Lee tr, 2nd edn, Penguin Classics 1974) 65–66. This approach is immanent because Socrates is able to demonstrate that there is a

78 *Intention, Supremacy and Judicial Review*

Immanent critique may initially be defined by contrasting it with an external form of critique. External critique seeks to evaluate how closely an object adheres to criteria which are external to it. For example, imagine that a critique of a legal system is undertaken in order to assess how closely it follows or departs from a particular conception of justice – say, a socialist view of equality. If it has not been claimed that this conception of justice is embodied in that legal system, then this would be an external form of critique because the criteria employed to evaluate the system are not claimed to be internal to it.

In contrast, immanent critique seeks to ascertain the degree to which the target of the critique actually embodies those values which are said to be inherent to it. Thus, to use a similar example, if a claim is made that a legal system embodies and gives effect to, say, a liberal democratic conception of justice, then a critique which assesses how much it adheres to that conception of justice would be an immanent critique.

Immanent critique, then, attempts to measure how closely reality and promise coincide. Its value is that it 'proceeds – so to speak – "from within" and hopes to avoid, thereby, the charge that its concepts impose irrelevant criteria of evaluation on the object'.[4] That is not to say that such an internal critique *per se* is preferable to an external one. This can be demonstrated by use of a simple illustration. Imagine that a government develops a policy to deprive a particular racial group, simply on the basis of their race, of their right to own property. If we assume that the stated aim of those who conceived this policy is to deprive this group of their property, would we then argue that it had some merit because it is able to live up to (or down to) this goal? One only needs to pose such a question to realise that the alignment of promise and reality is not in itself desirable and is not necessarily preferable to evaluation by external criteria.

The assumption on which immanent critique is based is that there should be a strong correlation between the target of the critique and the values which are said to underlie and justify it. It will often be the case that a 'lack of fit' between an object and its underlying values will lead to an assertion that either or both of them should be reformed so as to bring them closer:

> It is a common, though not necessary, theme of immanent critique that the exposure of contradictions internal to a system's own dynamics might trigger off a dialectical process whereby a new level of demands or expectations causes the system or group to move into a new higher gear. As such it is associated with reformist or radical tendencies.[5]

Indeed, the purpose of an immanent critique will often be to enable the critic to construct an argument for such reform. That is, the divergence exposed between

---

discrepancy between Cephalus' own concept of justice and the values which he believes underlie it. In proceeding in this way, Socrates is able to cause Cephalus to rethink what he means by justice.

4 Held, *Introduction to Critical Theory* (n 1) 184.

5 Ian Harden and Norman Lewis, *The Noble Lie: The British Constitution and the Rule of Law* (Hutchinson 1986) 10.

the target of the critique and the values which it is said to embody may lead to reform.

Immanent critique is not being used here to argue for reform of the practice judicial review. Rather, the aim is to evaluate how closely the *ultra vires* and common law theories align with judicial review in practice. The purpose is to determine whether it is appropriate to view either theory as the constitutional basis of judicial review. The targets of the critique, then, are the two theories posited as the basis of judicial review and they will be evaluated by reference to the operation of judicial review.

The critique is particularly appropriate to analyse the two competing theories. This is because, throughout the previous two chapters, we have seen evidence that protagonists on all sides of the debate believe that the proposed theories should match reality. For instance, critics of the *ultra vires* theory argue that it is unrealistic to suppose that Parliament specifically intends each of the standards of good administration to apply to the power that it grants and the supporters of that theory have amended it in response to such criticisms.[6] Moreover, the proponents of the common law theory posit it as an alternative to the *ultra vires* theory because they believe that it better reflects the reality that the standards of good administration are developed by the courts.[7] Indeed, as Bamforth writes: 'the degree to which any theory of judicial review can be considered plausible will depend to an extent on how well it fits the case law as a whole'.[8] Furthermore, though it is in a different context, Craig has explicitly recognised that theory and reality should coincide: 'If our theoretical constructs depart too much from reality, they risk becoming . . . empty vessels'.[9]

To undertake the critique, I will, first, identify relevant values underlying the *ultra vires* and common law theories. Next, I will evaluate the degree of fit between these values and judicial review in practice. Any discrepancies between the theories and the practice of judicial review will be noted and, in this way, the critique will be used to assess the degree to which the *ultra vires* theory and the common law theory can be considered to provide a suitable rationalisation of judicial review.

In describing judicial review in practice, I rely on the usual sources of legislation, case law and academic and judicial commentary. I make particular use of the observations and conclusions of the participants in the debate. For instance, when describing the practice of judicial review with which the *ultra vires* theory should be compared, the observations and conclusions of the leading *ultra vires* theorists – Elliott, Forsyth and Wade – are drawn on. Similarly, when describing the operation of judicial review with which the common law theory should be

6 Chapter Three p 33.
7 ibid p 35.
8 Nicholas Bamforth, 'Ultra Vires and Institutional Interdependence' in Christopher F Forsyth (ed), *Judicial Review and the Constitution* (Hart Publishing 2000) 116; see, also, 114: 'Perhaps the most preliminary criteria ask how well a particular theory fits the case law it is supposed to explain'.
9 Paul P Craig, *Public Law and Democracy in the United Kingdom and the United States of America* (OUP 1990) 167.

80 *Intention, Supremacy and Judicial Review*

compared, the observations and conclusions of the common law theorists, particularly Craig, are used. By so doing, I am attempting to ensure that the descriptions given of the practice of judicial review are appropriate ones with which to compare, respectively, the *ultra vires* theory and the common law theory.

Values underlying the two theories

We saw in Chapter Three that the *raison d'être* of both the *ultra vires* theory and the common law theory is to constitutionally justify judicial review in a way that accommodates the doctrine of parliamentary sovereignty.[10] Thus, adherence to the requirements of legislative sovereignty underpins both theories. It was also shown that the supporters of both theories state that the standards of good administration are developed and applied in accordance with the rule of law.[11] We can therefore state that both theories are also underpinned by the rule of law.

There is no agreement about what is required by the rule of law[12] and the two theories are largely silent on the particular version of the doctrine being relied upon. The intention here, though, is not to provide a comprehensive account of the doctrine. Even if such an exercise were possible, it would not be necessary for present purposes. As Craig writes: 'The detailed elaboration of the rule of law is a complex issue. It is wholly unrealistic to suggest that this can be explicated within the same debate as to the theoretical foundations of the subject'.[13] Rather, what is needed for the present critique is merely the identification of any requirements of the doctrine that are implicit in each of the theories and which are pertinent for the critique.

There is one particular characteristic which proponents of both theories would view as part of the rule of law and which is relevant for present purposes: that the law should be accessible. That is, the proponents of both theories appear to believe that the rule of law demands that the law be accessible, that a person's access to the courts should not be restricted without legitimate justification. For instance, Elliott writes: 'As a long line of authorities attests, the rule of law strongly favours citizens' access to the courts'.[14] In addition, Forsyth and Elliott describe access to the courts as a 'constitutional right' and they cite *Witham* as evidence for this.[15] Jowell also states that the rule of law requires 'access to

---

10 Chapter Three pp 30, 38 and 39.

11 ibid pp 33 and 35.

12 See, for example: Paul P Craig, 'Formal and Substantive Conceptions of the Rule of Law: An Analytical Framework' [1997] *PL* 467; Mark C Elliott, *The Constitutional Foundations of Judicial Review* (Hart Publishing 2001) 100; HWR Wade and Christopher F Forsyth, *Administrative Law* (11th edn, OUP 2014) 15.

13 Paul P Craig, 'Constitutional Foundations, the Rule of Law and Supremacy' [2003] *PL* 92, 95.

14 Mark C Elliott, 'The Ultra Vires Doctrine in a Constitutional Setting: Still the Central Principle of Administrative Law' [1999] *CLJ* 129, 151.

15 Christopher F Forsyth and Mark C Elliott, 'The Legitimacy of Judicial Review' [2003] *PL* 286, 298, 304. In *R v Lord Chancellor, ex p Witham* [1998] QB 575 (QBD), it was held, on the basis that access to the courts is a constitutional right, that the Senior Courts Act 1981 (SCA 1981)

Immanent critique and judicial review 81

justice not to be unfairly impeded'.[16] This requirement of accessibility is relevant because, as will be seen, it is able to provide particular guidance on how judicial review would operate if it were to fully adhere to either the *ultra vires* or common law theories.

With regard to parliamentary sovereignty, I argued in Chapter Four that it is implicit in both the *ultra vires* and common law theories that parliamentary sovereignty functions as a Dworkinian rule.[17] Yet, despite this shared understanding, I also argued that the two theories are underpinned by different conceptions of the doctrine. Under the *ultra vires* theory, sovereignty obliges the courts not to act contrary to the assumed intention of Parliament.[18] In contrast, parliamentary sovereignty under the common law theory simply requires the courts not to act contrary to the language used in primary legislation.[19] Despite these differences, it will be seen that the interpretative requirements of legislative sovereignty are largely the same under both theories.

The supporters of the common law theory expressly state that it implies no infringement of parliamentary sovereignty.[20] Indeed, they demonstrate their allegiance to it in two ways. First, they claim that, under the theory, the courts will apply any limits on public power which are expressly stated in an Act of Parliament.[21] Second, they contend that Parliament may exclude the standards of good administration by inserting into an Act of Parliament a clause, *written in unequivocal language*, stating that these standards, or any part of them, are not to apply in a particular situation. In such a case, they argue, the courts would hold that the standards do not apply.[22]

We may infer from this that the standards of good administration may *only* be completely excluded by such unequivocal language and that, without this, they will remain operative. This, in turn, leads to the conclusion that, under the common law theory, unless the language used points unequivocally in the opposite direction, Acts of Parliament are to be interpreted in the way which best accommodates the standards of good administration, and, by implication, the rule of law.

This conclusion may also be inferred from Craig's assertion that the foundation of the common law theory is based on a shared power between the courts and Parliament[23] and that 'The constitution assigns a role to the courts as well as

---

    s 130 did not give the Lord Chancellor the power to remove from litigants in person who were in receipt of income support the exemption from the payment of court fees.

16 Jeffrey L Jowell, 'Of Vires and Vacuums: The Constitutional Context of Judicial Review' [1999] *PL* 448, 455; see, also Jeffrey L Jowell, 'Is Equality a Constitutional Principle?' (1994) 47 *CLP* 1, 3.

17 Chapter Four pp 42–44.

18 ibid p 44.

19 ibid pp 44–45.

20 Chapter Three p 38.

21 ibid.

22 ibid.

23 'Constitutional Foundations, the Rule of Law and Supremacy' (n 13) 93.

82 *Intention, Supremacy and Judicial Review*

the legislator'.[24] The implication is that, while Parliament's role is to legislate, it is the courts' role to interpret that legislation and it will do this in a way which gives effect to the standards of good administration and the rule of law.[25]

Under the *ultra vires* theory, we are asked to assume that Parliament intends the courts to develop and apply the standards of good administration to public power derived from statute.[26] This is part of a wider assumption that Parliament intends to legislate in accordance with the rule of law.[27] While it was argued in Chapter Four that we cannot assume any particular intention of the legislature,[28] it is suggested here that we should adopt these assumptions for the purposes of undertaking an immanent critique of the *ultra vires* theory. The central place that they occupy within the theory means that we must accept them for the purposes of the critique. To decide otherwise would mean that we are not engaging with the theory on its own terms which would consequently mean that the critique would not be immanent.

Adopting these assumptions leads to the conclusion that parliamentary sovereignty under the *ultra vires* theory obliges the courts to interpret legislation in conformity with the rule of law. However, like the common law theory, this obligation can be displaced by 'clear contrary enactment',[29] that is, by statutory language that makes it plain that the rule of law is not to apply in a particular instance. Indeed, Elliott appears to confirm this when he writes: 'any irreconcilable conflict between the intention of Parliament and the rule of law must be resolved in favour of the former'.[30]

Thus, under both the common law and *ultra vires* theories, legislation is to be construed in the way that best accommodates the requirements of the rule of law. For present purposes, this requires legislation to be interpreted in a way which maintains access to the courts. This does not mean that the words used in the legislation can simply be overridden in order to achieve such an interpretation. Indeed, it is arguable that, for both theories, adherence to parliamentary sovereignty obliges us to find an interpretation that remains faithful to the statutory language. This is certainly the case with the common law theory which, as we have seen, requires the courts not to act contrary to the words used in primary legislation. It is also likely to be the case with the *ultra vires* theory. This is because this latter theory necessitates adherence to the intention of Parliament which, I suggest, surely means that statutory language must be abided by.

---

24 Paul P Craig, *Administrative Law* (7th edn, Sweet & Maxwell 2012) 18.

25 Indeed, we noted in Chapter Four Dicey's assertion: 'Parliament is supreme legislator, but from the moment Parliament has uttered its will as lawgiver, that will becomes subject to the interpretation put upon it by the judges of the land, and the judges . . . are influenced by the . . . general spirit of the common law', A V Dicey, *Introduction to the Study of the Law of the Constitution* (8th edn, Macmillan 1915) 273; Chapter Four p 46.

26 Chapter Three p 33.

27 ibid.

28 Chapter 4 pp 49–52.

29 Elliott, 'The Ultra Vires Doctrine in a Constitutional Setting: Still the Central Principle of Administrative Law', (n 14) 143.

30 ibid 153.

Immanent critique and judicial review 83

For both theories, then, legislation must be interpreted in a way that gives effect to the rule of law requirement that access to justice is maintained while remaining faithful to the statutory language used. The question arises as to when an interpretation breaches this limit so that – in the attempt to accommodate this requirement of the rule of law – fidelity to the statutory language is lost. Philosophical hermeneutics provides guidance here.

It was shown in Chapter Two that, when reading a text, the meaning that we take from it will always be conditioned by history of effect, by the operative force of the tradition we inhabit. This does not mean that we are free to give the text whatever meaning we choose. We must, rather, treat it like a conversation partner. For Gadamer, the primary advocate of philosophical hermeneutics, the aim in a genuine conversation is not simply to 'argue the other person down but [to] really consider the weight of the other's opinion'.[31] Similarly, we should not interpret a text in a way that simply overrides its meaning so that it conforms to our assumptions and opinions. Rather, we should interpret it through these assumptions while giving due weight to the language used.[32] Gadamer refers to this as a 'fusion of horizons' and suggests that it is an example of genuine understanding.[33] This is the approach I adopt here. Conformity with both the *ultra vires* and common law theories requires legislation to be read so as to maintain access to justice but only so far as is possible while still maintaining fidelity to the language used in the statute.

This cannot be an exact measurement: there will be differences of opinion about whether any particular interpretation is legitimate; that is, whether it achieves the correct balance between giving effect to the rule of law without simply making free with the statutory language. Probably the most we can say is that it is not legitimate to achieve an interpretation whereby the words used in the legislation are given a meaning which they cannot bear. This approach also seems appropriate because it echoes that suggested by the Court of Appeal with regard to the Human Rights Act 1998 (HRA 1998). Section 3(1) of the Act places an obligation on the courts to interpret primary or secondary legislation so that it is compatible with the Convention rights, 'so far as it is possible to do so'. Lord Woolf recommended that it should be circumscribed in the following way: 'if it is necessary in order to obtain compliance [with section 3(1)] to radically alter the effect of the legislation this will be an indication that more than interpretation is involved'.[34] I suggest a similar method here: the obligation to interpret legislation so as to accommodate the rule of law requirement that access to the courts

---

31 Hans-Georg Gadamer, *Truth and Method* (D G Marshall and Joel Weinsheimer trs, 2nd edn, Sheed and Ward 1989) 367. Chapter Two pp 23–24.

32 Allan appears to agree, arguing that we should find an interpretation that respects the 'semantic authority' of the language used: TRS Allan, 'Legislative Supremacy and Legislative Intention: Interpretation, Meaning and Authority' [2004] *CLJ* 685, 693.

33 Chapter Two pp 23–24.

34 *Poplar Housing and Regeneration Community Association Ltd v Donoghue* [2001] EWCA Civ 595, [2002] QB 48, 73. Lord Woolf's approach has been supported by Lord Hope: *R v A (No 2)* [2001] UKHL 25, [2002] 1 AC 45, 86–87. See also: *R v Secretary of State for the Home*

84   *Intention, Supremacy and Judicial Review*

should be maintained ought not be used to achieve a meaning which results in a substantial departure from the statutory language used. Adopting a different approach would mean that the courts would be legislating rather than interpreting. This would consequently mean that the language used in the statute was not being given appropriate weight but was, rather, being overridden in favour of the rule of law.

In summary, I have argued in this section that both the *ultra vires* theory and the common law theory are underpinned by the rule of law principle that the law should be accessible and by parliamentary sovereignty. I have also argued that, for the purposes of the immanent critique, the interpretative obligation required by parliamentary sovereignty is the same under both theories. This is, that legislation should be construed in the way that best accommodates the requirement that access to justice be maintained unless the statutory language clearly indicates otherwise. I have argued that this interpretive obligation does not allow the courts to simply override the meaning of the legislation; rather, legislation should be read to give effect to the rule of law only so far as is possible while maintaining fidelity to the statutory language.

Comparison: theories and practice

As noted above, the following sections will evaluate the *ultra vires* theory and the common law theory against six aspects of judicial review in practice: the scope of review; the permission stage; the time limits for bringing a claim; the sufficient interest requirement; the courts' treatment of ouster clauses; and the discretionary nature of remedies. These aspects of review have been chosen because they represent the main, relevant aspects of judicial review in practice or – in the case of ousters clauses and the discretionary nature of remedies – they are significant facets of the debate between the supporters of the two theories and, *prima facie*, indicate a significant divergence between practice and one or both of the theories.

The scope of judicial review

The scope of judicial review refers to the type of decisions that may be susceptible to the supervisory jurisdiction. I have noted that, according to the *ultra vires* theory, we must assume that when Parliament grants a public power it intends it to be exercised in accordance with the rule of law which includes the standards of good administration.[35] Indeed, as was shown in Chapter Four, Elliott argues that this is the only 'logical and plausible' assumption to make.[36] The *ultra vires* theory therefore requires that public power derived from statute should be susceptible to judicial review.

Department, ex p Anderson and Taylor [2002] UKHL 46, [2003] 1 AC 837; and *R (Wright) v Secretary of State for Health* [2009] UKHL 3, [2009] 1 AC 739 [39] (Baroness Hale).
35   Above p 80.
36   Chapter Four p 51.

Under the common law theory, the standards of judicial review are developed and applied pursuant to an inherent jurisdiction of the courts to control the exercise of public power.[37] Thus, the common law theory requires that all public power should be susceptible to judicial review. The common law theory also requires that the courts apply any limits on the exercise of public power expressly stated in an Act of Parliament.[38]

It was also shown in Chapter Four that Forsyth, a leading *ultra vires* theorist, explains review of non-statutory power as being a common law jurisdiction to ensure that monopolistic power is exercised reasonably and fairly.[39] Craig, the primary advocate of the common law theory, writes that he does not 'object to this line of argument'.[40] Indeed, at times, he implies that an exercise of monopoly power will, for that reason, mean that the activity in question is subject to the supervisory jurisdiction.[41] That is, supporters of both the *ultra vires* and common law theories contend that the exercise of monopolistic power should be susceptible to judicial review.[42]

When looking at judicial review in practice, I begin with the position under the HRA 1998. A claim for judicial review may be founded on an allegation that a public authority has acted in a way which is incompatible with the Convention rights.[43] That is, the scope of judicial review extends to ensuring that public authorities act in conformity with the Convention rights. There are two types of public authorities under the HRA 1998: pure (also known as 'core') public authorities and hybrid public authorities. The former will be those 'bodies that are obviously public in nature, such as government departments and ministers, local authorities, NHS Trusts, coroners, police, prisons, bodies such as the Parole Board, Legal Services Commission, and the General Medical Council'.[44] Such bodies are obliged to act consistently with the Convention rights in all that they do.[45] A hybrid public authority is one which is not a public body *per se* but which

---

37 ibid p 56.

38 Chapter Three p 38.

39 Chapter Four pp 56–57.

40 Paul P Craig, 'Ultra Vires and the Foundations of Judicial Review' [1998] *CLJ* 63, 77.

41 Paul P Craig, 'Contracting Out, the Human Rights Act and the Scope of Judicial Review' (2002) 118 *LQR* 551, 559. Strictly speaking, Craig is discussing whether a function should be considered to be a public function under the Human Rights Act 1998. He does, however, use a non-HRA judicial review case (*R v Disciplinary Committee of the Jockey Club, ex p Aga Khan* [1993] 1 WLR 909 (CA)) to illustrate his point.

42 Taggart writes: 'the historical justification given for the *Datafin*-style extension of judicial review to non-statutory bodies by both supporters and detractors of the ultra vires doctrine is rather ancient case law controlling abuse of de facto monopolistic power by individuals and entities', Michael Taggart, 'Ultra Vires as Distraction' in Christopher F Forsyth (ed), *Judicial Review and the Constitution* (Hart Publishing 2000) 428.

43 HRA 1998 s 6(1) states: 'It is unlawful for a public authority to act in a way which is incompatible with a Convention right'. Section 7 allows a claimant to bring proceedings, including making a claim for judicial review, where it is alleged that s 6(1) has been infringed.

44 John Wadham *et al*, *Blackstone's Guide to the Human Rights Act 1998* (6th edn, OUP 2011) 52.

45 HRA 1998 s 6(1).

86   *Intention, Supremacy and Judicial Review*

undertakes 'functions of a public nature'.[46] These bodies are required to act in conformity with the Convention rights only when undertaking such functions.[47]

In other cases, when delineating the boundaries of judicial review, it is the nature of the function or decision being challenged which is relevant rather than the nature of the body performing that function.[48] The courts draw a distinction between public and private law so that the overarching relevant factor in determining whether a power is susceptible to judicial review is whether it is public in nature. This is evident in the following statement from Lord Donaldson's judgment in *ex p Datafin*:

> the only *essential* elements are what can be described as a public element, which can take many different forms, and the exclusion from the jurisdiction of bodies whose sole source of power is a consensual submission to its jurisdiction (emphasis added).[49]

Public power is, then, susceptible to judicial review whereas private power, epitomised by power derived from contract, is not. However, the meaning of 'public power' is uncertain. To be sure, Lloyd LJ has stated that, 'to refer to "public law" in this context is to beg the question'.[50] Moreover, participants on both sides of the debate acknowledge that what is meant by 'public power' is not clear.[51]

---

46 Section 6(3)(b). It has become common to use the terms 'hybrid public authority' or 'functional public authority' as convenient shorthand when referring to such bodies. However, Oliver makes the point that this shorthand is misleading because it focuses on the nature of the body rather than the nature of the activity: Dawn Oliver, 'Functions of a Public Nature under the Human Rights Act' [2004] *PL* 329, 337–339.

47 Section 6(5).

48 For example, in *Aga Khan* (n 41) 930, Farquharson LJ made it clear that a finding that the Jockey Club was not susceptible to judicial review in that case did not mean that it would never be susceptible to judicial review. See, also, *R (Beer) v Hampshire Farmer's Market Ltd* [2003] EWCA Civ 1056, [2004] 1 WLR 233 [16] (Dyson LJ); Sir Harry Woolf, 'Public Law – Private Law: Why the Divide? A Personal View' [1986] *PL* 220, 223; David Pannick, 'Who is Subject to Judicial Review and in Respect of What?' [1992] *PL* 1, 6; Dawn Oliver, 'The Frontiers of the State: Public Authorities and Public Functions under the Human Rights Act' [2000] *PL* 476, 480; Dawn Oliver, 'Public Law Procedures and Remedies – Do We Need Them?' [2002] *PL* 91, 95; Peter Cane, *Administrative Law* (4th edn, OUP 2004) 35.

49 *R v Panel on Take-Overs and Mergers, ex p Datafin* [1987] QB 815 (CA) 838. Similar sentiments were expressed by Lloyd LJ, 847. See, also, *R v Criminal Injuries Compensation Board, ex p Lain* [1967] 2 QB 864 (QBD) 882 (Lord Parker CJ); *Aga Khan* (n 41) 916 (Lord Bingham); *Mass Energy Ltd v Birmingham City Council* [1994] Env LR 298 (CA) 306–307 (Glidewell LJ); *Beer* (ibid) [16] (Dyson LJ); *R (Agnello) v Hounslow LBC* [2003] EWHC 3112 (Admin), [2004] LLR. 268 [20]–[30] (Silber J); CPR 54.1(2) states that a claim for judicial review is a claim to review the lawfulness of an enactment or the exercise of a *public* function. Academic comment to this effect may also be found; see, for instance: Sir John Laws, 'Law and Democracy' [1995] *PL* 72, 75, 76; Craig, *Administrative Law* (n 24) 836.

50 *Datafin* (ibid) 847. However, his Lordship proceeded to opine that he did not think that it does beg the question. Dyson LJ has also stated that the test for amenability to judicial review is 'question-begging', *Beer* (ibid) [16].

51 Christopher F Forsyth, 'Of Fig Leaves and Fairy Tales: The Ultra Vires Doctrine, the Sovereignty

It has sometimes been claimed that power will be susceptible to review if it is 'governmental' in nature[52] and this term is often taken to be synonymous with 'public power'.[53] Yet, again, there is uncertainty here. In *ex p Wachmann*, Simon Brown J stated that in order to be susceptible to judicial review a power must not only be public but also governmental, thereby suggesting that these are not equivalent terms.[54] This qualification aside, it seems reasonably clear that if a government body is exercising power which is obviously governmental – that is, power which is central to its role *qua* government body – then it may be challenged by way of judicial review.[55] Where the nature of the power is not obvious – for instance non-statutory power exercised by non-government bodies – the courts have devised a number of tests by which they may assess whether it is public power and so susceptible to the supervisory jurisdiction.

The courts may ask whether, if the function was not exercised by the body in question, the government would step in to exercise it.[56] They may also ask whether the body whose decision is being challenged is established 'under authority of the government';[57] whether, when exercising the function being challenged, the body in question 'might de facto be a surrogate organ of government';[58] or whether there has been an 'implied devolution of power'.[59] Alternatively, it may be asked whether the function being challenged is underpinned by statute,[60] or is part of a regulatory system supported by statutory powers.[61] It has also been suggested that a function may be considered to be

of Parliament and Judicial Review' [1996] *CLJ* 122, 135–136; Oliver, 'The Frontiers of the State: Public Authorities and Public Functions under the Human Rights Act' (n 48) 487; Craig, *Administrative Law* (n 24) 850; Wade and Forsyth, *Administrative Law* (n 12) 540–541. See, also, Michael J Beloff, 'The Boundaries of Judicial Review' in Jeffrey L Jowell and Dawn Oliver (eds), *New Directions in Judicial Review* (Stevens and Sons 1988) 5, 7; David Pannick, 'Who is Subject to Judicial Review and in Respect of What?' (n 48) 1; Nicholas Bamforth, 'The Scope of Judicial Review: Still Uncertain' [1993] *PL* 239, 239, 246; Stephen H Bailey, 'Judicial Review of Contracting Decisions' [2007] *PL* 444, 446, 451, 462.

52 *Aga Khan* (n 41) 923 (Lord Bingham), 931 (Farquharson LJ).

53 In *Datafin* (n 49), the Court of Appeal held that the Panel was exercising governmental, and thus public, power and was for that reason susceptible to judicial review. Craig also seems to indicate that a body will be engaging in an activity that has a 'public law element' if it 'partakes in some manner of "governing"', *Administrative Law* (n 24) 854.

54 *R v Chief Rabbi of the United Congregations of Great Britain and the Commonwealth, ex p Wachmann* [1992] 1 WLR 1036 (QBD) 1042. See, also, a similar distinction drawn by Lord Nicholls between 'public function' and 'governmental function' in *Aston Cantlow and Wilmcote with Billesley Parochial Church Council v Wallbank* [2003] UKHL 37, [2004] 1 AC 546 [10].

55 Wade and Forsyth, *Administrative Law* (n 12) 538.

56 *R v Advertising Standards Authority, ex p Insurance Services* (1990) 9 Tr LR 169 (QBD) 177; *Wachmann* (n 54) 1042–1043 (Simon Brown J); *R v Football Association Ltd, ex p Football League Ltd* [1993] 2 All ER 833 (QBD) 848–849 (Rose J).

57 *Lain* (n 49) 884 (Diplock LJ); quoted with approval in *Datafin* (n 49) 849 (Lloyd LJ).

58 *Aga Khan* (n 41) 932 (Hoffmann LJ).

59 *Datafin* (n 49) 849 (Lloyd LJ).

60 *Football League Ltd* (n 56) 846 (Rose J).

61 *Wachmann* (n 54) 1042 (Simon Brown J). The courts may ask whether the function in question is 'woven into a system of governmental control . . . or integrated into a system of statutory

88 Intention, Supremacy and Judicial Review

governmental or public if it is monopolistic.[62] However, it should be noted that all these various tests are indicative only.[63] That is, the presence of any, or all, of the factors noted above is not conclusive that the power being exercised is public in nature. As Dyson LJ has noted: 'there is no simple litmus test of amenability to judicial review'.[64]

I have noted that supporters of both the *ultra vires* theory and the common law theory contend that all monopolistic power should be susceptible to judicial review.[65] Yet, they also concede that the courts do not review all exercises of such power.[66] For instance, it has been stated that the Jockey Club has 'near monopolistic powers' but is not susceptible to judicial review.[67] Furthermore, as was argued in Chapter Four, it is not clear what is meant by monopolistic power in this context.[68]

So, with regard to the scope of judicial review, the courts will supervise the exercise of all public power (as implicit in the common law theory), including public power derived from statute (as per the *ultra vires* theory). Indeed, the courts have adopted a number of tests to ascertain whether a particular exercise of power is public in nature or not when the matter it is not clear.

The courts do not, though, appear to review monopolistic power simply on the basis that it is monopolistic. Thus, in this respect, the scope of judicial review differs from that suggested by supporters of the two theories. This, it may be argued, does not, in itself, invalidate either the common law theory or the *ultra vires* theory. As noted in Chapter Three, the purpose of the theories is to rationalise the review of public power derived from statute.[69] The argument that the courts should review monopolistic power is made with regard to non-statutory public power and is thus supplementary to the central claims of the *ultra vires* and common law theories which, *sticto senso*, apply only to statutorily derived public power.

Permission stage

In any claim for judicial review, the permission of the court is needed before the claim may proceed.[70] Judicial review, then, is a two-stage procedure consisting of a permission stage followed by a substantive hearing. At first instance, the decision

---

regulation', *R v London Metal Exchange, ex p Albatross Warehousing BV* [2000] All ER (D) 452 (QBD, 30 March 2000) [27] (Richards J).

62 *Football League Ltd* (n 56) 846, 847 (Rose J); *R v Disciplinary Committee of the Jockey Club, ex p Massingberd-Mundy* [1993] 2 All ER 207 (DC) 222 (Roch J).

63 *Datafin* (n 49) 838; *Massingberd-Mundy* (ibid) 221 (Roch J).

64 *Beer* (n 48) [12].

65 Above p 85.

66 Chapter Four p 57. See, also, Lord Woolf of Barnes, '*Droit Public* – English Style' [1995] *PL* 57, 63; Wade and Forsyth, *Administrative Law* (n 12) 545.

67 *Massingberd-Mundy* (n 62) 222 (Roch J).

68 Chapter Four p 57.

69 Chapter Three pp 30–31, 33 and 38–39.

70 This is required by the SCA 1981 s 31(3) and CPR 54.4.

about whether permission will be granted is normally made without a hearing; the judge will simply consider the claim on the basis of the claim form and the defendant's written response.[71] So, at this stage of the judicial review process, the court may summarily decide that a claim should not be permitted to proceed.

The fact that the decision about permission is generally made without a hearing also means that it is usually taken without testing the evidence and without hearing oral representation in support of the claim.[72] Given this, it would be consistent with the rule of law principle underlying both the *ultra vires* and common law theories – that access to the courts be maintained – for the courts to adopt a light touch approach at this stage. That is, where there is a claim that limits on the exercise of public power have been breached, including the standards of good administration, both theories require that the claim should be permitted to proceed to full hearing, at least where that claim, *prima facie*, has some merit.

Furthermore, the requirement that access to the courts be maintained is necessary, *a fortiori*, where limits on the exercise of public power are said to be derived from Parliament. Both theories require limits on public power expressly stated in an Act of Parliament to be enforced by the courts.[73] The *ultra vires* theory additionally requires that any limits on public power which it is presumed are intended by Parliament – namely, the standards of good administration – should also be enforced by the courts.[74] For the courts not to grant permission for a claim to proceed to full hearing where a *prima facie* case has been made that these express or presumed limits have been breached would be an infringement of parliamentary sovereignty. Thus, it is submitted that both theories require that permission should be given where it appears that there has been a breach of any express limits on the exercise of public power contained in an Act of Parliament. The *ultra vires* theory also requires that permission should be granted if there is a *prima facie* case that the presumed limits on the exercise of statutory public power, the standards of good administration, have been infringed.

In practice, a claim may be rejected at the permission stage because there is an alternative path by which it may be pursued, such as a right of appeal or alternative dispute resolution,[75] or because the issue in question is a private law matter.[76] In addition, under section 31(3C) of the Senior Courts Act 1981 (SCA

---

71 54A PD 8.4.

72 54A PD 8.5.

73 Above pp 81–82.

74 Above p 82.

75 *R v Inland Revenue Commissioners, ex p Preston* [1985] AC 835 (HL) 852 (Lord Scarman); *R v Secretary of State for the Home Department, ex p Swati* [1986] 1 All ER 717 (CA) 723–724 (Lord Donaldson); *R (Cowl and Others) v Plymouth City Council (Practice Note)* [2001] EWCA Civ 1935, [2002] 1 WLR 803 [14]; *R (Sivasubramaniam) v Wandsworth County Court* [2002] EWCA Civ 1738, [2003] 1 WLR 475 [47]; Andrew P Le Sueur, Jeffrey L Jowell and Lord Woolf of Barnes, *De Smith, Woolf and Jowell's Principles of Judicial Review* (5th edn, Sweet & Maxwell 1999) 565; Craig, *Administrative Law* (n 24) 882; Mark C Elliott, *Beatson, Matthews and Elliott's Administrative Law: Text and Materials* (4th edn, OUP 2011) 466–467; Michael Fordham, 'Permission Principles' [2006] *JR* 176, para 3.

76 *O'Reilly v Mackman and Others* [1983] 2 AC 237 (HL).

90 *Intention, Supremacy and Judicial Review*

1981), as amended by section 84 of the Criminal Justice and Courts Act 2015, the court may consider whether the outcome for the applicant would 'have been substantially different if the conduct complained of had not occurred', and must consider this question if asked to do so by the defendant. Under section 31(3D), the court must refuse permission to proceed with a claim if it appears 'highly likely that the outcome for the applicant would not have been substantially different'. Section 31(3E) permits that court to 'disregard the requirement in subsection (3D) for reasons of exceptional public interest'.

Claims may also be rejected at the permission stage because the claimant does not have sufficient interest in the matter to which the claim relates, or because the claim has been made out of time. I deal with these two issues in their separate sections below.

The main criterion determining whether permission is granted is whether the claimant has an arguable case.[77] Latham J states: 'In considering . . . whether . . . there is material which justifies the grant of leave to move, I recognise that the applicant *only* has to establish that his case is arguable' (emphasis added).[78] Arguability has been defined as meaning that the judicial review should have a 'realistic prospect of success'.[79] However, a case may be considered arguable, even if not deemed to have a realistic prospect of success, if the issues raised are sufficiently important.[80] Lord Scarman seems to echo this when he states that, at this stage, the claimant must show that there is 'a *prima facie* case or reasonable grounds for believing that there has been a failure of public duty'.[81] Similarly, Lord Diplock states:

> If, on a quick perusal of the material then available, the court thinks that it discloses what might on further consideration turn out to be an arguable case in favour of granting to the applicant the relief claimed, it ought, in the exercise of a judicial discretion, to give him leave to apply for that relief.[82]

The authors of the Bowman report simply contend that the purpose of the permission stage is to filter out cases which are 'hopeless'[83] and that there should be a presumption in favour of granting permission.[84]

---

77 *Inland Revenue Commissioners v National Federation of Self-Employed and Small Businesses Ltd* [1982] AC 617 (HL) 644 (Lord Diplock); Sir Jeffrey Bowman *et al*, *Review of the Crown Office List: A Report to the Lord Chancellor* (Lord Chancellor's Department 2000) Chapter 7, paras 12, 14; Wade and Forsyth, *Administrative Law* (n 12) 552; Fordham, 'Permission Principles' (n 75) para 2. Varda Bondy and Maurice Sunkin, 'Accessing Judicial Review' [2008] *PL* 647, 651–652.

78 *R v Provincial Court of the Church in Wales, ex p Williams* [1998] EWHC Admin 998 [8].

79 *Sharma v Brown-Antoine* [2006] UKPC 57, [2007] 1 WLR 780 [14] (Lord Bingham); Michael Fordham, 'Arguability Principles' [2007] *JR* 219, para 3.

80 *R (Gentle) v Prime Minister* [2006] EWCA Civ 1078 (CA) [22]–[23]; Fordham, 'Arguability Principles' (ibid) para 5.

81 *National Federation of Self-Employed and Small Businesses Ltd* (n 77) 653.

82 ibid 644.

83 *Review of the Crown Office List* (n 77) Chapter 7, para 12.

84 ibid Chapter 7, para 13. See, also, Andrew P Le Sueur and Maurice Sunkin, 'Applications for Judicial Review: The Requirement of Leave' [1992] *PL* 102, 127–128.

Immanent critique and judicial review   91

This approach would appear to conform to the requirements of the two theories that a light touch be taken at the permission stage: that a case should be granted permission to proceed where there is _prima facie_ evidence that the limits on public power have been infringed. However, Craig writes that the test has become stricter over time and that the courts need to be convinced that a case 'really was arguable'.[85] He states that the success rate in gaining permission has 'declined markedly over the years' and that this is, in part, because of a 'more rigorous test' being employed by the courts.[86] If so, this suggests that the courts are not, or not in all cases, adopting the light touch approach required by the two theories.

Further, there is evidence that, at the permission stage, the courts also apply criteria that are not consistent with the light touch approach. For instance, Lord Diplock has stated that the aim of the permission stage is to 'prevent the time of the court being wasted by busybodies with misguided or trivial complaints of administrative error'.[87] Moreover, the courts appear to reject claims at the permission stage for being 'frivolous or vexatious' or because the claimant is not '_bona fide_'.[88]

There is also evidence that the permission stage is used to manage and ration the resources of the court. Indeed, Le Sueur and Sunkin suggest that a primary purpose of this stage is to protect the courts from being swamped with claims.[89] One of the most explicit judicial statements to this effect has been made by Lord Donaldson:

> the public interest normally dictates that if the judicial review jurisdiction is to be exercised, it should be exercised very speedily and, given the constraints imposed by limited judicial resources, this necessarily involves limiting the number of cases in which leave to apply should be given.[90]

It would seem, then, that the courts will employ the permission stage to keep the volume of cases which are allowed to proceed to the full hearing at a manageable level.

---

85 _Administrative Law_ (n 24) 865. Bondy and Sunkin note that in 2006 only 22% of claims were given permission to proceed. This may be, however, because many of the more meritous claims are now settled early: 'Accessing Judicial Review' (n 77) 648, 656–657.
86 ibid 867.
87 _National Federation of Self-Employed and Small Businesses Ltd_ (n 77) 643.
88 In research by Le Sueur and Sunkin, these are two of the reasons given in their research sample for refusing permission: 'Applications for Judicial Review: The Requirement of Leave' (n 84) 119–125. See, also, Sir Harry Woolf: 'This requirement [of leave] undoubtedly deters frivolous applications', 'Public Law – Private Law: Why the Divide? A Personal View' (n 48) 230.
89 'Applications for Judicial Review: The Requirement of Leave' (n 84) 104–105. The Bowman report also seems to suggest this as a purpose of the permission stage. It states that the permission stage 'provides a useful tool for case management', _Review of the Crown Office List_ (n 77) Chapter 7, para 12. See, also, Tom Cornford and Maurice Sunkin, 'The Bowman Report, Access and the Recent Reforms of the Judicial Review Procedure' [2001] _PL_ 11, 15; and Craig, _Administrative Law_ (n 24) 868.
90 _R v Panel on Take-Overs and Mergers, ex p Guinness Plc_ [1990] 1 QB 146 (CA) 177–178.

92 *Intention, Supremacy and Judicial Review*

Using the permission stage to filter out 'trivial complaints of administrative error' or claims considered to be 'frivolous or vexatious' may be questionable with regard to the requirements of the *ultra vires* and common law theories. This is because such criteria may be taken to mean that the unlawfulness complained of is of such a trifling nature that it should not be used to waste the time and resources of the courts. If so, then this is not compatible with the theories which require that there should be access to the courts where there is a *prima facie* case that limits on public power or rule of law values, including the standards of good administration, have been infringed, even where the infringement may be seen as 'trivial'.

Of course, it may be argued that granting permission for trivial cases to proceed will deny access to the courts for more deserving cases and thus, for those cases, infringe the principle that access to the courts should be maintained. This argument is rejected here. Rather, it is contended that the principle requires that there should be sufficient judicial resources to maintain such access for all potential claimants.

I have also noted that the courts may refuse permission for a claim to proceed because the claimant is not '*bona fide*'. In assessing whether this requirement is commensurate with the *ultra vires* and common law theories, we must look at the purpose of review under these theories. It may be that the purpose of judicial review is to secure a public law right owed to the claimant. If so, then it might also be appropriate to insist that the claimant has acted with good faith and that she must, for instance, act fairly in order to claim a right to be treated fairly.

However, I have argued above that, where a *prima facie* claim is made that limits on the exercise of public power have been breached, then both the *ultra vires* and common law theories require that permission should be granted for the claim to proceed to full hearing. This is especially the case where the limits are said to be the express or presumed intention of Parliament.[91] This suggests that, for both theories, the purpose of judicial review is not to secure a public law right owed to an individual; it is, rather, to ensure that those exercising public power do so according to the grounds of judicial review. Sedley J would appear to agree: 'Public law is not at base about rights, even though abuses of power may and often do invade private rights; it is about wrongs – that is to say misuses of public power'.[92] For this reason, we may infer that, under both theories, the *fides* of the claimant are irrelevant in assessing whether permission for a claim to proceed to full hearing should be granted. It is, for instance, just as much of an infringement of parliamentary sovereignty for the courts to allow the exercise of public power in breach of the limits expressly contained in primary legislation where the claimant is *mala fides* as it is where she is *bona fides*.[93] This, I suggest, means that taking

---

91 Above p 89.

92 *R v Somerset County Council and ARC Southern Limited, ex p Dixon* [1998] Env. LR 111 (QBD) 121. See, also, 'public law . . . at heart, is the restraint of abuses of power', Sir Stephen Sedley, *The Hamlyn Lectures: Freedom, Law and Justice* (Sweet & Maxwell 1999) 33.

93 Having said this, the status of the claimant is not irrelevant; as will be shown below, a claimant must demonstrate sufficient interest in the matter to which the claim relates before permission will be granted.

into account the good or bad faith of the claimant when determining whether permission should be granted is not consistent with either the *ultra vires* theory or the common law theory.

I have also recorded that it is sometimes claimed that the permission stage is a necessary expedient to manage and ration access to the courts. This may mean either of two things. It may simply mean that it is a way to protect the courts from having to give a full substantive hearing to cases which are not arguable and have no prospect of success.[94] If this is the case, it does not necessarily conflict with the two theories. However, it may mean that, when deciding whether permission to proceed to full hearing should be granted in any particular case, the courts should take into account the fact that there are 'limited judicial resources'.[95] If so, then, as Himsworth states, it is objectionable that, 'access to justice in vindication of the rule of law should depend on the availability of judges and courts'.[96] Furthermore, and more pertinently for present purposes, to prevent cases from proceeding in order to lighten the courts' caseload would be to introduce a criterion which is external to the two theories and which is contrary to the principle – inherent in both theories – that access to the courts should be maintained. On the evidence available, it is not possible to conclude which of these two meanings, or indeed whether either meaning, accurately represents the approach of the courts.[97]

Time limits

The time limit for bringing a claim in judicial review is set by Part 54.5 of the Civil Procedure Rules. In addition, section 31(6) of the SCA 1981 states that the court may refuse permission to continue, or may withhold a remedy, if it considers there to have been 'undue delay' and 'if it considers that the granting of the relief sought would be likely to cause substantial hardship to, or substantially prejudice the rights of, any person or would be detrimental to good administration'.

---

94 This was certainly the conclusion reached by the Bowman report which found that the permission stage prevents approximately 1,000 court days being wasted on 'unmeritorious claims', *Review of the Crown Office List* (n 77) Chapter 7, para 11. It is also implicit in the judgment of Charles J in *S (A Minor) v Knowsley Borough Council and Others* [2004] EWHC 491 (Fam), [2004] 2 FLR 716 [72]; see, also, Fordham, 'Permission Principles' (n 75) para 1. For criticism that the Bowman report overestimated the saving in court time that the permission stage makes see: Lee Bridges, George Meszaros and Maurice Sunkin, 'Regulating the Judicial Review Caseload' [2000] *PL* 651, 665.

95 Text to n 90.

96 Chris Himsworth, 'No Standing Still on Standing' in Peter Leyland and Terry Woods (eds), *Administrative Law Facing the Future: Old Constraints and New Horizons* (Blackstone Press 1997) 209.

97 The statistical evidence that exists is inconclusive; research by Bridges *et al* finds that throughout the 1980s and early 1990s the percentage of cases granted leave decreased as the caseload increased which would suggest that the courts do, indeed, ration access to the courts. However, a sample of cases from 1994–1995 showed that the percentage increased despite an increase in the caseload: 'Regulating the Judicial Review Caseload' (n 94).

94   *Intention, Supremacy and Judicial Review*

As already noted, both the *ultra vires* and common law theories are underpinned by the rule of law principle that access to the courts be maintained.[98] I have already argued that this means that, under both theories, the courts should grant permission for all claims where a *prima facie* case has been made that limits on public power have been breached.[99] Here, the principle of accessibility also suggests that the courts should hear all claims where it is alleged that these limits have been breached, regardless of the time that has elapsed since the alleged infringement. To conclude otherwise would reduce claimants' access to the courts.

Of course, it may be argued that there are practical constraints which require a claim to be heard within a certain time frame. For instance, one might claim that, if the decision in question has resulted in physical construction work being undertaken, and perhaps even finished, then to entertain a claim that the decision is unlawful is to entertain an irrelevance. There are a number of replies that can be made to such an argument. First, any practical considerations would not apply to all judicial review cases and so it would not be necessary to adopt a universally applicable time limit. Moreover, where a decision has been acted on, and is such that it cannot be undone, there is nothing to prevent the courts from granting a declaration that the decision was unlawful. The advantage of this is that it will not require the decision-maker to undo what has been done in the way that, say, a quashing order, may do. Lord Donaldson suggested just such a course with regard to the Panel on Take-Overs and Mergers. The Panel performs a regulatory role on the London Stock Exchange with regard to the take-over and merger of companies. His Lordship suggested that, given the nature of the Panel's activities, the relationship between the Panel and the courts should be 'historic rather than contemporaneous' and that, if the courts were to be involved, it should be in retrospect by way of declaratory order.[100] Such a course of action would be consistent with the access to law requirement inherent in both existing theories of judicial review while satisfying any practical concerns that could be raised.

A similar contention may be made with regard to section 31(6) of the SCA 1981 allowing the courts to deny permission to proceed with a claim or a remedy if there has been 'undue delay' in making the claim. I argued above that it is implicit in both the *ultra vires* theory and the common law theory that statutory requirements such as this should be interpreted, where possible, in conformity with the principle that access to the courts be maintained, provided that such an interpretation does not ascribe to the statutory language a meaning that the words are not able to bear. With this in mind, I suggest that there will be few cases where the potential for substantial prejudice or hardship to any person, or detriment to the administration of justice (the conditions precedent for which the

---

98 Above pp 80–81.

99 Above p 89.

100 *Datafin* (n 49) 842. However, in this case the court held that there were no grounds on which to grant the claim for judicial review.

Immanent critique and judicial review 95

courts may refuse permission or relief for undue delay), cannot be avoided by the granting of a declaration.

In practice, the Civil Procedure Rules state that a claim for judicial review must be filed 'promptly; and . . . in any event not later than 3 months after the grounds to make the claim first arose'.[101] Hence, a claim may be made within three months but rejected because it was not made promptly.[102] The three-month time limit cannot be extended simply by the parties' agreement,[103] though the courts may, for good reason, grant an extension.[104] Where a claim relates to a decision made by the Secretary of State or a local planning authority under the planning Acts, the claim form must be filed within six weeks of the decision being challenged.[105] If a claim is brought in relation to a matter governed by the Public Contracts Regulations 2015, the time limit is 30 days. It is worth noting here that these time limits are not required by primary legislation; rather, they are set by the Civil Procedure Rule Committee.[106]

So, in summary, while the principle that access to the courts should be maintained, implicit in both the *ultra vires* theory and the common law theory, suggests that there should be no time limit within which claims for judicial review must be made, in practice very short time limits do exist.[107]

Sufficient interest

Section 31(3) of the SCA 1981 states: 'the court *shall not* grant leave to make . . . an application [for judicial review] unless it considers that the applicant has

---

101 CPR 54.5.
102 See, for example, *R v Swale Borough Council, ex p Royal Society for the Protection of Birds* [1991] 1 PLR 6 (QBD).
103 CPR 54.5(2).
104 CPR 3.1(2)(a). It would appear from the case law that there are two conditions to be met before the courts will exercise this discretion. First, that the issue raised is one of general or public importance (*R v Secretary of State for the Home Department, ex p Ruddock and Others* [1987] 1 WLR 1482 (QBD) 1485 (Taylor J); *R v Secretary of State for Foreign and Commonwealth Affairs, ex p World Development Movement Ltd* [1995] 1 WLR 386 (QBD) 402–403 (Rose LJ); *R v Secretary of State for Trade and Industry, ex p Greenpeace Ltd* [2000] Env LR 221 (QBD) 263–264 (Maurice Kay J); *R (M) v School Organisation Committee, Oxford CC* [2001] EWHC Admin 245 [21]–[22] (Jackson J)). Second, that either the parties to the case, or third parties, would not be adversely affected by the granting of relief (*Greenpeace Ltd* (ibid) 258, 259, 261, 262–263 (Maurice Kay J); *R (M) v School Organisation Committee, Oxford CC* (ibid) [23]–[32] (Jackson J)). Academic comment about when the courts will exercise their discretion can also be found: Alistair Lindsay, 'Delay in Judicial Review Cases: A Conundrum Solved' [1995] *PL* 417, 423–425; Woolf, 'Public Law – Private Law: Why the Divide? A Personal View' (n 48) 231; Craig, *Administrative Law* (n 24) 871; Elliott, *Beatson, Matthews and Elliott's Administrative Law* (n 75) 475.
105 CPR 54.5(5).
106 Civil Procedure Act 1997 s 2.
107 Bondy and Sunkin write that the time limit requiring a judicial review claim to be brought promptly or within three months is 'very tight, especially when contrasted with general limitation periods', Vera Bondy and Maurice Sunkin 'Judicial Review Reform: Who is Afraid of Judicial Review? Debunking the Myths of Growth and Abuse.' UK Const. L. Blog (10 January 2013) (available at http://ukconstitutionallaw.org).

96 Intention, Supremacy and Judicial Review

a sufficient interest in the matter to which the application relates' (emphasis added). This sufficient interest requirement is also known as the requirement that a claimant should have standing or *locus standi*. For a claim brought under the HRA 1998, only a person who is a victim of the unlawful act complained of – that is, a victim of an act by a public authority which is not compatible with the Convention rights – may bring proceedings.[108]

In the past there were different tests for sufficient interest depending on which remedy the claimant was seeking. It is likely that there is now only one test regardless of the remedy being sought.[109]

It will be noted that the standing provision under section 31(3) explicitly *prohibits* the courts from granting permission for a claim to proceed unless the claimant has sufficient interest in the matter to which the claim relates. Similarly, under the HRA 1998, the courts *should not* permit a person to proceed with a claim unless assured that she is a victim of the unlawful act complained of. When making an assessment on these points, though, the interpretive obligation under both the *ultra vires* and common law theories requires the courts to give the SCA 1981 and the HRA 1998 the meaning that best accommodates the rule of law, including the principle that access to the courts should be maintained.[110] However, this obligation does not permit an interpretation which the statutory language cannot support.[111]

The general practice of the courts when considering whether a claimant's interest is sufficient has been given by Lord Donaldson:

> The first stage test, which is applied upon the application for leave, will lead to a refusal if the applicant has no interest whatsoever and is, in truth, no more than a meddlesome busybody. If, however, the application appears to be otherwise arguable and there is no other discretionary bar, such as dilatoriness on the part of the applicant, the applicant may expect to get leave to apply, leaving the test of interest or standing to be re-applied as a matter of discretion on the hearing of the substantive application. At this second stage, the strength of the applicant's interest is one of the factors to be weighed in the balance.[112]

---

108 Section 7(1): 'A person who claims that a public authority has acted (or proposes to act) in a way which is made unlawful by section 6(1) may . . . bring proceedings . . . *but only if he is (or would be) a victim of the unlawful act*' (emphasis added).

109 This seems to be the majority view in *National Federation of Self-Employed and Small Businesses Ltd* (n 77). See, also, *R v Felixstowe Justices, ex p Leigh* [1987] QB 582 (DC) 597 (Watkins LJ); and *Dixon* (n 92) 120 where Sedley J stated: 'The time is past when doctrinal niceties, as opposed to substantive merits, could distinguish locus for prohibition from locus for mandamus or certiorari'. The view that there is a uniform test for sufficient interest regardless of which remedy is being sought is also one shared by academics on both sides of the debate: Wade and Forsyth, *Administrative Law* (n 12) 587; Craig, *Administrative Law* (n 24) 778–779.

110 Above pp 82–83.

111 ibid.

112 *R v Monopolies and Mergers Commission, ex p Argyll Group Plc* [1986] 1 WLR 763 (CA) 774. The

Immanent critique and judicial review 97

Refusing permission for a claim to proceed only where the claimant 'has no interest whatsoever' would seem to be consistent with the obligation under both theories: it appears to represent an interpretation of the requirement that a claimant have sufficient interest in a way that maintains access to the courts.

While Lord Donaldson's statement may broadly represent the approach of the courts, there are examples of where a claim has been rejected for insufficient interest, even when it cannot be said that the claimant has no interest in the matter whatsoever. For example, in *R (Bulger) v Secretary of State for the Home Department*,[113] the parent of a murdered child did not have sufficient interest to challenge the Lord Chief Justice's recommended tariff setting the period of detention that the juvenile murderers should serve. This was so even though his Lordship had invited the victim's family to make representations before recommending the tariff. In *R v Director of the Serious Fraud Office, ex p Johnson*,[114] the claimant did not have sufficient interest to challenge a notice served on his wife to answer questions in relation to an investigation against him. In cases such as these, the courts do not appear to be adopting an approach which attempts to maintain access to the courts and so cannot be said to be acting in conformity with the requirements of both theories.

In addition, there are indications that the courts make an assessment of the genuineness of the claimant's concern when considering the sufficient interest question. So, in *R (Chandler) v Secretary of State for Children, Schools and Families*[115] the court held that the claimant lacked sufficient interest to challenge the establishment of an academy school on the ground that the public procurement regime had not been complied with. Chandler was a parent of secondary school aged children in the area of the proposed school. The court held that she lacked sufficient interest because her challenge was motivated by political opposition to academy schools rather than an interest in the public procurement regime. In *Walton v Scottish Ministers*, Lord Hope stated that the genuineness of the claimant's concern, as well as the sufficiency of his knowledge, were relevant factors when evaluating the sufficiency of his interest.[116] These considerations of the genuineness of the claimant's concern are not new.[117] Yet, they potentially conflict with the requirement of both theories that the sufficient interest condition be interpreted in such a way that access to the courts is maintained where there is a *prima facie* case of unlawfulness. Preventing a case from proceeding because the claimant's concern in the matter being challenged is perceived to

---

Bowman report suggested that there should be a presumption in favour of finding that a claimant has sufficient interest: *Review of the Crown Office List* (n 77) Chapter 7, para 29.

113 [2001] EWHC Admin 119, [2001] 3 All ER 449.

114 [1993] COD 58.

115 [2009] EWCA Civ 1011, [2010] PTSR 749.

116 [2012] UKSC 44, [2013] PTSR 51 [153].

117 See, for instance, *R v Secretary of State for Foreign and Commonwealth Affairs, ex parte Rees-Mogg* [1994] QB 552 (DC) 561–562 where the court accepted that the applicant had sufficient interest because of his 'sincere concern for constitutional issues'.

98 *Intention, Supremacy and Judicial Review*

be insufficiently genuine, or because she is thought to be acting for an ulterior motive (as in the *Chandler* case), is not consistent with this requirement.

It will be noted that Lord Donaldson also states that, after granting permission to proceed with a claim, the court may make an assessment of whether a claimant has sufficient interest at the substantive hearing. This two-stage approach was suggested by the House of Lords in *Inland Revenue Commissioners v National Federation of Self-Employed and Small Businesses.*[118] However, section 31(3) of the SCA 1981 requires the sufficiency of the claimant's interest to be assessed at the permission stage.[119] Once this stage has been passed, there is no statutory obligation that a claimant's interest in the matter be reassessed. In itself, this does not necessarily mean that it cannot be revisited at the substantive stage: 'it is clear that the statutory rules . . . do not require [standing] to be dealt with finally at [the permission] stage; neither do they preclude the raising of standing issues at a later stage'.[120] Nevertheless, in the absence of a statutory necessity to the contrary, both the *ultra vires* theory and the common law theory require that access to the courts should be maintained.[121] Consequently, this means that, if, at the substantive hearing, a case is made that limits on public power have been breached then the claimant's interest is irrelevant. For this reason, any reassessment, at the substantive hearing, of the claimant's personal interest in the matter to which the claim relates is contrary to both theories.[122]

Generally speaking, though, the test of sufficient interest is not determined solely by reference to the individual's personal interest in the subject matter of the claim; provided she is not motivated by malice or ill will, a claimant who has insufficient private interest will be given permission to proceed to the substantive hearing if the matter she raises is one of genuine public interest.[123] Wade and Forsyth have noted that this changes the meaning of sufficient interest:

---

118 *National Federation of Self-Employed and Small Businesses* (n 77).

119 Elliott appears to agree: 'the text of s 31(3) suggests that [the sufficient interest requirement] is resolved at the permission stage', *Beatson, Matthews and Elliott's Administrative Law* (n 75) 500; see, also, 515–516.

120 Himsworth, 'No Standing Still on Standing' (n 96) 204.

121 Above p 81–83.

122 It may be that this type of reassessment happens less since the introduction of the Civil Procedure Rules in 2000. Previously, the decision on whether to grant permission was made after hearing only the claimant's case. One factor in allowing the issue of sufficient interest to be considered again at the main hearing may have been to allow the defendant to challenge the claimant's interest. Given that the permission stage is now an *inter partes* procedure, the justification to re-visit the issue of sufficient interest may have diminished. Craig also seems to suggest that the adoption of a two-stage approach to standing was due in part to the fact that prior to the introduction of the Civil Procedure Rules the permission stage was an *ex parte* procedure: *Administrative Law* (n 24) 779–780.

123 *R (Feakins) v Secretary of State for the Environment, Food and Rural Affairs* [2003] EWCA Civ 1546, [2004] 1 WLR 1761 [21]–[23] (Dyson LJ). See, also, *National Federation of Self-Employed and Small Businesses* (n 77) 630 where Lord Wilberforce suggested that the matter is not simply an assessment of the personal interest of the claimant but is to be assessed 'together with the legal and factual context of the case'. Similarly, *World Development Movement Ltd* (n 104) 395–396 (Rose LJ). Bowman also states that the current law allows a finding of sufficient

The novel aspect of the second-stage test, as thus formulated, is that it does not appear to be a test of standing but rather a test of the merits of the complaint. The essence of standing, as a distinct concept, is that an applicant with a good case on the merits may have insufficient interest to be allowed to pursue it. The . . . new criterion would seem virtually to abolish the requirement of standing in this sense. However remote the applicant's interest, even if he is merely one taxpayer objecting to the assessment of another, he may still succeed if he shows a clear case of default or abuse. The law will now focus upon public policy rather than private interest.[124]

The test, then, is no longer merely an evaluation of the claimant's personal interest in the case but is also an assessment of its nature and strength. Where there is a 'clear case of default or abuse' – that is, where there is a clear case that, in the exercise of public power, the standards of good administration or any express statutory limits, have been breached – the courts will not block a case on sufficient interest grounds.[125]

Similarly, a group representing the interests of its members or acting on behalf of people who are affected by a decision may, for that reason alone, be found to have a sufficient interest to pursue a claim.[126] Cane refers to these two situations as, respectively, 'associational standing' and 'surrogate standing'.[127] An example of the former is to be found in *Inland Revenue Commissioners v National Federation of Self-Employed and Small Businesses*[128] where the Federation brought

interest where the claim is brought in the public interest: *Review of the Crown Office List* (n 77) Chapter 7, paras 28–29. Wade and Forsyth summarise the situation thus: 'the real question is whether the applicant can show some substantial default or abuse, and not whether his personal rights or interests are involved', *Administrative Law* (n 12) 588.

124 ibid 587–588 (citation omitted). While Wade and Forsyth are specifically referring to the reassessment of sufficient interest at the substantive hearing, their general point is applicable here; namely that the test has altered from one of assessing the claimant's interest to assessing the strength of the case. Cane similarly argues that the more liberal approach to standing, 'contains within it the seeds of the death of standing as an independent requirement of success in an application for judicial review', Peter Cane, 'Standing, Legality and the Limits of Public Law' [1981] *PL* 322, 332. For an argument in favour of this liberal approach to the sufficient interest requirement, see John McGarry, 'The Importance of an Expansive Test of Standing' [2014] *JR* 60.

125 There is some evidence that the courts adopt a varying approach here. Mills writes that the 'degree of private interest required depends on the degree of public interest in the proceedings', Alex Mills, 'Reforms to Judicial Review in the Criminal Justice and Courts Act 2015: Promoting Efficiency of Weakening the Rule of Law?' [2015] *PL* 583, 585; this varying standard has been advocated by Lord Reed in *AXA General Insurance Ltd and Others v HM Advocate and Others* [2011] UKSC 46, [2012] 1 AC 868 [170] and *Walton v Scottish Ministers* (n 116) [93]. See, also, Stephen H Bailey, 'Reflections on Standing for Judicial Review in Procurement Cases' (2015) 4 *PPLR* 122, 127.

126 Ligere suggests that the courts might be more likely to find that the representative claimant has sufficient interest in such cases if the courts consider the case to be deserving: Edite Ligere, '*Locus Standi* and the Public Interest: A Hotchpotch of Legal Principles' [2005] *JR* 128, paras 9–12.

127 Peter Cane, 'Standing up for the Public' [1995] *PL* 276, 276.

128 *National Federation of Self-Employed and Small Businesses* (n 77).

100 *Intention, Supremacy and Judicial Review*

an action against the Inland Revenue Commissioners on behalf of its members. An example of the latter can be found in *R v Secretary of State for Social Services, ex p Child Poverty Action Group*[129] where the Child Poverty Action Group could be said to be acting on behalf of 'unidentified claimants, who could be deprived of benefits by the secretary of state'.[130]

The courts have also indicated that a relevant consideration in deciding that a claimant has sufficient interest is that, otherwise, a challenge may be made by a claimant who has less expertise or who is not as well resourced.[131] Similarly, the likely absence of another responsible challenger has also been held to be a factor in holding that a claimant has standing.[132]

For present purposes, the question with all these cases – public interest claims, group claims and claims where it is unlikely that there will be an alternative responsible or resourced claimant – is whether the position taken by the courts is consistent with the *ultra vires* and common law theories.

It is perfectly possible to construe the sufficient interest obligation under section 31(3) of the SCA 1981 in such a way that it will only be satisfied if the claimant is personally affected by the decision to which the claim relates. Such an interpretation would mean public interest and group claims would not necessarily satisfy the sufficient interest requirement. This is because, with regard to the former, a matter may be of public interest but may not personally affect the claimant. With regard to the latter, a group bringing a case may not be able to maintain that it is, in itself, affected by the subject matter of the claim. This will certainly be true of surrogate standing where the group acts on behalf of individuals who are not necessarily its members. It may also be true of associational standing, particularly if the group is incorporated and so has a legal personality which is distinct to that of its members. In such a situation, it may be argued that the corporation is not affected by the matter simply because its members are affected. A personal interest test would also prohibit the courts from taking into account the likely absence of another responsible or well-resourced challenger. This is because a claimant does not become more affected by the matter to which the claim relates simply because there is no other suitable challenger.

On the other hand, it is not an explicit requirement, or a necessary implication, of section 31(3) that the claimant should be personally affected by the subject matter of the claim. This means that a broad interpretation, which allows claims even where the claimant cannot be said to have a personal interest, does not give the provision a meaning which the words are not capable of bearing. In addition, such an interpretation would place a high priority on maintaining access to the courts where there has been *prima facie* evidence of an unlawful exercise of public power.[133]

---

129 [1990] 2 QB 540 (CA).
130 Craig, *Administrative Law* (n 24) 783.
131 *R v Inspectorate of Pollution, ex p Greenpeace (No 2)* [1994] 4 All ER 329 (QBD) 350 (Otton J).
132 *World Development Movement* (n 104) 395 (Rose LJ).
133 It is worth noting that one could argue that access to the courts includes a right not to pursue a claim, or to have it pursued on one's behalf. This could also lead to the conclusion that surrogate

The same conclusion is also suggested by contrasting the standing requirement under the SCA 1981 with that under the HRA 1998. Under the latter statute, in order to bring a claim, a claimant must be a victim of the unlawful act complained of.[134] The plain inference of this is that the victim requirement under the HRA 1998 *is* a personal interest test: 'The use of the term "victim" . . . implies that only those who are *actually affected* by alleged breaches may apply to the Court' (emphasis in original).[135] This precludes, for instance, public interest challenges. The lack of a similar demand, in section 31(3) of the SCA 1981, that the claimant be a victim of the unlawful act which forms the basis of the claim, implies that the sufficient interest test under this provision is not necessarily a personal interest one.[136]

In summary, it is submitted that the approach of the courts in allowing public interest claims, group claims and claims taking into account the likelihood and quality of alternative possible challenges, is consistent with the *ultra vires* and common law theories. Similarly, blocking claims only where a claimant has no interest whatsoever and allowing claims to proceed where they raise a matter of genuine public interest is also commensurate with both theories. However, taking account of the genuineness of the claimant's interest, or her motivations, appears to conflict with the requirements of both theories that access to the courts should be maintained where there is a *prima facie* case of unlawfulness. In addition, any re-evaluation of the claimant's personal interest at the substantive hearing is contrary to both the *ultra vires* and common law theories.

Ouster clauses

As seen in Chapter Four, ouster clauses are legislative provisions which seek to limit or exclude the courts' supervisory jurisdiction. I observed that, broadly speaking, there are two types of ouster clauses: total ouster clauses and limited time clauses. The former seek to wholly prohibit the courts from reviewing the

---

claims should not be allowed to proceed without the express permission of those affected. Miles neatly sums up this view in the following way: 'the (paternalistic) belief of a third party that his or her actions will help a certain class of person should not be allowed to override the wishes of those intended beneficiaries. Since it is often difficult to know whether the beneficiaries of the proposed litigation will approve of the action, it is better as a default position to bar such actions. The burden should be on the applicant to show why the case should go ahead. And on this view, in the absence of positive evidence of victim approval, the applicant's ideological concerns are not in themselves sufficient to justify litigation', Joanna Miles, 'Standing under the Human Rights Act 1998: Theories of Rights Enforcement and the Nature of Public Law Adjudication' [2000] *CLJ* 133, 149–150.

134 Text to n 108.

135 Elliott, *Beatson, Matthews and Elliott's Administrative Law* (n 75) 528.

136 It is widely accepted that the 'victim' test under the HRA 1998 is narrower than the sufficient interest test under s 31(3) of the SCA 1981: Miles, 'Standing under the Human Rights Act 1998' (n 133) 134; Craig, *Administrative Law* (n 24) 787; Elliott, *Beatson, Matthews and Elliott's Administrative Law* (ibid) 530; Peter Leyland and Gordon Anthony, *Textbook on Administrative Law* (7th edn, OUP 2013) 206–207.

102 *Intention, Supremacy and Judicial Review*

exercise of the power in question. The latter allow judicial review for a specified period after which review is prohibited.[137]

I have argued above that, under both theories, there is an interpretive obligation that Acts of Parliament should be given the meaning that best corresponds to the rule of law. This, in turn, necessitates an interpretation that most effectively maintains access to the courts. Yet, I have also argued that this obligation does not permit statutory language to be overridden.[138] This means that, if it is plain that an ouster clause excludes judicial review in relation to a particular power, both the *ultra vires* theory and the common law theory require that there should be no exercise of the supervisory jurisdiction in respect of that power.

I noted in Chapter Four that, in practice, the courts have a different approach to the two types of ouster clauses. While they find that limited time clauses prohibit the courts from reviewing the exercise of power outside of the time allowed by the clause, they typically find that total ouster clauses do not prohibit the courts from judicially reviewing the exercise of the power in question.[139] I argued that the courts' interpretation of total ouster clauses conflicts with the requirements of parliamentary sovereignty.[140] Here, I wish to evaluate how closely the treatment of such clauses adheres to the requirements of the *ultra vires* and common law theories.

It is plain that the unequivocal meaning of total ouster clauses is that the jurisdiction of the courts should be excluded in relation to the power to which the clause relates. Support for this assertion can be found in the work of commentators on both sides of the debate. Wade and Forsyth, two of the leading *ultra vires* theorists, state that the courts' interpretation of ouster clauses is often contrary to 'the plain meaning of the words'.[141] Likewise, Elliott, another supporter of the *ultra vires* theory, writes of the decision in the *Anisminic* case,[142] where it was held that the ouster clause in the Foreign Compensation Act 1950 did not exclude the courts' jurisdiction: 'In no sense can it be maintained that the House of Lords simply gave effect to the plain meaning of the preclusive provision in *Anisminic*'.[143] Similarly, Craig, the chief advocate of the common law theory, writes that when an Act of Parliament contains such a clause, 'the legislature has stated in *clear* terms that it does not wish the courts to intervene with the decisions made' (emphasis added).[144] So, by relying on the assessment of the advocates of both the *ultra vires* and common law theories, we can conclude

---

137 Chapter Four p 62.

138 Above pp 82–83.

139 Chapter Four pp 62–63.

140 ibid pp 64–68.

141 *Administrative Law* (n 12) 609; see, also, 614.

142 *Anisminic Ltd v Foreign Compensation Commission* [1969] 2 AC 147 (HL).

143 Elliott, *The Constitutional Foundations of Judicial Review* (n 12) 31, 121.

144 'Ultra Vires and the Foundations of Judicial Review' (n 40) 68; see, also, 69; and Craig, *Administrative Law* (n 24) 892. See, also, Philip A Joseph, 'The Demise of Ultra Vires – A Reply to Christopher Forsyth and Linda Whittle' (2002) 8 *Canta LR* 463, 476 and John Chu, 'One Controversy, Two Jurisdictions: A Comparative Evaluation of the Ultra Vires and Common Law Theories of Judicial Review' [2009] *JR* 347, para 13.

that the courts' treatment of total ouster clauses conflicts with the requirements of both theories.

Remedies

I noted above that, under the *ultra vires* theory, when the courts apply the standards of good administration to the exercise of public power derived from statute, they do so pursuant to a presumed intention of Parliament.[145] I argued that the theory also obliges the courts not to act contrary to the intention of Parliament.[146] For these reasons, if the standards of good administration are breached in the exercise of power derived from statute, the *ultra vires* theory requires that a remedy must be granted as of right. If this were not the case, and the courts were able to withhold a remedy, they would be acting contrary to the intention of Parliament and thereby infringing sovereignty.

The position is different with regard to other types of public power such as *de facto* public power or power derived from the Royal prerogative. Under the *ultra vires* theory, the application of the standards of good administration to such power is required by the common law.[147] Because of this, the theory does not necessarily require that a remedy be granted when the courts find that the exercise of such power infringes these standards.

Under the common law theory, the courts should apply any limits on public power which are expressly stated in an Act of Parliament.[148] As such, if a court finds that such limits have been breached, a remedy should be granted. For all other cases, the standards of good administration are applied to all public power pursuant to a common law inherent jurisdiction of the courts.[149] Thus, with regard to such limits, the common law theory does not necessarily require that a remedy be granted when the courts find that public power has been exercised in breach of these standards.

In practice, section 31(2A) of the SCA 1981, as inserted by section 84 of the Criminal Justice and Courts Act 2015, obliges the court to refuse relief 'if it appears . . . highly likely that the outcome for the applicant would not have been substantially different if the conduct complained of had not occurred'. The court may, though, disregard this requirement, under subsection (2B), if it 'is appropriate to do so for reasons of exceptional public interest'. It is not yet clear how the courts will interpret this requirement. On the face of it, it seems to conflict with those aspects of both the common law and *ultra vires* theories which require a remedy to be granted where there has been a breach of the standards of good administration. However, given that this instruction to refuse a remedy where it would make no difference to the claimant is contained in an Act of

145 Above p 82.
146 Above p 81.
147 Chapter Four pp 56–57.
148 Above p 81.
149 Chapter Four p 56; also Chapter 3 pp 34–35.

104   *Intention, Supremacy and Judicial Review*

Parliament, and given the primacy afforded to parliamentary sovereignty in the two theories, it would be consistent with both theories if these provisions of the SCA 1981were used to refuse a remedy. This is particularly so given the ability of the courts, under section 31(2B), to supply a remedy where there is exceptional public interest.

Outside of these requirements under section 31(2A)–(2C) of the SCA 1981, the granting of remedies is for the most part at the court's discretion.[150] Indeed, as noted in Chapter Four, Feldman contends that this discretion exists because unlawful decisions are not necessarily *void ab initio*.[151]

Whatever the basis of the courts' discretion with regard to remedies, in the main it is consistent with the common law theory. It is similarly consistent with the *ultra vires* theory as it applies to non-statutory public power. However, the discretion conflicts with the *ultra vires* theory as it relates to public power derived from statute. It also conflicts with the common law theory with regard to limits on public power expressly stated in an Act of Parliament.

It is worth acknowledging here, Forsyth's argument, as noted in Chapter Four, that, when the courts use their discretion to withhold a remedy, this does not confer legality on the unlawful act: the unlawful act still remains null and void.[152] If correct, then the discretionary nature of remedies does not necessarily conflict with either the *ultra vires* or common law theories. This is because, for example, an exercise of statutorily derived power which breaches the standards of good administration would be a nullity regardless of whether a remedy had been granted. It would not, therefore, be a breach of parliamentary sovereignty for the courts to refuse a remedy because that refusal, according to Forsyth, would have no legal effect. Yet, as I also noted in Chapter Four, the evidence suggests that the courts act as though the granting or withholding of remedies does have legal effect.[153]

Conclusion

Chapter Four consisted of a critical review of the arguments that are marshalled in support of the *ultra vires* theory and the common law theory. Among other things, I observed that it is implicit in those arguments that the theories should match the reality of the supervisory jurisdiction.[154] This led to the conclusion that it would be appropriate to systematically analyse, using immanent critique, the degree to which the theories coincide with the practice of judicial review. The purpose of this chapter has been to subject the two theories to such a critique. This has involved identifying the values that underlie the theories – the rule of

---

150 Chapter Four pp 69–70.
151 David Feldman, 'Error of Law and Flawed Administrative Acts' [2014] *CLJ* 275; Chapter Four p 71.
152 Christopher F Forsyth, 'The Rock and the Sand: Jurisdiction and Remedial Discretion' [2013] *JR* 360; Chapter Four pp 70–71.
153 Chapter Four p 71.
154 Chapter Four p 73.

law and parliamentary sovereignty – and using these to evaluate how closely the practice of judicial review adheres to the requirements of the two theories. I examined six aspects of judicial review.

With regard to the scope of judicial review, I noted that supporters of both theories argue that all monopolistic power should be susceptible to the supervisory jurisdiction. This, though, is not the case in practice; the courts will not necessarily review power on the basis that it is monopolistic. However, I argued that this divergence between the contention of supporters of both theories and review in practice does not in itself call into question the legitimacy of either theory. This is because the argument that the courts should review monopolistic power is made with regard to non-statutory power and so, strictly speaking, does not conflict with either theory which are posited to explain judicial review of public power derived from statute.

The operation of the permission stage does conflict with the requirements of both theories. I argued that denying permission for a case to proceed because the issue raised is frivolous; because the claimant is not *bona fide*; or to manage and ration judicial resources, is to take into account factors external to the *ultra vires* and common law theories and which are contrary to the requirement of both that access to the courts should be maintained. There are also instances where the courts do not take a 'light touch' approach at this stage as necessitated by each theory.

When looking at time limits, I argued that both theories require that a time limit should not be set. The principle that access to the courts be maintained – inherent in both theories – means that a claim should be permitted to proceed where there is an argument that implied or express limits on the exercise of public power have been breached regardless of the time that has elapsed since the alleged breach. It is worth repeating here that a time limit in judicial review cases is not demanded by primary legislation. Nevertheless, in practice, there is a very short time limit by which such claims must be brought. Generally, a claim must be made 'promptly and in any event not later than 3 months after the grounds to make the claim first arose'.[155] In planning cases and cases relating to decisions made under the Public Contracts Regulations 2015, the time limit is even shorter: respectively, a claim must be brought within six weeks and within 30 days.

I also suggested that the courts' approach to the sufficient interest requirement diverges from that required by the *ultra vires* and common law theories. The expansive approach adopted by the courts to the requirement of sufficient interest – whereby the courts will not block a claim in which there is a *prima facie* case that the standards of good administration have been breached regardless of the claimant's personal interest in the matter – is consistent with both theories. However, I argued that taking into account the genuineness of the claimant's concern, or her motivations in bringing a challenge, as well as a possible

155 Text to n 101.

106 *Intention, Supremacy and Judicial Review*

re-assessment of a claimant's personal interest at the substantive hearing stage, is contrary to both theories.

The courts' interpretation of total ouster clauses is also contrary to the requirements of both theories. This is because the plain and unequivocal reading of such provisions is that the jurisdiction of the courts should be excluded. Yet, the courts construe them so that the supervisory jurisdiction is unaffected.

Finally, I argued that the discretionary nature of remedies in judicial review cases conflicts with the demands of both theories, though it does so in different ways for each of them. It is contrary to the requirements of the common law theory where the basis of the claim is that a decision-maker has breached a limit on the exercise of public power which is expressly stated in an Act of Parliament. The discretion is contrary to the *ultra vires* theory in all cases where the power in question is derived from primary legislation.

So, the immanent critique undertaken in this chapter has revealed a number of discrepancies between judicial review in practice and the *ultra vires* and common law theories. These discrepancies bring into question the ability of either theory to supply a rationalised account of judicial review. Yet, as argued in Chapter Three, the *raison d'être* of both theories is to provide such an account: to explain judicial review in a way which accommodates the requirements of parliamentary sovereignty.[156] But, as I have argued in Chapter Four, the rationalisation provided by both theories is premised on the assumption that parliamentary sovereignty operates in the manner of a Dworkinian rule.[157] I challenge this assumption in the following chapter where I argue that parliamentary sovereignty functions as a principle rather than a rule. I explore the consequences of this assertion on the manner in which we may justify the exercise of judicial review in Chapter Seven.

---

156 Chapter Three pp 30, 38 and 39.
157 Chapter Four pp 42–44.

Bibliography

Allan TRS, 'Legislative Supremacy and Legislative Intention: Interpretation, Meaning and Authority' [2004] *Cambridge Law Journal* 685

Antonio R J, 'Immanent Critique as the Core of Critical Theory: Its Origins and Developments in Hegel, Marx and Contemporary Thought' (1981) 32(3) *The British Journal of Sociology* 330

Bailey S H, 'Judicial Review of Contracting Decisions' [2007] *Public Law* 444

— 'Reflections on Standing for Judicial Review in Procurement Cases' (2015) 4 *Public Procurement Law Review* 122

Bamforth N, 'The Scope of Judicial Review: Still Uncertain' [1993] *Public Law* 239

— 'Ultra Vires and Institutional Interdependence' in Christopher F Forsyth (ed), *Judicial Review and the Constitution* (Hart Publishing 2000)

Beloff M J, 'The Boundaries of Judicial Review' in Jeffrey L Jowell and Dawn Oliver (eds), *New Directions in Judicial Review* (Stevens and Sons 1988)

Bondy V and Sunkin M, 'Accessing Judicial Review' [2008] *Public Law* 647

— 'Judicial Review Reform: Who is Afraid of Judicial Review? Debunking the Myths of Growth and Abuse.' UK Const. L. Blog (10 January 2013) (available at http://ukconstitutionallaw.org)

Bowman Sir Jeffrey *et al*, *Review of the Crown Office List: A Report to the Lord Chancellor* (Lord Chancellor's Department 2000)

Bridges L, Meszaros G and Sunkin M, 'Regulating the Judicial Review Caseload' [2000] *Public Law* 651

Buchwalter A, 'Hegel, Marx, and the Concept of Immanent Critique' (1991) 29(2) *Journal of the History of Philosophy* 253

Cane P, 'Standing, Legality and the Limits of Public Law' [1981] *Public Law* 322

— 'Standing up for the Public' [1995] *Public Law* 276

— *Administrative Law* (4th edn, OUP 2004)

Chu J, 'One Controversy, Two Jurisdictions: A Comparative Evaluation of the Ultra Vires and Common Law Theories of Judicial Review' [2009] *Judicial Review* 347

Cornford T and Sunkin M, 'The Bowman Report, Access and the Recent Reforms of the Judicial Review Procedure' [2001] *Public Law* 11

Craig P P, *Public Law and Democracy in the United Kingdom and the United States of America* (OUP 1990)

— 'Formal and Substantive Conceptions of the Rule of Law: An Analytical Framework' [1997] *Public Law* 467

— 'Ultra Vires and the Foundations of Judicial Review' [1998] *Cambridge Law Journal* 63

— 'Contracting Out, the Human Rights Act and the Scope of Judicial Review' (2002) 118 *Law Quarterly Review* 551

— 'Constitutional Foundations, the Rule of Law and Supremacy' [2003] *Public Law* 92

— *Administrative Law* (7th edn, Sweet & Maxwell 2012)

Dicey A V, *Introduction to the Study of the Law of the Constitution* (8th edn, Macmillan 1915)

Elliott M C, 'The Ultra Vires Doctrine in a Constitutional Setting: Still the Central Principle of Administrative Law' [1999] *Cambridge Law Journal* 129

— *The Constitutional Foundations of Judicial Review* (Hart Publishing 2001)

— *Beatson, Matthews and Elliott's Administrative Law: Text and Materials* (4th edn, OUP 2011)

108 *Intention, Supremacy and Judicial Review*

Feldman D, 'Error of Law and Flawed Administrative Acts' [2014] *Cambridge Law Journal* 275

Fordham M, 'Permission Principles' [2006] *Judicial Review* 176

— 'Arguability Principles' [2007] *Judicial Review* 219

Forsyth C F, 'Of Fig Leaves and Fairy Tales: The Ultra Vires Doctrine, the Sovereignty of Parliament and Judicial Review' [1996] *Cambridge Law Journal* 122

— 'The Rock and the Sand: Jurisdiction and Remedial Discretion' [2013] *Judicial Review* 360

— and Elliott M C, 'The Legitimacy of Judicial Review' [2003] *Public Law* 286

Gadamer H-G, *Truth and Method* (D G Marshall and Joel Weinsheimer trs, 2nd edn, Sheed and Ward 1989)

Gottlieb A, 'Philosopher's Martyr: Socrates' in Ray Monk and Frederic Raphael (eds), *The Great Philosophers: From Socrates to Turing* (Phoenix 2001)

Harden I and Lewis N, *The Noble Lie: The British Constitution and the Rule of Law* (Hutchinson 1986)

Held D, *Introduction to Critical Theory: Horkheimer to Habermas* (University of California Press 1980)

Himsworth C, 'No Standing Still on Standing' in Peter Leyland and Terry Woods (eds), *Administrative Law Facing the Future: Old Constraints and New Horizons* (Blackstone Press 1997)

Joseph P A, 'The Demise of Ultra Vires – A Reply to Christopher Forsyth and Linda Whittle' (2002) 8 *Canterbury Law Review* 463

Jowell J L, 'Is Equality a Constitutional Principle?' (1994) 47 *Current Legal Problems* 1

— 'Of Vires and Vacuums: The Constitutional Context of Judicial Review' [1999] *Public Law* 448

Laws Sir John, 'Law and Democracy' [1995] *Public Law* 72

Le Sueur A P and Sunkin M, 'Applications for Judicial Review: The Requirement of Leave' [1992] *Public Law* 102

Le Sueur A P, Jowell J L and Woolf Lord, *De Smith, Woolf and Jowell's Principles of Judicial Review* (5th edn, Sweet & Maxwell 1999)

Leyland P and Anthony G, *Textbook on Administrative Law* (7th edn, OUP 2013)

Ligere E, '*Locus Standi* and the Public Interest: A Hotchpotch of Legal Principles' [2005] *Judicial Review* 128

Lindsay A, 'Delay in Judicial Review Cases: A Conundrum Solved' [1995] *Public Law* 417

McGarry J, 'The Importance of an Expansive Test of Standing' [2014] *Judicial Review* 60

Miles J, 'Standing under the Human Rights Act 1998: Theories of Rights Enforcement and the Nature of Public Law Adjudication' [2000] *Cambridge Law Journal* 133

Mills A, 'Reforms to Judicial Review in the Criminal Justice and Courts Act 2015: Promoting Efficiency of Weakening the Rule of Law?' [2015] *Public Law* 583

Oliver D, 'The Frontiers of the State: Public Authorities and Public Functions under the Human Rights Act' [2000] *Public Law* 476

— 'Public Law Procedures and Remedies – Do We Need Them?' [2002] *Public Law* 91

— 'Functions of a Public Nature under the Human Rights Act' [2004] *Public Law* 329

Pannick D, 'Who is Subject to Judicial Review and in Respect of What?' [1992] *Public Law* 1

Plato, *The Republic* (D Lee tr, 2nd edn, Penguin Classics 1974)

Sedley Sir Stephen, *The Hamlyn Lectures: Freedom, Law and Justice* (Sweet & Maxwell 1999)

Taggart M, 'Ultra Vires as Distraction' in Christopher F Forsyth (ed), *Judicial Review and the Constitution* (Hart Publishing 2000)

Wade HWR, and Forsyth C F, *Administrative Law* (11th edn, OUP 2014)

Wadham J, Mountfield H, Prochaska E and Brown C, *Blackstone's Guide to the Human Rights Act 1998* (6th edn, OUP 2011)

Woolf Lord, 'Public Law – Private Law: Why the Divide? A Personal View' [1986] *Public Law* 220

— '*Droit Public* – English Style' [1995] *Public Law* 57

6 The principle of parliamentary sovereignty

In Chapter Four, I argued that parliamentary sovereignty is assumed to function as a Dworkinian rule in both the *ultra vires* and the common law theories. This conception will be challenged in this chapter. I argue, in the first section, that, in practice, parliamentary sovereignty operates as a principle rather than a rule. I follow this, in the second section, by examining some potential criticisms of this argument.

I first contended that parliamentary sovereignty functions as a principle in the PhD dissertation on which this monograph is based. I then made the argument in a journal article.[1] As will be evident in the following, the idea that the legislative competence of Parliament is less absolute, and more flexible, than is commonly thought, is one that has increasingly gained greater traction.

Parliamentary sovereignty as a principle

In Chapter Two, I noted Dworkin's position that, unlike rules, principles operate in a non-conclusive way. They do not compel or demand a particular result but merely indicate a possible direction; they will be balanced, one against another, when reaching a particular decision. Because of this, they possess a flexibility that rules do not. As will be shown, when we conceive of legislative supremacy in this way, it seems to fit the actual, extant relationship between the legislature and the courts.

I begin by observing that, while the *ultra vires* theory is premised on an *assumption* of parliamentary sovereignty operating as a rule, as argued in Chapter Four,[2] its supporters often explain the *reality* in a manner that is suggestive of a principle. Elliott's account of the courts' treatment of ouster clauses is an example of this. I have noted, in previous chapters, that ouster clauses are provisions in

---

1 John McGarry, 'The Principle of Parliamentary Sovereignty' (2012) 32(4) *LS* 577. My argument has since been supported by Sir John Laws who writes that his own contention regarding parliamentary sovereignty 'marches with the reasoning of John McGarry in a very interesting recent article . . . Legislative sovereignty is not a doctrine set in stone. It is an evolving legal construct: a principle, not a rule', Sir John Laws, *The Hamlyn Lectures: The Common Law Constitution* (CUP 2014) 28.
2 Chapter Four pp 43–44.

The principle of parliamentary sovereignty 111

primary legislation that appear to curtail the courts' judicial review jurisdiction. There are two basic types, limited time and total. The former permit a decision to be reviewed within a particular time frame – often six weeks – after which review is prohibited. The latter prohibit review entirely. Generally, the courts faithfully adhere to limited time ouster clauses whereas they commonly rule that total ouster clauses do not inhibit the exercise of the supervisory jurisdiction.[3]

As discussed in Chapter Four, Elliott states that, when faced with a total ouster clause, the courts take its plain meaning and weigh this against the principle that access to the courts should be maintained: 'Two countervailing forces are . . . at work. The courts must attempt to find the right constitutional balance between the prima facie meaning of the provision and the strong preference for access to justice which the rule of law embodies'.[4] By this reasoning, a finding that such clauses do not exclude the supervisory jurisdiction is simply the result of balancing two competing interests. He uses the same argument to explain why the courts adhere to limited time ouster clauses. That is, because the potential infringement of the 'access to the courts' principle is less severe, the courts can give effect to the plain meaning of the legislation.[5] This depiction of the courts being engaged in a balancing of competing interests is indicative, not of a rule, but of a Dworkinian principle.

A similar conclusion is implicit within Forsyth and Elliot's explication of the decision in *R v Lord Chancellor, ex p Witham*.[6] The judgment of the court – which was, in the main, given by Laws J – was that the Lord Chancellor did not have the power to remove, from litigants in person, the exemption from paying court fees. The Lord Chancellor had purported to act under section 130 of the Supreme Court Act 1981 (now known as the Senior Courts Act 1981). However, his actions were ruled to be unlawful because, the court determined, access to the courts is a constitutional right. Forsyth and Elliott state: 'it is clear that Laws J envisages an interaction between . . . "common law" rights and the words of a statute and that the outcome of that interaction is the actual meaning given to statute'.[7] This description of an interaction between common law rights and legislation corresponds with my suggestion that the courts are engaging in a balancing of competing principles.

Of course, one could simply view these instances as the modification of a rule

---

3 ibid pp 62–63.

4 Mark C Elliott, 'The Ultra Vires Doctrine in a Constitutional Setting: Still the Central Principle of Administrative Law' [1999] *CLJ* 129, 151; Chapter Four p 64.

5 Chapter Four, ibid.

6 [1998] QB 575 (QBD).

7 Christopher F Forsyth and Mark C Elliott, 'The Legitimacy of Judicial Review' [2003] *PL* 286, 304.Taggart seems to envisage a similar interaction: 'in accordance with the "folk ways" of common lawyers statutes are read in accordance with . . . values [of the rule of law], and the judges have fashioned administrative law so as to give expression to them', Michael Taggart, 'Ultra Vires as Distraction' in Christopher F Forsyth (ed), *Judicial Review and the Constitution* (Hart Publishing 2000) 427.

112   *Intention, Supremacy and Judicial Review*

by a principle. Dworkin's use of the New York case of *Riggs v Palmer*[8] to illustrate the qualities of principles appears to demonstrate just such an occurrence. Here, the New York court decided that a grandson who was named in his grandfather's will could not inherit because he had murdered his grandfather in order to do so. The court conceded that a literal reading of the pertinent statute would have allowed the grandson to inherit. Yet, they determined that the statute, the rule, should be qualified by the principle that 'No one should be permitted to profit by his own fraud, or to take advantage of his own wrong, or to found any claim upon his own iniquity, or to acquire property by his own crime'.[9] The court reasoned: 'all laws as well as all contracts may be controlled in their operation and effect by general, fundamental maxims of the common law'.[10] It is, then, perfectly consistent with Dworkin's overall thesis that a rule can be amended by a principle.[11] In our case this would mean that legislative supremacy may still be considered to be a rule, albeit one that is qualified by the principle that access to the courts should be maintained.

Indeed, such a qualification may be thought to be merely a more comprehensive account of the rule of parliamentary sovereignty. Again, Dworkin certainly allows for this to take place – for a fuller account of any rule, including its exceptions, to be given in order to create a more accurate description of it.[12] This new, more comprehensive statement of the rule of legislative supremacy could read as follows:

> The courts will faithfully adhere to all legislation, including legislation that prohibits the courts from reviewing a decision after a specified period of time. They will not, however, give effect to legislation which substantially infringes the rights of access to the courts.

Yet, this is not how Elliott rationalises the treatment of ouster clauses. He writes of it being a balancing of 'countervailing forces'.[13] Also, with Forsyth, he explains the *Witham* case as an 'interaction' between legislation and rights.[14] These descriptions are characteristic of principles rather than rules. Furthermore, the case for viewing parliamentary sovereignty as a principle is strengthened if

---

8 115 N.Y. 506, 22 N.E. 188 (1889), cited in Ronald Dworkin, *Taking Rights Seriously* (Duckworth & Co 1977) 23.

9 ibid 511.

10 ibid.

11 *Taking Rights Seriously* (n 8) 37. Dworkin has been criticised on this point because the idea that rules may be qualified by principles seems to be inconsistent with the conclusive character that he attributes to them. Hart, for instance, writes of Dworkin's use of *Riggs v Palmer*: 'This is an example of a principle winning in competition with a rule, but the existence of such competition surely shows that rules do not have an all-or-nothing character, since they are liable to be brought into such conflict with principles which may outweigh them', HLA Hart, *The Concept of Law* (3rd edn, OUP 2012) 262 (Postscript).

12 *Taking Rights Seriously* (ibid) 24–25.

13 Text to n 4.

14 Text to n 7.

The principle of parliamentary sovereignty 113

we suppose that a number of elements of, say, a limited time ouster clause were different. Such clauses often deal with decisions affecting the planning, control or acquisition of land and, as I have already noted, they often leave six weeks during which the determination in question may be challenged.[15] Let us imagine, though, that a citizen's liberty is at stake and that a limited time clause allows just three days for a decision affecting that liberty to be challenged. It is easy to envisage that the courts would not adhere as closely to such a clause as they do to the usual six-week version. Such variability, if true, suggests that parliamentary sovereignty is not a rule. This is because, unlike with rules, we could not – even in theory – identify all the exceptions to the principle that the variation represents and thereby give a more comprehensive statement of it.[16]

Moreover, parliamentary sovereignty – that is, the maxim that the courts should faithfully adopt and apply Acts of Parliament – has a quality that is possessed by principles but not by rules: the dimension of weight. The relative weight, or importance, of principles will determine how a conflict between two or more of them will be resolved.[17] So, the weighting that an Act of Parliament has will determine the degree to which it is complied with by the courts when it conflicts with a competing principle. We know that parliamentary sovereignty has this dimension of weight because adherence to a particular statute will vary according to its characteristics.

One such characteristic is subject matter. A legislative provision may be accorded greater weight than another because it deals with an issue perceived to be of more importance. We can see this clearly with the European Communities Act 1972 (ECA 1972). The traditional view of parliamentary sovereignty is that Parliament may not bind a successor.[18] This means that where two Acts of Parliament are in conflict, the earlier one should be impliedly repealed by the later one as much as is necessary to resolve the conflict.[19] Yet, in the *Factortame*[20] case, the House of Lords granted an interim injunction to prevent the Merchant Shipping Act 1988 taking effect because it conflicted with European Community law, which was incorporated into UK law by the ECA 1972. This meant that the ECA 1972 was not impliedly repealed by the later statute – the Merchant Shipping Act 1988 – but was used to grant an injunction preventing that later

---

15 Paul P Craig, *Administrative Law* (7th edn, Sweet & Maxwell 2012) 890; HWR Wade and Christopher F Forsyth, *Administrative Law* (11th edn, OUP 2014) 619. For example, see the Acquisition of Land Act 1981 s 23 and the Town and Country Act 1990 s 287.

16 Dworkin, *Taking Rights Seriously* (n 8) 25. Allan makes the point in the following way: 'A principle's weight will vary infinitely within an infinite range of facts and circumstances: it is precisely this elastic quality which eludes the straight-jacket nature of rules', TRS Allan, *Law, Liberty and Justice: The Legal Foundations of British Constitutionalism* (Clarendon Press 1993) 93.

17 *Taking Rights Seriously* (ibid) 26.

18 *Vauxhall Estates v Liverpool Corporation* [1932] 1 KB 733 (KBD) 743 (Avory J); *Ellen St Estates v Minister of Health* [1934] 1 KB 590 (CA) 595 (Scrutton LJ), 597 (Maugham LJ).

19 *Thoburn v Sunderland City Council* [2002] EWHC 195 (Admin), [2003] QB 151 [37] (Laws LJ). Laws' definition, and examples, of constitutional statutes has been criticised; see, for example: T St J N Bates, 'Editorial: Constitutional Statutes' (2007) 28 *Stat LR* iii, iii–iv.

20 *R v Secretary of State for Transport, ex p Factortame and Others (No 2)* [1991] 1 AC 603 (HL).

114 *Intention, Supremacy and Judicial Review*

Act being applied. In short, there was a conflict between the requirements of two statutes and the significance of the ECA 1972 meant that it was afforded greater weight than, and was able to override, the relevant provisions of the Merchant Shipping Act 1988.

In *Thoburn v Sunderland City Council*, Laws LJ also suggested that adherence to a statute will vary according to its substance.[21] He stated: 'There are now classes or types of legislative provision which cannot be repealed by mere implication'.[22] He continued: 'Ordinary statutes may be impliedly repealed. Constitutional statutes may not'.[23] We may infer that constitutional statutes are of such consequence that the implied repeal rule does not apply to them because they will outweigh any conflicting legislation. He also stated: 'The courts may say – have said – that there are certain circumstances in which the legislature may only enact what it desires to enact if it does so by *express, or at any rate specific, provision*' (emphasis added).[24]

More recently, in the Supreme Court, Lord Neuberger PSC and Lord Mance JSC referred to Laws' discussion of the distinction between ordinary and constitutional statutes, and of the assertion that the latter cannot be impliedly repealed by the former, as providing 'important insights'. Indeed, they suggest that there may be a hierarchy among constitutional statutes (not simply between constitutional and ordinary statutes) such that one constitutional statute – or, to adopt their phrase, constitutional instrument – should not be taken to impliedly repeal another considered to be more important.[25] As Elliott writes, this approach 'signals a shift away from a bright-line distinction between ordinary and constitutional legislation, and instead embraces a more nuanced approach that is capable of accommodating varying degrees of constitutional fundamentality'.[26] Lords Neuberger and Mance also state that the common law recognises certain principles as being fundamental to the rule of law and which, they suggest, the courts will assume that Parliament does not intend to abrogate unless there is a clear indication to the contrary.[27] Presumably, this clear indication would be provided by express words.

Where explicit language is used in any competing legislation, this may alter the weight attributed to it, and thereby result in a different outcome. Lord Denning MR has made this clear with regard to the ECA 1972:

---

21 *Thoburn* (n 19) [60]–[64].

22 ibid [60].

23 ibid [63].

24 ibid [60].

25 *Regina (HS2 Action Alliance Ltd and Others) v Secretary of State for Transport* [2014] UKSC 3, [2014] 1 WLR 324 [207]–[208].

26 Mark C Elliott 'Constitutional Legislation, European Union Law and the Nature of the United Kingdom's Contemporary Constitution' (2014) 10(3) *ECLR* 379, 388.

27 *HS2 Action Alliance* (n 25) [207]. See, also, Mark C Elliott, 'The Principle of Parliamentary Sovereignty in Legal, Constitutional, and Political Perspective' in Jeffrey L Jowell, Dawn Oliver and Colm O'Cinneide (eds), *The Changing Constitution* (8th edn, OUP 2015) 48.

The principle of parliamentary sovereignty 115

If the time should come when our Parliament deliberately passes an Act –
with the intention of repudiating the Treaty or any provision in it – or inten-
tionally of acting inconsistently with it – *and says so in express terms* – then
I should have thought that it would be the duty of the courts to follow the
statute of our Parliament (emphasis added).[28]

That is, the ECA 1972 may be overridden by competing legislation if the language used in that legislation is sufficiently categorical.

In fact, the explicitness of statutory language is another characteristic that
influences the weight which legislation is perceived to possess: the more explicit
the language, the more likely it is that it will be adhered to. For instance,
Viscount Simonds stated, in response to an argument that the jurisdiction of the
court to grant a declaration had been excluded, 'It is a principle not by any means
to be whittled down that the subject's recourse to Her Majesty's courts for the
determination of his rights is not to be excluded *except by clear words*' (emphasis
added).[29] Likewise, with regard to the courts' jurisdiction to safeguard liberty,
Lord Scarman said: 'If Parliament intends to exclude effective judicial review of
the exercise of a power in restraint of liberty, *it must make its meaning crystal
clear*' (emphasis added).[30] Elliott, one of chief supporters of the *ultra vires*
theory, makes a similar point with regard to legislation which confers authority
on Ministers and other executive bodies:

Unless the legislation provides in *crystal-clear terms* to the contrary, the
effects of the principle of legality is to yield an interpretation of the statute
that withholds from the constitutional actor any authority to act incompatibly with common law constitutional principles (emphasis added).[31]

A similar conclusion may be taken from the opinion of Lord Reid in *Anisminic
Ltd v Foreign Compensation Commission*.[32] It was shown in Chapter Four that, in
this case, the House of Lords decided that an ouster clause would not prohibit
them from exercising their supervisory jurisdiction.[33] Lord Reid stated that, if
Parliament wished to exclude the courts, he would expect to find, 'something
much more specific than the bald statement that a determination shall not be
called in question in any court of law'.[34] The clear implication is that if Parliament
had used more explicit language to try to preclude the supervisory jurisdiction, it is more likely that the courts would have adhered to it. Indeed, with

---

28 *Macarthys v Smith* [1979] ICR 785 (CA) 789.
29 *Pyx Granite Co v Ministry of Housing and Local Government* [1960] AC 260 (HL) 286.
30 *Khawaja v Home Secretary* [1984] AC 74 (HL) 111.
31 'The Principle of Parliamentary Sovereignty in Legal, Constitutional, and Political Perspective'
    (n 27) 56. See, also, Elliott 'Constitutional Legislation, European Union Law and the Nature of
    the United Kingdom's Contemporary Constitution' (n 26) 389 and 392.
32 [1969] 2 AC 147 (HL).
33 Chapter Four pp 62–63.
34 [1969] 2 AC 147 (HL) 170.

116 *Intention, Supremacy and Judicial Review*

regard to statutory provisions which attempt to exclude the courts' jurisdiction, Denning LJ has stated: 'I find it very well settled that the remedy by certiorari is never to be taken away by any statute *except by the most clear and explicit words*' (emphasis added).[35] More recent judgments have also made it clear that the courts' supervisory jurisdiction cannot be removed by statutory implication.[36]

A similar variability can be seen with regard to fundamental rights. The term 'fundamental rights' includes human rights and other important constitutional principles.[37] In *R v Secretary of State for the Home Department, ex p Brind*,[38] Lord Bridge rejected the suggestion that primary enabling legislation must be read so as to only permit the making of regulations by the Home Secretary that conform to such rights – in that case, those guaranteed by the European Convention on Human Rights and Fundamental Freedoms (ECHR).[39] However, in other cases, the courts have stated that infringements of fundamental rights must be authorised by explicit statutory language or by necessary implication.[40] Indeed, writing extra-judicially, Laws states:

> it is now surely uncontentious – elementary – that [fundamental] rights protected by the common law could not be abrogated by statute *save by crystal clear provisions leaving no room for doubt* as to what the legislative intention was (emphasis added).[41]

This has also been recognised by Jowell. He writes that Parliament may legislate to exclude a constitutional principle but that, 'to command . . . acceptance [by the courts], Parliament will have to make itself clear . . . ambiguity may not be enough to coax the courts into agreeing to displace democracy's foundational features'.[42]

---

35 *R v Medical Appeal Tribunal, ex p Gilmore* [1957] 1 QB 574 (CA) 583.

36 For example: Lord Phillips in *R (Savasubramaniam) v Wandsworth County Court* [2002] EWCA Civ 1738, [2003] 1 WLR 475 [44] and Laws LJ in *R (Cart) v Upper Tribunal* [2009] EWHC 3052 (Admin), [2010] 2 WLR 1012 [32].

37 Craig, *Administrative Law* (n 15) 576–579. Two such important constitutional principles may be that there should be reasonably free access to the courts and that citizens should be allowed freedom of movement. The former has been held to be a 'constitutional right', *Witham* (n 6) 585, 586 (Laws J). Similarly, it has been stated that the latter is a 'fundamental value of the common law', *R v Secretary of State for the Home Department, ex p McQuillan* [1995] 4 All ER 400 (QBD) 421 (Sedley J).

38 [1991] 1 AC 696 (HL).

39 ibid 748. See, also, Sir John Laws, 'Is the High Court the Guardian of Fundamental Constitutional Rights?' [1993] *PL* 59, 62.

40 *Witham* (n 6) 585–586 (Laws J); *R v Secretary of State for the Home Department, ex p Simms and Another* [2000] 2 AC 115 (HL) 131 (Lord Hoffmann); *International Transport Roth GmbH v Secretary of State for the Home Department* [2002] EWCA Civ 158, [2003] QB 728 [74] (Laws LJ); *R (Jackson) v Attorney-General* [2005] UKHL 56, [2006] 1 AC 262 [159] (Baroness Hale).

41 Sir John Laws, 'Constitutional Guarantees' (2007) 16 *Com Lawyer* 24, 28; see, also, Laws, *The Common Law Constitution* (n 1) 21, 70.

42 Jeffrey L Jowell, 'Of Vires and Vacuums: The Constitutional Context of Judicial Review' [1999] *PL* 448, 458.

The principle of parliamentary sovereignty 117

Lord Hoffmann has given a rationale for this approach. He stated in *ex p Simms*:

> Parliamentary sovereignty means that Parliament can, if it chooses, legislate contrary to fundamental principles of human rights . . . But the principle of legality means that Parliament must squarely confront what it is doing and accept the political cost. Fundamental rights cannot be overridden by general or ambiguous words. This is because there is too great a risk that the full implications of their unqualified meaning may have passed unnoticed in the democratic process.[43]

Alternatively, it may be argued that the greater protection given to such rights is part of a growing intolerance, among the judiciary, of inhumanity.[44] If so, this increased intolerance is manifested in the increased willingness to intervene to protect citizens' fundamental rights.

It is worth noting here that this greater protection of rights seems to symbiotically mirror the development of irrationality whereby the courts adopt a sliding scale of review depending on the issue at stake. Laws writes:

> it cannot in reality be doubted that in an area such as national economic policy the courts' perception of what will count as good judicial review grounds is quite different from the approach taken in the recent authorities to the role of the judges in cases touching fundamental or constitutional rights.[45]

So, a decision that infringes some fundamental right – in order to be found to be rational – must be justified by reference to some equally important competing

---

43 *Simms* (n 40) 131. A similar justification is implicit in the judgment of Laws LJ in *Thoburn* (n 19) [63]: 'For the repeal of a constitutional Act or the abrogation of a fundamental right to be effected by statute, the court would apply this test: is it shown that the legislature's *actual* – not imputed, constructive or presumed – intention was to effect the repeal or abrogation? I think the text could only be met by express words in the later statute, or by words so specific that the inference of an actual determination to effect the result contended for was irresistible' (emphasis in original). See, also, *Jackson* (n 40) [159] (Baroness Hale).

44 Charles Banner and Richard Moules, 'Public Law in the House of Lords: Emerging Trends and Guidance on Petitions for Leave to Appeal' [2007] *JR* 24, paras 2–8.

45 Sir John Laws, 'Wednesbury' in Christopher F Forsyth and Ivan Hare (eds), *The Golden Metwand and the Crooked Cord: Essays on Public Law in Honour of Sir William Wade QC* (Clarendon Press 1998) 189, 196. See, also, *R v Ministry of Defence, ex p Smith* [1996] QB 517 (CA) 554 (Lord Bingham); *R v Department of Education and Employment, ex p Begbie* [2000] 1 WLR 1115 (CA) 1130 (Laws LJ); *R v Lord Saville of Newdigate and Others, ex p A and Others* [2000] 1 WLR 1855 (CA) [37]; TRS Allan, 'Fairness, Equality, Rationality: Constitutional Theory and Judicial Review' in Christopher F Forsyth and Ivan Hare (eds), *The Golden Metwand and the Crooked Cord: Essays on Public Law in Honour of Sir William Wade QC* (Clarendon Press 1998) 15–37, 33; Sir Stephen Sedley, 'The Rocks of the Open Sea: Where is the Human Rights Act Heading?' in Luke Clements and Philip A Thomas (eds) *Human Rights Act: A Success Story?* (Blackwell Publishing 2005) 9.

118 *Intention, Supremacy and Judicial Review*

requirement of the public interest. Such justification is not necessary where the issue is, say, one that simply affects matters of public finance.

These reasons, though, while important and pertinent, merely supply a rationale for the courts' approach. They do not alter the contention that there is a varying standard determined, in part, by the language used.

In summary, then, the explicitness of the language deployed in a statute, in combination with its substance, or subject matter, will determine the authority attributed to it. Such fluid variability is not consistent with parliamentary sovereignty conceived of as a rule but *is* commensurate with a principle.

The degree to which judges will adhere to a legislative provision is not, of course, wholly determined by its own characteristics; it will also depend on the weight ascribed to any competing principle or statute. This can be demonstrated if we contrast legislation which infringes the common law privilege against self-incrimination with legislation which attempts to exclude access to the courts. With regard to the former, the privilege has been curtailed by a number of statutory enactments. For instance, the registered keeper of a motor vehicle is obliged by statute to identify the driver of that vehicle at a certain time and place even though the provision of such information may lead to criminal charges being brought against her.[46] With the latter, though, the courts' treatment of total ouster clauses demonstrates that this type of legislation will not usually be adhered to. We may infer from this differential treatment that the privilege against self-incrimination is perceived to be less important than the principle that access to the courts should be maintained. This means that legislation that infringes the latter is less likely to be faithfully complied with when compared with legislation infringing the former.

The extent to which legislation will be adopted is also reliant on the degree to which a competing principle will be infringed. Allan is surely correct when he writes: 'Statutes, properly enacted, are entitled to great respect, but not unlimited deference: the warmth of their judicial reception may legitimately vary with the gravity of their assault, if such it be, on settled rights and expectations'.[47] More significantly for present purposes, the same sentiment has been expressed by Elliott, a leading *ultra vires* protagonist: 'The *more important* the value and the *greater the extent* of its disturbance by the legislation in question, the *less certain*

---

46 Road Traffic Act 1988 s 172. The privilege against self-incrimination is also protected by the ECHR Art 6. In *JB v Switzerland* [2001] ECHR 31827/96, para 64, the European Court of Human Rights stated: 'the right to remain silent and the privilege against self-incrimination are generally recognised international standards which lie at the heart of the notion of a fair procedure under Article 6(1) of the Convention. The right not to incriminate oneself in particular presupposes that the authorities seek to prove their case without resort to evidence obtained through methods of coercion or oppression in defiance of the will of the person charged'. However, in *Mawdsley v Chief Constable of the Cheshire Constabulary* [2003] EWHC 1586 (Admin), [2004] 1 WLR 1035 [40]–[41] Owen J decided that the Road Traffic Act 1988 s 172 was not a disproportionate response to the problem of driving with excess speed and so did not breach Art 6.

47 *Law, Liberty and Justice* (n 16) 269.

The principle of parliamentary sovereignty 119

we can be that a court would straightforwardly enforce the legislation' (emphases in original).[48]

This variability is, again, evident when we consider the treatment of ouster clauses and, in particular, the difference in approach between limited time and total ouster clauses. Both of these provisions infringe the principle that access to the courts should be maintained. However, the infringement represented by limited time clauses is minimal and so they are faithfully adhered to. In contrast, total ouster clauses amount to a substantial infringement and so are not usually complied with by the courts.

A similar fluidity is implicit in the Court of Appeal's judgment in *R (Jackson) v Attorney-General*.[49] This case involved a challenge to the Hunting Act 2004, which had been enacted under the procedure laid down in the Parliament Acts 1911 and 1949. These allow a Bill to be passed without the consent of the House of Lords. The case turned on whether the 1949 Act was valid. Parliament had enacted it using the procedure established in the 1911 Act. The later statute amended the earlier one to produce the system under which the Hunting Act 2004 was passed. The appellants argued that the 1911 Act could not be used to amend itself. This claim was rejected. The Court of Appeal did, however, state: 'the greater the scale of the constitutional change proposed by any amendment, the more likely it is that it will fall outside the powers contained in the 1911 Act'.[50] When the case reached the House of Lords, a number of their Lordships rejected this part of the Court's judgment,[51] though Lord Carswell did, 'incline very tentatively to the view that [the Court of Appeal's] instinct might be right'.[52] The significance for present purposes is that the Court of Appeal seems to rely on an intuitive acceptance that obedience to legislation may vary in proportion to the degree of infringement of prior constitutional principles. To be sure, this is a sentiment that has been echoed by Laws LJ: 'the issue is whether the right is violated, or if it is whether the extent of the statute's intrusion is acceptable or justified'.[53]

The contention that something more is required to effect major constitutional alterations is not novel. MacCormick writes:

> If we looked at historical precedents such as those involved in the Reform Acts and the Parliament Acts, we would note that changes connected with

---

48 'The Principle of Parliamentary Sovereignty in Legal, Constitutional, and Political Perspective' (n 27) 62. Ringhand similarly writes: 'The deeper or more serious the departure from . . . fundamental principles, the less weight should be given to any apparent textual intent to deviate from them', Lori A Ringhand, 'Fig Leaves, Fairy Tales, and Constitutional Foundations: Debating Judicial Review in Britain' (2005) 43(3) *Columbia Journal of Transnational Law* 865, 891.

49 [2005] EWCA Civ 126, [2005] QB 579.

50 ibid [100].

51 *Jackson* (n 40) [96] (Lord Steyn), [127] (Lord Hope), [131] (Lord Rodger), [158] (Baroness Hale), [194] (Lord Brown).

52 ibid [178].

53 *International Transport Roth GmbH* (n 40) [74].

120 *Intention, Supremacy and Judicial Review*

the power of change, concerning the composition of Parliament and of the electorate, *have always required express legislative change* (emphasis added).[54]

He notes that in *Nairn v University of Saint Andrews*[55] legislation which permitted universities to confer degrees on women did not, of itself, entitle women to vote in University Constituencies even though the right to do so was possessed by university graduates.[56] Express legislation would be needed to effect such a substantial change.

An indication of the interaction between, on the one hand, the importance of the principle in combination with the degree of infringement, and, on the other, the explicitness of the legislative language used, is also given in *R v Secretary of State for the Home Department, ex p Leech*.[57] The question for the court was the degree to which a prisoner's civil rights could be infringed by prison rules made under the authority of an Act of Parliament. Steyn LJ stated: 'in relation to rule-making powers alleged to arise by necessary implication, it can fairly be said that *the more fundamental the right interfered with, and the more drastic the interference, the more difficult becomes the implication*' (emphasis added).[58] In short, the more important the principle is conceived to be, or the more serious its infringement, then the more explicit the statutory language, or the more necessary the implication, will need to be before that infringement will be permitted. This, again, suggests a fluidity that is not consistent with the all-or-nothing characteristic of a rule but *is* consistent with principles.

Principles are not, though, simply identifiable by their flexibility, even if this may be – as has proved to be the case here – the primary method by which they are distinguished from rules. They may also be recognised as being, 'a requirement of justice or fairness or some other dimension of morality'.[59] This applies to the doctrine of legislative supremacy. The doctrine promotes a claim that is analogous to fairness or justice: that, in a representative democracy, political morality requires that the enactments of the elected legislature should be afforded significant consideration. Indeed, Dworkin makes it clear that political fairness necessitates judges giving appropriate weight to public opinion as it is manifested in the legislative enactments of elected representatives.[60]

---

54 Neil MacCormick, *Questioning Sovereignty* (OUP 1999) 86.
55 [1909] AC 147 (HL).
56 *Questioning Sovereignty* (n 54) 86–87.
57 [1994] QB 198 (CA).
58 ibid 209.
59 Dworkin, *Taking Rights Seriously* (n 8) 22.
60 Ronald Dworkin, *Law's Empire* (Hart Publishing 1998) 342; Ronald Dworkin, 'Political Judges and the Rule of Law' in Ronald Dworkin, *A Matter of Principle* (OUP 1985) 16. Likewise, Allan writes: 'fairness – meaning the appropriate distribution of political power – finds its constitutional expression in the enactment and application of statute', *Law, Liberty and Justice* (n 16) 12. In a similar vein, Goldsworthy states: 'One of the most fundamental of all rights is that of ordinary people to participate, on equal terms, in the political decision-making that affects their lives as much as anyone else's', Jeffrey Goldsworthy, *The Sovereignty of Parliament: History and Philosophy* (OUP 1999) 263.

The principle of parliamentary sovereignty 121

Parliamentary sovereignty, then, operates as a principle. It is an aspect of political fairness. It has a weight which varies according to the subject matter of, and the language used in, a particular statute. Furthermore, it will be balanced against competing principles according to the latter's importance and the degree of infringement.

Commentators will often explicate this balancing of competing interests in terms of interpretation. Elliott himself explains the courts' treatment of ouster clauses in this way: as an interpretation 'which is consistent with the rule of law'.[61] Similar arguments have been made with regard to the ECA 1972: that it simply established a rule of construction to the effect that future legislation should be interpreted to conform with European Community law.[62] In many cases, this may seem to be an adequate way to describe the balance achieved between legislation and, say, a fundamental right: the former will appear to be construed in a way that is commensurate with the latter. The result will contain elements of both the statute and the fundamental right.

It is, however, difficult to accept the treatment of ouster clauses as simple interpretation when, as even Elliott concedes, the resulting construction of such provisions is the very opposite of their plain meaning.[63] Likewise, it is not easy to conceive of how the granting of an injunction to prevent a statute being applied – as in *Factortame* – can be considered to be a mere act of interpretation. To be sure, many would agree with Wade's view that *Factortame* represented 'much more than an exercise in construction'.[64]

It is unsurprising that legislative supremacy is usually assumed to be a rule. For the most part it will appear to behave in an all-or-nothing fashion. Its importance means that it will usually outweigh any competing principle. It is only when a similarly important principle is at stake – such as a fundamental right – that its character as a principle becomes apparent.

Categorising parliamentary sovereignty as a principle appears to permit a better, more accurate narrative of the relationship between the legislature and the courts. By this account, Parliament is still seen as the pre-eminent legal body within the constitution. However, the courts are credited with possessing a more autonomous role than is sometimes the case with established conceptions of

---

61 'The Ultra Vires Doctrine in a Constitutional Setting' (n 4) 153; Mark C Elliott, *The Constitutional Foundations of Judicial Review* (Hart Publishing 2001) 122, 123.

62 Sir John Laws, 'Law and Democracy' [1995] *PL* 72, 89. See, also, a summary of this view given by Craig: Paul P Craig, 'Sovereignty of the United Kingdom Parliament after *Factortame*' (1991) 11 *YBEL* 221, 251.

63 Chapter Four p 64.

64 HWR Wade, 'Sovereignty – Revolution or Evolution' (1996) 112 *LQR* 568, 570; also, 568, 573, 575; Elliott, *The Constitutional Foundations of Judicial Review* (n 61) 82. In the recent case of *Benkharbouche v Embassy of the Republic of Sudan* [2015] EWCA Civ 33, [2015] 3 WLR 301, the Court of Appeal upheld the decision of the Employment Appeal Tribunal to disapply provisions of the State Immunity Act 1978 to the extent that they conflicted with Art 47 of the Charter of Fundamental Rights of the European Union protecting their right to an effective remedy for a breach of rights protected by EU law. There was no suggestion that such disapplication amounted to a mere interpretation of the 1978 statute.

122 *Intention, Supremacy and Judicial Review*

legislative supremacy. Their role is no longer simply to apply legislation but to balance it against competing considerations.

I should, for the avoidance of doubt, explicitly state that this modified understanding of parliamentary sovereignty is not simply superficial; it alters the substance of the doctrine. This is evident when we contrast it with a traditional view of the doctrine given by Dicey:

> The principle then of Parliamentary sovereignty may, looked at from its positive side, be thus described: Any Act of Parliament, or any part of an Act of Parliament, which makes a new law, or repeals or modifies an existing law, will be *obeyed by the courts*. The same principle, looked at from its negative side, may be thus stated: There is no person or body of persons who can, under the English Constitution, make rules which override or derogate from an Act of Parliament, or which (to express the same thing in other words) will be *enforced by the courts in contravention of an Act of Parliament* (emphases added).[65]

As I have argued, under this new conception of sovereignty, Acts of Parliament are not simply obeyed by the courts; they are, or can often be, balanced against other statutes or competing principles that are inherent in the English legal system.

I should also be clear about whether this new understanding of parliamentary sovereignty amounts to a hard-edged limit to the legislative competence of Parliament. Such an approach has been suggested by some.[66] For instance, Lord Woolf has stated: 'I . . . would consider there were advantages in making it clear that ultimately there are even limits on the supremacy of Parliament which it is the courts' inalienable responsibility to identify and uphold'.[67] Moreover, this seemed to be the result in *Anisminic* where the House of Lords reached a decision contrary to that plainly required by the Foreign Compensation Act 1950. In fact, Wade explicitly makes the connection between the sentiment expressed by Lord Woolf and the decision in *Anisminic*:

> Lord Woolf's suggestion that the courts might refuse to enforce an Act abolishing judicial review was only saying what the House of Lords had said, though in a much more involved way, in *Anisminic* and what Lord Woolf himself had held in the *Al Fayed* case when disregarding the ouster clause.[68]

It also seems to be the result in *Factortame* where the House of Lords 'disapplied' the relevant provisions of the Merchant Shipping Act 1988.

---

65 A V Dicey, *Introduction to the Study of the Law of the Constitution* (8th edn, Macmillan 1915) 4.
66 See Chapter Four p 63.
67 Lord Woolf of Barnes, '*Droit Public* – English Style' [1995] *PL* 57, 69.
68 HWR Wade 'Constitutional Realities and Judicial Prudence' in Christopher F Forsyth (ed), *Judicial Review and the Constitution* (Hart Publishing 2000) 431.

The principle of parliamentary sovereignty 123

Yet, even the *Factortame* decision does not amount to a hard-edged limit to the scope of Parliament's legislative ability. I have argued that the courts will adhere to an Act of Parliament which is contrary to European Union law if the statutory language used is sufficiently explicit.[69] This suggests flexibility rather than a clear boundary. Furthermore, the imposition of sharp limits is not necessary. Indeed, to do so would be contrary to the variability which, I am suggesting, the doctrine of legislative supremacy encompasses. Laws LJ has, again, captured this variability, and its reliance on differing factors, in the *Thoburn* case:

> This development of the common law regarding constitutional rights, and as I would say constitutional statutes, is highly beneficial. It gives us most of the benefits of a written constitution, in which fundamental rights are accorded special respect. But it preserves the sovereignty of the legislature and the flexibility of our uncodified constitution. It accepts the relation between legislative supremacy and fundamental rights is *not fixed or brittle*: rather the courts (in interpreting statutes and, now, applying the Human Rights Act 1998) *will pay more or less deference to the legislature*, or other public decision maker, *according to the subject in hand* (emphases added).[70]

I am not, then, necessarily talking about the courts ruling that a particular statute is invalid – so-called constitutional review. Rather, I am suggesting that, in any particular case, the courts will balance the effect of an Act of Parliament against any competing principles. In some circumstances, very explicit statutory language may enable an infringement of even the most fundamental rights.[71] It may, for instance, be possible to legislate to exclude access to the courts if the legislation is sufficiently explicit and the issue in question is, say, one of national security.

This new understanding of legislative supremacy has implications for the manner in which the exercise of judicial review may be justified, as will be explored in the next chapter. First, though, I wish to consider some possible criticisms of this new conception of parliamentary sovereignty.

---

69 Above pp 114–115.

70 *Thoburn* (n 19) [64]. It should be noted, however, that Laws LJ has also stated that the ability of Parliament to override fundamental or constitutional rights by using express legislative language is a 'brightline rule whose edge is sharp', *International Transport Roth GmbH* (n 40) [75].

71 However, Allan writes: 'If it is true that Parliament may override such rights by "express, focussed provision", that is because it is rightly presumed to intend their protection unless there are powerful reasons against it. And the stronger the right, as a matter of general principle, and the weaker the reasons suggested for infringing or restricting it, the more clearly expressed and focused the relevant provision must be; *in some cases there will be no language appropriate to authorise executive action whose legality could be affirmed only at the cost of constitutional breakdown*' (emphasis added), TRS Allan, 'The Constitutional Foundations of Judicial Review: Conceptual Conundrum or Interpretative Inquiry?' [2002] *CLJ* 87, 103 (citation omitted). See, also, Allan, *Law, Liberty and Justice* (n 16) 143.

124   *Intention, Supremacy and Judicial Review*

Potential criticisms

The thesis advanced above, that parliamentary sovereignty operates in the manner of a principle rather than a rule, may no doubt be subject to many criticisms. In this section, I anticipate and address some of them.

One possible criticism of my contention is that it assumes that parliamentary sovereignty is limited. Indeed, I have argued that there are circumstances in which the courts may refuse to give effect to Acts of Parliament. I have supported this argument with, among other things, curial and extra-curial judicial statements to this effect. I should acknowledge, though, that judges are not united on this point. For example, while, in the *Jackson* case, Baroness Hale, Lord Steyn and Lord Hope appeared to view Parliament's legislative competence as limited,[72] Lord Bingham seemed to support the orthodox view:

> The bedrock of the British constitution is . . . the supremacy of the Crown in Parliament. . . . Then, as now, the Crown in Parliament was unconstrained by any entrenched or codified constitution. It could make or unmake any law it wished.[73]

Similarly, in a lecture, Lord Neuberger expressed his support for the traditional, absolute view of parliamentary sovereignty and questioned the contrary position taken by Baroness Hale and Lords Steyn and Hope in *Jackson*.[74] There are, of course, numerous other examples where judges, and academics, have argued that Parliament's law-making ability is absolute rather than limited. Lord Hope has acknowledged that the judges are not agreed on the matter: 'The question of whether the principle of the sovereignty of the United Kingdom Parliament is absolute or may be subject to limitation in exceptional circumstances is still under discussion'.[75] There is no way of knowing which of these two contrasting views is correct until the courts are called upon to rule directly on the matter. I suggest, though, that there is sufficient support among senior judges and academics to make the idea of a Parliament with limited law-making abilities more than fanciful.

A second potential criticism of the claim advanced in this chapter is to be found in Allan's contention that 'statute consists only of rules'.[76] This is because legislative provisions are 'uniquely authoritative in the resolution of particular cases . . . Where it applies to a state of facts, a statute gives a definitive answer'.[77] By this reasoning, an Act of Parliament will operate in the all-or-nothing fashion that is characteristic of rules. In addition, Allan argues that it is not possible for a statute

---

72 *Jackson* (n 40) Lord Steyn [102], Lord Hope [104], Baroness Hale [159].
73 ibid [9]; see also [27].
74 Lord Neuberger of Abbotsbury, 'Who are the Masters Now?' Second Lord Alexander of Weedon Lecture, 6 April 2011, paras 13–51 and 73–74.
75 *AXA General Insurance Ltd v HM Advocate* [2011] UKSC 46, [2012] 1 AC 868 [50].
76 *Law, Liberty and Justice* (n 16) 93
77 ibid.

The principle of parliamentary sovereignty 125

to be a principle because principles have no real existence apart from their weight and it is not possible for the legislature to specify the weight to be attributed to a principle.[78] This can only be determined in the context of a particular case, when one principle is balanced against another, rather than by legislative fiat.[79]

Allan may well be correct in claiming that the weight of any particular principle cannot be established by a legislative act. Yet, this does not mean that a legislature cannot create principles whose weight is then ascertained in particular cases by the courts. This is surely the position with Articles 8–11 of the ECHR, the so-called qualified rights. These were created by a legislative act, the drafting and ratifying of the Convention, and their application in any particular case – including the way they are balanced against other competing principles and rights – is a matter for the courts.[80]

Further, my argument above demonstrates that a statutory provision is not always 'uniquely authoritative in the resolution of particular cases'. It may, in an individual case, be outweighed by a competing principle or statute. This, in turn, suggests that, contrary to Allan's assertion, statutes *do* have the dimension of weight. I have claimed that the weight attributed to a legislative provision will be dependent on a number of factors, including the explicitness of the language used and the subject matter of the legislation. Allan seems to acknowledge that Acts of Parliament are inevitably subject to interpretation by reference to common law standards.[81] What is such interpretation if it is not the balancing of competing principles so as to accommodate the requirements of the common law and the requirements of statute?

In addition, Allan himself contends that Dworkin's ideal of 'law as integrity' necessitates an interplay between fairness – which requires adherence to properly enacted legislation – and justice. As a result of this interplay, a judge will interpret legislation to give effect to the demands of justice and, where she considers the iniquity of a statute to be grave, she may be excused from her obligation to enforce it.[82] In short, while Allan claims that statutes can only be rules, he seems to recognise that they have a fluidity, and may be balanced in a way, that is characteristic of principles.

Another criticism that may be made of my conception of parliamentary sovereignty is that it merely reflects the practice of the courts. Of course, in one sense, this is desirable. It is surely inherent in any theory that it should closely correspond to the practice for which it is proposed as an explanation. Indeed, this is the rationale on which the immanent critique undertaken in Chapter Five was based. Yet, it may be argued that to alter our conception of parliamentary sovereignty so that it more closely correlates with the practice of the courts robs it of its

---

78 ibid 93–94.
79 ibid.
80 A point with which Allan seems to agree: ibid 150–151. Similarly, Raz states: 'Legal principles, like other laws, can be enacted or repealed by legislatures and administrative authorities', Joseph Raz, 'Legal Principles and the Limits of Law' (1972) 81 *Yale LJ* 823, 848; also 854, n 55.
81 See, for example, *Law, Liberty and Justice* (ibid) 79.
82 ibid 130–134.

126 *Intention, Supremacy and Judicial Review*

normative value, that is, as a standard for guiding individual judicial decisions and against which such decisions may be meaningfully evaluated. It might be thought to be more appropriate to conceive of parliamentary sovereignty as having fixed, hard and fast limits and to question any decision that does not adhere to these rather than altering the theory to match the practice.

There is, then, a tension between two distinct requirements. On the one hand, it is desirable that theory and practice should correspond and, where this does not happen, that the theory should be evaluated and amended if necessary. On the other hand, we need to avoid a situation where we simply alter the theory to conform to each judicial decision and thereby neutralise its normative value.

In a similar way, one may question whether it is justifiable to argue, as I have done here, that a constitutional fundamental – the meaning of parliamentary supremacy – has altered because the practice of the courts has changed. I suggest that it is. Legislative supremacy is not simply a legal requirement. The degree to which the courts adhere to an Act of Parliament is a political fact and, in determining the way in which it operates, it is surely the reality of the courts' actions that counts.[83] If judicial practice is steady and sustained in one direction – and that direction is contrary to the meaning traditionally given to parliamentary supremacy – then it is reasonable to conclude that the meaning has altered. As Wade writes: 'All law students are taught that Parliamentary sovereignty is absolute. *But it is the judges who have the last word*' (emphasis added).[84] So, if the courts consistently treat parliamentary sovereignty as though it is a principle – as I have suggested – then it cannot be plausibly argued that it does not function as such.[85]

We may, of course, challenge the legitimacy of the courts' actions and argue that it is not justifiable for them to unilaterally alter such a fundamental rule of the constitution. This appears to be the view of Goldsworthy: 'the courts can initiate change, *provided that the other branches of government are willing to accept*

---

83 I echo Wade here who writes: 'For it is reality that counts: if the courts of the newly made independent country have in fact thrown off their allegiance [to the UK Parliament], it is futile to talk of continuing sovereignty', HWR Wade, 'The Basis of Legal Sovereignty' [1955] *CLJ* 172, 196.

84 HWR Wade, *The Hamlyn Lectures: Constitutional Fundamentals* (Stevens 1980) 65. See, also: Laws LJ who states that it is the courts 'to which the scope and nature of parliamentary sovereignty are ultimately confided': *Thoburn* (n 19) [60]; Lord Steyn, '[T]he supremacy of Parliament . . . is a construct of the common law. The judges created this principle. If that is so, it is not unthinkable that circumstances could arise where the courts may have to qualify a principle established on a different hypothesis of constitutionalism', *Jackson* (n 40) [102]; and Geoffrey Marshall, 'Parliamentary Sovereignty: The New Horizons' [1997] *PL* 1, 4. For contrary views see Richard Ekins, 'Acts of Parliament and the Parliament Acts' (2007) 123 *LQR* 91, 102–103 and Michael Gordon, 'The Conceptual Foundations of Parliamentary Sovereignty: Reconsidering Jennings and Wade' [2009] *PL* 519, 534–539.

85 Craig writes: 'Given that the content of the rule of recognition [ie parliamentary sovereignty] is based upon factual acceptance by those who operate the system, and that it only exists if this is present, then it follows that the content of this rule could alter if the practice of those who operate the system itself changes', Paul P Craig, *Public Law and Democracy in the United Kingdom and the United States of America* (OUP 1990) 225–226.

it' (emphasis added).[86] Furthermore, it may be that, if the executive or legislative branches of government insist on adherence to a more traditional conception of sovereignty, the courts would heed this. Such a demand has not yet occurred. Until it does, it is safe to conclude that the courts do 'have the last word' and that their decisions indicate that parliamentary supremacy does operate in the non-conclusive fashion of a principle.

There is an associated political question, here, concerning the appropriate relationship between the legislature and the courts: is it legitimate for the unelected judiciary to decide that legislation enacted by the democratic arm of government – Parliament – should be overridden by a competing value perceived to be more important?

A possible answer to this question may be found in the work of Lakin. He suggests that the British constitution rests, not on parliamentary sovereignty, but on the principle of legality. This means that political power – including legislative power – may be exercised only in accordance with the principles that justify that power, though there may be disagreement about what those principles are. That is, the principle of legality determines the powers of Parliament.[87] Thus, it may be argued, when treating parliamentary sovereignty[88] as a principle and balancing Acts of Parliament against competing principles or statutes, the courts are not acting illegitimately; they are simply keeping Parliament within the bounds of its power as determined by the principle of legality.

We may ask how legislative supremacy, as a non-conclusive principle, should be balanced against other standards. I have argued that the doctrine possesses the dimension of weight. The question here is what factors should govern the weight attributed to any particular statutory provision. The practice of the courts indicates two: the explicitness of the language used and the subject matter of the statute. However, one could argue that other factors should also be taken into account. For example, it might be appropriate for the courts to take notice of the degree of support – parliamentary or public – that the legislation in question commanded during, or subsequent to, its enactment. Indeed, Lord Phillips seems to suggest that the courts should take into account public hostility when deciding how to respond to legislation which infringes a constitutional principle:

---

86 Goldsworthy, *The Sovereignty of Parliament* (n 60) 245; also, more generally, 236–279. Likewise, Forsyth writes: 'An unelected branch of government cannot remake the constitution on its own', Christopher F Forsyth, 'Showing the Fly the Way Out of the Flybottle: The Value of Formalism and Conceptual Reasoning in Administrative Law' [2007] *CLJ* 325, 346. Lord Millett goes further, requiring legislative rather than judicial activism: 'This is not to say that the doctrine of Parliamentary supremacy is sacrosanct, but only that any change in a fundamental constitutional principle should be the consequence of deliberate legislative action and not judicial activism, however well meaning', *Ghaidan v Godin-Mendoza* [2004] UKHL 30, [2004] 2 AC 557 [57].

87 Stuart Lakin, 'Debunking the Idea of Parliamentary Sovereignty: The Controlling Factor of Legality in the British Constitution' (2008) 28 *OJLS* 709.

88 I should note that Lakin contends that his argument makes talk of parliamentary sovereignty obsolete: 'Given that Parliament derives its powers from law, we have a *normative reason* to erase the concept of sovereignty from our constitutional landscape', ibid 731.

128 *Intention, Supremacy and Judicial Review*

If Parliament did the inconceivable, we might do the inconceivable as well. One is envisaging a situation where a strong majority in Parliament enacted legislation that *produced a complete public outcry* because it was opposed to some fundamental constitutional principle. Then one might say that the Supreme Court might react. But if you reach that situation, you might be in a constitutional crisis and we are nowhere near that situation (emphasis added).[89]

This, though, raises questions about whether the courts could accurately evaluate the strength of any support. It may be possible to ascertain the strength of parliamentary support by reference to the record of votes that a statute received during its enactment. It may also be possible to gauge the degree of public support if the legislation was preceded by a referendum, but not possible otherwise. We may additionally question how much significance should be attributed to such support.

We may also ask how the courts should assess the importance to be attributed to one statute when compared with others or with any applicable principles.[90] There is room for disagreement about the correctness of any outcome. Dworkin acknowledges this when discussing the balancing of competing principles: 'This cannot be, of course, an exact measurement, and the judgment that a particular principle or policy is more important than another will often be a controversial one'.[91] There is, then, scope for legitimate differences of opinion when determining the relative weights to be ascribed to any pertinent factors or, indeed, when assessing which factors should be considered pertinent.

Of course, there may be no disagreement; a particular decision may remain comparatively unexamined and be accepted as being naturally or logically inevitable. For instance, the so-called right of access to the courts is seemingly recognised as fundamental by those judges who have commented on it. Consequently, this right has been able to outweigh legislative provisions that seek to deny it. Yet, the very description of some rights as fundamental, and the relative weights that may be attributed to them, is itself a value choice, influenced by personal, political or ideological prejudices. It would not be difficult to imagine that while judges describe access to the courts as fundamental, legislators or government officials

---

89 Lord Phillips, Interview, *The Today Programme*, BBC Radio 4 (2 August 2010). I should note that this conflicts with Dicey's assertion: 'the courts will take no notice of the will of the electors. The judges know nothing about any will of the people except in so far as that will is expressed by an Act of Parliament, and would never suffer the validity of a statute to be questioned on the ground of its having been passed or kept alive in opposition to the wishes of the electors', Dicey, *Introduction to the Study of the Law of the Constitution* (n 65) 28.

90 Similarly, Loughlin asks: 'What . . . are these foundational constitutional principles? What is it within the background, education, training and experience of the judiciary which enables them to not only identify the principles (the relatively easy bit) but also to unpack them and set them to work to resolve particular social disputes concerning the appropriate exercise of public power?', Martin Loughlin, 'Whither the Constitution?' in Christopher F Forsyth (ed), *Judicial Review and the Constitution* (Hart Publishing 2000) 426.

91 *Taking Rights Seriously* (n 8) 26.

The principle of parliamentary sovereignty   129

may disagree. Further, any such choice may – deliberately or unintentionally – be presented as fundamental in order to disguise the fact that a value judgement is being made and to avoid drawing attention to any contestable assumptions in what would otherwise appear to be inexorable judicial reasoning.

One attraction of parliamentary supremacy conceived of as a rule is that these issues remain hidden and the application of statute can appear to be objective: judges can simply claim to be acting neutrally, in conformity with Parliament's intention. This may be contrasted with the position advanced in this chapter whereby legislative supremacy is categorised as a principle. Here, the claim to be acting objectively becomes less tenable. Rather, as I have argued in the preceding paragraphs, it becomes apparent that judges are making value choices and that there may be legitimate differences of opinion about the outcome of any particular case. The advantage of recognising the existence of such value judgements is that we are perhaps better able to reveal, and comment upon, the assumptions on which they are made.

I should note a final potential criticism of the argument that the conduct of the courts indicates that parliamentary supremacy operates as a principle not a rule. This is that it presupposes that such a rational explanation of the courts' behaviour is possible. It also assumes that the resolution of any particular case is derived from – and supplements – a coherent body of rules and principles. Indeed, Dworkin's notion of 'law as integrity' appears to take this as the purpose of judicial reasoning.[92] These are, though, presumptions that could be challenged.

For instance, we may begin with the alternative assumption that in any body of law there will inevitably be conflicting and contradictory decisions. These may be capable of offering support to a number of different theories and so we should be slow to conclude that they support any particular one.[93] It would also mean that we should not necessarily presume that all judicial determinations can or should be explained in a seamlessly coherent way. Rather, we can simply argue that those cases that do not adhere to the rule of parliamentary sovereignty were wrongly decided. Indeed, as Altman notes, there is no way of determining whether decisions which depart from one theory represent the emergence of a new trend or should be considered to be insignificant blips.[94] In short, those cases on which I have relied to advance my argument may simply be anomalies rather than signs of an amended theory of parliamentary sovereignty.

---

92 A concise account of this is given in *Law's Empire* (n 60) 225. See, also: *Taking Rights Seriously* (ibid) 115–118; and Ronald Dworkin, 'How Law is like Literature' in Ronald Dworkin, *A Matter of Principle* (OUP 1985) 151–152 and 158–162.

93 Waldron captures this perfectly when he writes of Duncan Kennedy's work: 'Kennedy thinks the background is so riven with contradiction as to be capable of offering spurious support for everything and determinate support for nothing in legal reasoning', Jeremy Waldron, 'Did Dworkin Ever Answer the Crits?' in Scott Hershovitz (ed), *Exploring Law's Empire: The Jurisprudence of Ronald Dworkin* (OUP 2006) 155.

94 Andrew Altman, 'Legal Realism, Critical Legal Studies and Dworkin' (1986) 15 *Phil Pub Aff* 205, 226.

Conclusion

In this chapter, I have argued that the doctrine of parliamentary sovereignty may be perceived as a Dworkinian principle. This differs from the conception which is inherent in both the *ultra vires* and common law theories where parliamentary sovereignty is assumed to operate in the fashion of a rule.

I have contended that Acts of Parliament may be balanced against competing principles derived from the common law or from other legislation. The weight, or importance, attributed to any statute will be dependent on a number of factors, including the explicitness of the language used in, and the subject matter of, the legislation. This, it has been submitted, better captures the relationship between Parliament and the courts.

In the next chapter, I examine the implications of this new conception of parliamentary sovereignty for the constitutional justification of judicial review.

Bibliography

Allan TRS, *Law, Liberty and Justice: The Legal Foundations of British Constitutionalism* (Clarendon Press 1993)

— 'Fairness, Equality, Rationality: Constitutional Theory and Judicial Review' in Christopher F Forsyth and Ivan Hare (eds), *The Golden Metwand and the Crooked Cord: Essays on Public Law in Honour of Sir William Wade QC* (Clarendon Press 1998)

— 'The Constitutional Foundations of Judicial Review: Conceptual Conundrum or Interpretative Inquiry?' [2002] *Cambridge Law Journal* 87

Altman A, 'Legal Realism, Critical Legal Studies and Dworkin' (1986) 15 *Philosophy and Public Affairs* 205

Banner C and Moules R, 'Public Law in the House of Lords: Emerging Trends and Guidance on Petitions for Leave to Appeal' [2007] *Judicial Review* 24

Craig P P, *Public Law and Democracy in the United Kingdom and the United States of America* (OUP 1990)

— 'Sovereignty of the United Kingdom Parliament after *Factortame*' (1991) 11 *Yearbook of European Law* 221

— *Administrative Law* (7th edn, Sweet & Maxwell 2012)

Dicey A V, *Introduction to the Study of the Law of the Constitution* (8th edn, Macmillan 1915)

Dworkin R, *Taking Rights Seriously* (Duckworth & Co 1977)

— 'How Law is like Literature' in Ronald Dworkin, *A Matter of Principle* (OUP 1985)

— 'Political Judges and the Rule of Law' in Ronald Dworkin, *A Matter of Principle* (OUP 1985)

— *Law's Empire* (Hart Publishing 1998)

Ekins R, 'Acts of Parliament and the Parliament Acts' (2007) 123 *Law Quarterly Review* 91

Elliott M C, 'The Ultra Vires Doctrine in a Constitutional Setting: Still the Central Principle of Administrative Law' [1999] *Cambridge Law Journal* 129

— *The Constitutional Foundations of Judicial Review* (Hart Publishing 2001)

— 'Constitutional Legislation, European Union Law and the Nature of the United Kingdom's Contemporary Constitution' (2014) 10(3) *European Constitutional Law Review* 379

— 'The Principle of Parliamentary Sovereignty in Legal, Constitutional, and Political Perspective' in Jeffrey L Jowell, Dawn Oliver and Colm O'Cinneide (eds), *The Changing Constitution* (8th edn, OUP 2015)

Forsyth C F, 'Showing the Fly the Way Out of the Flybottle: The Value of Formalism and Conceptual Reasoning in Administrative Law' [2007] *Cambridge Law Journal* 325

— and Elliott M C, 'The Legitimacy of Judicial Review' [2003] *Public Law* 286

Goldsworthy J, *The Sovereignty of Parliament: History and Philosophy* (OUP 1999)

Gordon M, 'The Conceptual Foundations of Parliamentary Sovereignty: Reconsidering Jennings and Wade' [2009] *Public Law* 519

Hart HLA, *The Concept of Law* (3rd edn, OUP 2012)

Jowell J L, 'Of Vires and Vacuums: The Constitutional Context of Judicial Review' [1999] *Public Law* 448

Lakin S, 'Debunking the Idea of Parliamentary Sovereignty: The Controlling Factor of Legality in the British Constitution' (2008) 28 *Oxford Journal of Legal Studies* 709

Laws Sir John, 'Is the High Court the Guardian of Fundamental Constitutional Rights?' [1993] *Public Law* 59

132 *Intention, Supremacy and Judicial Review*

— 'Law and Democracy' [1995] *Public Law* 72

— 'Wednesbury' in Christopher F Forsyth and Ivan Hare (eds), *The Golden Metwand and the Crooked Cord: Essays on Public Law in Honour of Sir William Wade QC* (Clarendon Press 1998)

— 'Constitutional Guarantees' (2007) 16 *The Commonwealth Lawyer* 24

— *The Hamlyn Lectures: The Common Law Constitution* (CUP 2014)

Loughlin M, 'Whither the Constitution?' in Christopher F Forsyth (ed), *Judicial Review and the Constitution* (Hart Publishing 2000)

MacCormick N, *Questioning Sovereignty* (OUP 1999)

McGarry J, 'The Principle of Parliamentary Sovereignty' (2012) 32(4) *Legal Studies* 577

Marshall G, 'Parliamentary Sovereignty: The New Horizons' [1997] *Public Law* 1

Neuberger Lord, 'Who are the Masters Now?' Second Lord Alexander of Weedon Lecture, 6 April 2011

Phillips Lord, Interview, *The Today Programme*, BBC Radio 4 (2 August 2010)

Raz J, 'Legal Principles and the Limits of Law' (1972) 81 *Yale Law Journal* 823

Ringhand L A, 'Fig Leaves, Fairy Tales, and Constitutional Foundations: Debating Judicial Review in Britain' (2005) 43(3) *Columbia Journal of Transnational Law* 865

St J N Bates T, 'Editorial: Constitutional Statutes' (2007) 28 *Statute Law Review* iii

Sedley Sir Stephen, 'The Rocks of the Open Sea: Where is the Human Rights Act Heading?' in Luke Clements and Philip A Thomas (eds) *Human Rights Act: A Success Story?* (Blackwell Publishing 2005)

Taggart M, 'Ultra Vires as Distraction' in Christopher F Forsyth (ed), *Judicial Review and the Constitution* (Hart Publishing 2000)

Wade HWR, 'The Basis of Legal Sovereignty' [1955] *Cambridge Law Journal* 172

— *The Hamlyn Lectures: Constitutional Fundamentals* (Stevens 1980)

— 'Sovereignty – Revolution or Evolution?' (1996) 112 *Law Quarterly Review* 568

— 'Constitutional Realities and Judicial Prudence' in Christopher F Forsyth (ed), *Judicial Review and the Constitution* (Hart Publishing 2000)

— and Forsyth C F, *Administrative Law* (11th edn, OUP 2014)

Waldron J, 'Did Dworkin Ever Answer the Crits?' in Scott Hershovitz (ed), *Exploring Law's Empire: The Jurisprudence of Ronald Dworkin* (OUP 2006)

Woolf Lord, '*Droit Public* – English Style' [1995] *Public Law* 57

7 The constitutional legitimacy of judicial review

In the first section of this chapter, the implications of the argument made in Chapter Six, that parliamentary sovereignty functions as a principle, will be used to evaluate the way in which we may justify the exercise of judicial review. This will be followed, in the second section, by an examination of whether the standards of good administration could be said to be judicial creations whose development and application is conditioned by history of effect. I also consider the direct and indirect influence of legislation on the exercise of the supervisory jurisdiction.

The constitutional legitimacy of judicial review

I noted in Chapter Three that the *raison d'être* of the *ultra vires* theory is to provide an explication of the supervisory jurisdiction that accommodates legislative supremacy.[1] Its proponents do this by arguing that we must assume that the standards of good administration are developed and applied pursuant to an assumed intention of Parliament.[2]

The common law theory was produced in response, and as an alternative, to the *ultra vires* theory. It is an attempt to provide a more realistic account of judicial review. Its supporters claim that the standards of good administration are judicial creations and are developed and applied pursuant to an inherent jurisdiction of the courts.[3] They too, though, endeavour to accommodate parliamentary supremacy, claiming that legislation which excludes the supervisory jurisdiction will be adhered to by the courts. Yet, the contention advanced in the previous chapter – that parliamentary sovereignty operates as a principle rather than a rule – brings into question the need to provide such reconciliation between it and the exercise of judicial review. In this section, I use the *ultra vires* theory as a foil by which we can evaluate whether this is now necessary.

The *ultra vires* theory is based on an argument that Parliament either intends those exercising statutory public power to do so in accordance with the standards of good administration or that it intends the standards not to apply. If it is the

---

1 Chapter Three p 30.
2 ibid pp 31–32.
3 ibid pp 34–35.

134 *Intention, Supremacy and Judicial Review*

latter, the supporters of the theory contend, the application of these standards would amount to a breach of parliamentary sovereignty. It is to avoid this result that they argue that the application of the standards to statutory public power must be assumed to be authorised by the legislature.[4]

This conclusion is premised on a particular view of parliamentary sovereignty: that the doctrine enables the legislature to exclude the standards of good administration. This sentiment is captured by Forsyth:

> if the making of . . . vague regulations is within the powers granted by a sovereign Parliament, on what basis may the courts challenge Parliament's will and hold that the regulations are invalid? If Parliament has authorised vague regulations, those regulations cannot be challenged without challenging Parliament's authority to authorise such regulations.[5]

So, if the legislature did sanction the making of vague regulations, or any other breach of the standards of good administration, under the *ultra vires* theory, the courts would be obliged to adhere to this. Furthermore, this sanction need not be expressly communicated but may simply be assumed. This is, again, reflected in Forsyth's assertion: 'what an all powerful Parliament does not prohibit, it must authorise either expressly or *impliedly*' (emphasis added).[6]

This premise, though, does not hold under the modified version of legislative supremacy. I have submitted that it is not necessarily the case that the courts will adhere to an Act of Parliament. I have argued, rather, that a legislative provision may be balanced against, and outweighed by, any competing principles interpreted as germane and appropriate. I have also argued that the weight attributed to an Act of Parliament when balanced against any competing principles will be dependent on a number of factors including the importance of the legislation and any competing principles, the degree of infringement of any competing principles and the explicitness of the statutory language. This has obvious implications for the reliance on the assumed intention of the legislature at the heart of the *ultra vires* theory: if it is accurate to assert, as I have done, that the weight of legislation will be dependent on the explicitness of the language used, then an *assumed* intention of Parliament is, *a fortiori*, more likely to be outweighed by a rival principle.

In short, this new view of parliamentary sovereignty does not necessarily oblige the courts to comply with an express or implied intention of the legislature that the standards of good administration should not apply to statutory public power. Rather, any attempt to legislate in this way would be balanced against a competing principle to the effect that these standards should apply. Because of this, the application of the standards need not be justified by reference to legislative intent.

---

4 ibid p 31.

5 Christopher F Forsyth, 'Of Fig Leaves and Fairy Tales: The Ultra Vires Doctrine, the Sovereignty of Parliament and Judicial Review' [1996] *CLJ* 122, 133–134.

6 ibid 133. See, also, Chapter Four p 43.

Constitutional legitimacy 135

It is worth repeating here that the *ultra vires* theorists concede that the standards of good administration are, in reality, judicial creations.[7] Their argument that their application must, as a matter of logic, be legitimised by reference to legislative intent is based on a version of parliamentary sovereignty operating as a rule. This is no longer necessary when we conceive of the doctrine as a principle.[8] Indeed, the altered conception of legislative supremacy being suggested here would mean that there is now no need to legitimise the application of the standards of good administration by reference to Parliament at all. The standards can simply be acknowledged as common law standards and their application to public power – whether statutory or otherwise – as an instance of the inherent jurisdiction of the courts.

Moreover, it is inherent in the notion of parliamentary sovereignty conceived of as a principle that it will be balanced against other principles and that, while these may be derived from the legislature, this is not necessarily the case. As has been argued with regard to fundamental rights, legislation will be evaluated against standards which are derived from the common law. It is worth noting here that some of those who advocate that we now have a qualified version of legislative supremacy, where importance is attributed to fundamental rights and constitutional statutes, contend that this is a common law development.[9]

This rejection of the *ultra vires* theory is not, though, a wholesale acceptance of the common law theory as devised by Craig. This is because he, too, implies that parliamentary sovereignty operates as a rule. It was shown in Chapter Three that he argues that Parliament may legislate to exclude judicial review altogether.[10] Yet, as has been argued here, and as the example of the courts' treatment of ouster clauses illustrates,[11] this is not the case. Rather, any attempt to do so will be balanced against the principle that the exercise of public power should be supervised by the courts.

It is interesting to note here that the proponents of the *ultra vires* theory have argued that the abandonment of a presumed intention of Parliament as the basis of judicial review would mean that we must also abandon parliamentary sovereignty.[12] However, the revised view of parliamentary sovereignty, operating as a principle, that I have advanced has not been driven by the rejection of a presumed

---

7 Chapter Three p 33.
8 Bamforth's observation seems apposite here: 'If the constitutional justification for characterising judicial review as being based on the ultra vires principle is the need to defend parliamentary sovereignty (or at least to give the appearance of doing so), it is difficult to see why ultra vires should remain if . . . sovereignty does not', Nicholas Bamforth, 'Ultra Vires and Institutional Interdependence' in Christopher F Forsyth (ed), *Judicial Review and the Constitution* (Hart Publishing 2000) 126. We might paraphrase this and state that it is difficult to see why the *ultra vires* theory is necessary if sovereignty is no longer conceived of as a rule.
9 *Thoburn v Sunderland City Council* [2002] EWHC 195 (Admin), [2003] QB 151 [59]–[60], [62], [64], [69] (Laws LJ); *R (Jackson) v Attorney-General* [2005] UKHL 56, [2006] 1 AC 262 [102] (Lord Steyn).
10 Chapter Three p 38.
11 Chapter Four pp 62–68; Chapter Five pp 101–103.
12 Forsyth, 'Of Fig Leaves and Fairy Tales' (n 5) 123, 127–129; Christopher F Forsyth, 'Heat

136 *Intention, Supremacy and Judicial Review*

intention of the legislature as the basis of review; rather, it has been derived from observations of the operation of the courts.

Moreover, this revised view allows us to fully acknowledge, without recourse to a fictional legislative intent, what everyone knows to be true: that the standards of good administration are judicial creations. That is not to say, though, that statute does not play a part. In the next section, I examine the extent to which the development and application of the standards of good administration is guided by, among other things, statute.

The standards of good administration

I argued in Chapter Two that understanding always involves application.[13] This means that understanding what the standards of good administration are thought to require – and how they should be balanced against any competing principles or statutory requirements – can only occur in the context of a particular case. I also argued that each act of applying, say, the principle of rationality will further determine its meaning.[14] For this reason, such application is an example of practical knowledge – it can only be fully realised in the concrete situation.[15] Given this, it will be guided by experience and history of effect.[16] The former of these will guide in two ways.

First, when deciding how to apply a rule or principle, Gadamer submits that we should 'assume its completeness'.[17] That is, we should envisage it as a coherent whole and choose the application that best fits that whole. Dworkin refers to this as the 'adjudicative principle of integrity'.[18] In imagining this whole, we should be directed by our experience of previous applications. These may be acquired directly or vicariously. So, when deciding what fairness requires in a particular case, a judge should draw on her previous experiences of this principle being applied. These may be direct, through cases with which she has been personally involved, or indirect, through, say, law reports. The greater the number of these experiences that the judge has, the more nuanced and thorough her image of the whole is likely to be. Consequently, this will mean that she has become better able to determine how the case before her best fits with this sense of a coherent whole.

Second, it was shown in Chapter Two that, for Gadamer, experiences also help one to develop the faculties of judgement, tact and taste – that is, our way of knowing what is required in the particular situation.[19] This means that, as well

---

and Light: A Plea for Reconciliation' in Christopher F Forsyth (ed), *Judicial Review and the Constitution* (Hart Publishing 2000) 400–404.

13 Chapter Two pp 10–16.
14 ibid pp 12–14.
15 ibid pp 13–14.
16 ibid pp 14–15 and 16.
17 ibid p 15.
18 Ronald Dworkin, *Law's Empire* (Hart Publishing 1998) 225; Chapter Two p 19.
19 Chapter Two p 14.

Constitutional legitimacy 137

as allowing us to construct a detailed image of the whole, experiences will also guide us in deciding which application of the principle in the instant case best fits with that whole. Again, the greater the number of experiences we have, the more developed these faculties will be which, in turn, may mean that we are better able to apply the principle. So, the greater experience that a judge has of when the courts have found a decision to be contrary to the requirements of fairness, then the more likely it is that he will have better developed his faculties of tact, taste and judgement and, consequently, be better able to assess whether the decision in the case before him is unfair.

Some commentators appear to appreciate the potential value and benefit of acquired experience with regard to judicial review. They recognise, for instance, that it is desirable to have judges in the Administrative Court who have a background in, and therefore extensive experience of, administrative law. The advantage of this is that a consistency of approach may be maintained in exercising the variety of judicial discretions that this area of law contains.[20]

The development and application of the standards of good administration will also be conditioned by history of effect. I noted in Chapter Two that this is the phrase used by Gadamer to describe the conditioning force that the tradition we inhabit will have on all acts of interpretation. This tradition will provide us with the assumptions, beliefs, prejudices and values that govern the way we interpret the world. Its ongoing conditioning effect will often occur through taken-for-granted assumptions which may become explicit or remain permanently hidden.[21]

History of effect will guide judges in their evaluation of what justice, fairness, the rule of law and the standards of good administration require in any particular case. Further, it will influence their assessment of what weight any principle has in relation to another and, consequently, how different principles – and legislation – should be balanced against each other.

Indeed, the advocates of both the common law and *ultra vires* theories explicate the development and application of the standards of good administration in a Dworkinian/Gadamerian way.[22] The common law theorists state that the development of these standards is 'normatively justified' by reference to 'justice, the rule of law, etc,'[23] and that the courts will decide what is required in a manner 'that [provides] the best constructive interpretation of the community's legal

---

20 Sir Harry Woolf, 'Judicial Review: A Possible Programme for Reform' [1992] *PL* 221, 224–225; Sir Jeffrey Bowman *et al, Review of the Crown Office List: A Report to the Lord Chancellor* (Lord Chancellor's Department 2000) 18, 19, 50. However, the workload of the Court may make it difficult that only judges with such experience hear administrative law cases: Maurice Sunkin, 'Withdrawing: A Problem in Judicial Review?' in Peter Leyland and Terry Woods (eds), *Administrative Law Facing the Future: Old Constraints and New Horizons* (Blackstone Press 1997) 226.

21 Chapter Two pp 16–18.

22 Chapter Four pp 58–59.

23 Paul P Craig, 'Competing Models of Judicial Review' [1999] *PL* 428, 429, 431; Chapter Three p 35.

138 *Intention, Supremacy and Judicial Review*

practice judged in the light of previous case law'.[24] Wade and Forsyth, who are leading supporters of the *ultra vires* theory, write:

> Faced with the fact that Parliament freely confers discretionary powers with little regard to the dangers of abuse, the courts must attempt to strike a balance between the needs of fair and efficient administration and the need to protect the citizen against oppressive government. Here they must rely on their own judgement, sensing what is required by the interplay of forces in the constitution.[25]

This reliance on 'the interplay of forces in the constitution' appears to be echoed by Elliott who writes: 'in effecting judicial review, the courts are seeking to give effect to a body of norms which lies at the core of the British legal culture'.[26] The supporters of both theories, then, seem to implicitly acknowledge that the standards of good administration are derived from, and conditioned by, an evolving cultural and legal tradition.

Legislation, though, still plays a part in the creation and application of the standards of good administration. Indeed, it has both a direct and an indirect effect. With regard to the former, Forsyth and Elliott point out that the exercise of public power, and, consequently, the way in which the standards of good administration govern that exercise, will often take place within a statutory structure: 'it is impossible to make sense of judicial review without considerable recourse to the legislative frameworks within which administrative power subsists'.[27] For instance, the determination of whether a discretion has been exercised fairly will regularly be made against a particular statutory background.[28] Similarly, the assessment of whether a decision-maker has taken account of all relevant considerations, and ignored all irrelevant ones, is frequently made by reference to legislation.[29] And, of course, one can only judge whether an exercise of public power is contrary to the objects and purpose of an Act of Parliament by reference to the statute in question.[30] In short, 'the boundaries of a statutory decision-maker will be set predominantly by statute'.[31]

The indirect effect of legislation refers to the effect it will have on elements of the tradition we inhabit. This tradition will change over time and will, itself, be

---

24 Paul P Craig, 'Legislative Intent and Legislative Supremacy: A Reply to Professor Allan' (2004) 24 *OJLS* 585, 590; Chapter Three p 35.

25 HWR Wade and Christopher F Forsyth, *Administrative Law* (11th edn, OUP 2014) 16.

26 Mark C Elliott, *The Constitutional Foundations of Judicial Review* (Hart Publishing 2001) 104; Chapter Four p 59.

27 Christopher F Forsyth and Mark C Elliott, 'The Legitimacy of Judicial Review' [2003] *PL* 286, 300.

28 ibid 300–302.

29 ibid 303.

30 ibid. In *Padfield v Minister of Agriculture* [1968] 2 WLR 92 the House of Lords concluded that a statutory discretion must be exercised in a way that is consistent with the overall purpose and objects of the Act granting the power.

31 Forsyth and Elliott, 'The Legitimacy of Judicial Review' (ibid) 305.

Constitutional legitimacy 139

subject to a number of influences. Legislation will often be one of these. It is well known that legislation can, to a varying extent, alter the social and moral mores of society. For instance, laws decriminalising homosexuality or criminalising driving while under the influence of alcohol will no doubt have affected attitudes towards these activities. Legislation does not simply alter the law; it will often have a conditioning and educatory effect and will, over time, modify our assumptions and prejudices.

More pertinently for present purposes, it is possible to argue that the greater protection afforded to fundamental rights in recent years is, at least in part, the result of a number of statutes in which the protection of rights has been put at a premium. These include: the Equal Pay Act 1970; the European Communities Act 1972 (ECA 1972); the Sex Discrimination Act 1975; the Race Relations Act 1976; the Disability Discrimination Act 1995; and the Human Rights Act 1998 (HRA 1998). As Jowell writes:

> The elucidation of constitutional rights and constitutional principle should not ... be seen as an achievement of the judiciary alone. Parliament itself has played a significant role in protecting rights, for example by initiating and extending legislation seeking to prohibit unjustified discrimination and the incorporation of the provisions of the European Convention on Human Rights through the Human Rights Act 1998.[32]

Indeed, Lord Browne-Wilkinson described statutes that prohibit discrimination on the grounds of gender or race as 'pioneering legislation *designed to produce a social*, as much as a legal, change' (emphasis added).[33] The same can hardly be considered to be less true of the HRA 1998. In fact, in the preface to the White Paper that preceded the Act, the then Prime Minister, Tony Blair, predicted that the HRA 1998 'will enhance the awareness of human rights in our society'.[34]

Such rights-based legislation will shape the tradition in a number of ways. They will, for instance, create a greater consciousness of rights. It is certainly the case that there is a greater judicial awareness here. For example, while it would appear that there are no mentions of the ECHR in domestic courts before 1970,[35] by 1993 Bratza could write that 'A recent search reveals that the Convention has been referred to in the judgments of domestic courts and Tribunals over 200 times'.[36] A similar exercise today would, I suggest, return results in the thousands.

This greater recognition is almost inevitably accompanied by an increase in rights discourse, in the media and within society more generally. Consequently,

---

32 Jeffrey L Jowell, 'Parliamentary Sovereignty Under the New Constitutional Hypothesis' [2006] *PL* 562, 576.

33 *Nagarajan v London Regional Transport* [2000] 1 AC 501 (HL) 509.

34 Home Office, *Rights Brought Home: The Human Rights Bill* (Cm 3782, 1997) 1.

35 Michael J. Beloff and Helen Mountfield, 'Unconventional Behaviour? Judicial Uses of the European Convention in England and Wales' [1996] *EHRLR* 467, 474.

36 Quoted in 'Unconventional Behaviour?' (ibid) 494.

140   *Intention, Supremacy and Judicial Review*

this leads to a better understanding of such rights and of the rationale on which they are founded. This will, in turn, cultivate an assumption that they should be protected because they truly are fundamental.

Rights-based legislation will also engender a greater predilection, and confidence, to challenge executive action which infringes rights. This can also be said of the ECA 1972. As the *Factortame* case demonstrates, the ECA 1972 has even made it legitimate to disapply primary legislation.[37]

The influence is not, of course, all one way. The assumptions and prejudices inherent in the tradition will condition the treatment by the courts of legislation affecting that tradition. To be sure, this has been one of the main themes of this chapter and Chapter Six. Legislation will be construed in such a way so as to give effect to principles and values inherent in the common law. Indeed, as the treatment of total ouster clauses demonstrates, the courts may ascribe a meaning to legislation which is contrary to its 'plain meaning' when that legislation conflicts with principles inherent in the legal tradition.

Conclusion

I argued in Chapter Four[38] that there is an assumption inherent in both the *ultra vires* and common law theories – that legislative supremacy is implicitly conceived of as operating in the manner of a rule. Indeed, it is this conception that leads to the assertion, by the *ultra vires* theorists, that the exercise of the supervisory jurisdiction must be justified by reference to legislative intent. I have argued in this chapter that, when we view parliamentary sovereignty as a principle, it is not necessary to legitimise judicial review in this way. Rather, the standards of good administration can be accepted to be what commentators on all sides agree they are in reality: judicial creations. Their development and application, including the way they are balanced against each other and against competing principles, is conditioned by history of effect.

Legislation still has, however, a substantial part to play. It will, in a broad sense, shape and influence the tradition from which the principles are derived. More directly, it will create a statutory framework within which the exercise of public power and, consequently, the supervisory jurisdiction, operates.

This new approach to legitimising judicial review, and the conception of parliamentary sovereignty on which it is based, avoids some of the more questionable aspects and assumptions of the *ultra vires* and common law theories. It does not rely on a fiction of legislative intent, as in the *ultra vires* theory, or assume that parliamentary sovereignty requires adherence to the intention, as well as the legislation, of Parliament. It does not deny the courts a legitimate law-making role. There is no necessity to assert, as supporters of both the *ultra vires* and common law theories do, that the courts will adhere to legislation which attempts to exclude the supervisory jurisdiction, an assertion which fails to acknowledge that

---

37 *R v Secretary of State for Transport, ex p Factortame and Others (No 2)* [1991] 1 AC 603 (HL).
38 Chapter Four pp 42–44.

Constitutional legitimacy 141

the courts have ignored such provisions in cases such as *Anisminic*.[39] In fact, my alternative justification of judicial review does not attempt to ignore, or explain as consistent with absolute conceptions of unlimited legislative competence, decisions where the courts protect fundamental rights from statutory infringement, interpret ouster clauses so as to maintain access to the courts or apply European Union law in preference to an Act of Parliament.

Rather, this new theory of judicial review, and the conception of parliamentary sovereignty on which it is based, attempts to provide a rationalisation of the relationship between Parliament and the courts which better reflects the reality demonstrated in the decisions of the latter. In doing so, it assumes that the courts have an independent constitutional role which views them as guardians of legislative supremacy and other fundamental constitutional norms and as attempting to reach an appropriate accommodation between the two where there is conflict. Indeed, this independent constitutional role means that they have an inherent jurisdiction which requires them to balance statute against competing principles, or to develop and apply the standards of good administration, and, what is more, that they exercise this jurisdiction without attempting to divine what parliamentarians would have done in their place.

This new theory, then, does not rely on fictions or fairy tales. It assumes that in a grown-up legal system such things are unnecessary and that they mask the legitimate, independent law-making role of the courts. As Laws LJ writes: 'We do not need the fig-leaf any more'.[40]

---

39 *Anisminic Ltd v Foreign Compensation Commission* [1969] 2 AC 147 (HL).
40 Sir John Laws, 'Law and Democracy' [1995] *PL* 72, 79.

142 *Intention, Supremacy and Judicial Review*

Bibliography

Bamforth N, 'Ultra Vires and Institutional Interdependence' in Christopher F Forsyth (ed), *Judicial Review and the Constitution* (Hart Publishing 2000)

Beloff M J and Mountfield H, 'Unconventional Behaviour? Judicial Uses of the European Convention in England and Wales' [1996] *European Human Rights Law Review* 467

Bowman Sir Jeffrey *et al*, *Review of the Crown Office List: A Report to the Lord Chancellor* (Lord Chancellor's Department 2000)

Craig P P, 'Competing Models of Judicial Review' [1999] *Public Law* 428

— 'Legislative Intent and Legislative Supremacy: A Reply to Professor Allan' (2004) 24 *Oxford Journal of Legal Studies* 585

Dworkin R, *Law's Empire* (Hart Publishing 1998)

Elliott M C, *The Constitutional Foundations of Judicial Review* (Hart Publishing 2001)

Forsyth C F, 'Of Fig Leaves and Fairy Tales: The Ultra Vires Doctrine, the Sovereignty of Parliament and Judicial Review' [1996] *Cambridge Law Journal* 122

— 'Heat and Light: A Plea for Reconciliation' in Christopher F Forsyth (ed), *Judicial Review and the Constitution* (Hart Publishing 2000)

— and Elliott M C, 'The Legitimacy of Judicial Review' [2003] *Public Law* 286

Home Office, *Rights Brought Home: The Human Rights Bill* (Cm 3782, 1997)

Jowell J L, 'Parliamentary Sovereignty Under the New Constitutional Hypothesis' [2006] *Public Law* 562

Laws Sir John, 'Law and Democracy' [1995] *Public Law* 72

Sunkin M, 'Withdrawing: A Problem in Judicial Review?' in Peter Leyland and Terry Woods (eds), *Administrative Law Facing the Future: Old Constraints and New Horizons* (Blackstone Press 1997)

Wade HWR and Forsyth C F, *Administrative Law* (11th edn, OUP 2014)

Woolf Sir Harry, 'Judicial Review: A Possible Programme for Reform' [1992] *Public Law* 221

Index

absolute knowledge 17
access to the courts 80–1, 82, 83–4, 89, 92, 93, 94, 95, 96, 97, 98, 100, 102, 111, 112; competing principles 118, 123; constitutional or fundamental principle 116, 128–9; *see also* ouster clauses
alcohol 139
Allan, TRS 1, 2, 21, 22, 32, 33, 35, 45, 50, 51, 55, 59, 64, 65, 67, 68, 83, 113, 117, 120, 123, 124–5
Altman, A 22–3, 129
Anthony, G 101
Antonio, RJ 77
application and interpretation 10–16, 17, 21–2, 136
associational standing 99–100
Austin, J 59

Bailey, SH 48, 87, 99
Bamforth, N 35, 38, 44, 56, 68, 79, 87, 135
Banner, C 117
Barber, NW 66
Barendt, E 61
Bates, TStJN 113
Beloff, MJ 139
Bingham, Lord 69, 86, 87, 90, 117, 124
Blair, Tony 139
Bondy, V 90, 91, 95
Bowman, Sir Jeffrey 90, 91, 93, 97, 98, 137
Bradley, AW 39, 61
Bridge, Lord 14, 116
Bridges, L 93
Brown, Lord 119
Browne-Wilkinson, Lord 139
Buchwalter, A 77

Cane, P 86, 99
Carnwath, Lord 69
Chu, J 1, 2, 50, 65, 102
common law theory 2, 15, 19–20, 23, 25, 29, 34–8, 133, 135, 137–8; collateral challenge 68–9; immanent critique 73, 77, 79–84; (ouster clauses) 101–3, 106; (permission stage) 88–93, 105; (remedies) 103–4, 106; (scope of judicial review) 85, 88, 105; (sufficient interest) 95–101, 105–6; (time limits) 93–5, 105; inherent jurisdiction 29–30, 34–6, 39, 56, 62, 133; language 45, 72, 81; non-statutory power 56, 73, 85, 88, 105; ouster clauses 63, 67–8, 72, 101–3; parliamentary sovereignty 36, 38, 39, 42, 43, 44–5, 46, 47–8, 52, 54, 72, 81, 82, 84, 140; query need for 54; rejection of parliamentary intent 36, 38, 47–8; review of non-statutory power 73; rule of law 20, 35, 38–9, 58, 59, 62, 72, 73, 80–4, 92, 96, 137; summary 38–9
completeness of text 15, 19
constitutional legitimacy of judicial review 16, 30, 133–6, 140–1; standards of good administration 18, 135, 136–40
contract law 36
Cornford, T 91
Cotterell, R 52
Craig, PP 1, 19–20, 32, 33, 34, 35, 36, 38, 44, 45, 47, 48, 49, 50, 52–3, 58, 59, 67–8, 73, 79, 80, 81–2, 85, 87, 89, 91, 95, 96, 98, 100, 102, 113, 116, 121, 126, 135, 137, 138

144 *Intention, Supremacy and Judicial Review*

Denning, Lord 114–15, 116
Dicey, AV 18, 42, 46, 47, 48, 52, 54, 82, 122, 128
Diplock, Lord 29, 37, 45, 61, 87, 90, 91
discrimination 139
Donaldson, Lord 86, 89, 91, 94, 96, 97, 98
Douzinas, C 14–15
drink-driving 139
Dworkin, R 19–23, 35, 42–3, 49, 50, 59, 60, 110, 112, 113, 120, 125, 128, 129, 136
Dyson, Lord 67, 70, 86, 88, 98
Dyzenhaus, D 65

Ekins, R 8, 51, 52, 126
Elliott, MC 1, 29, 31, 32, 33, 34, 35, 36, 47, 51, 53, 55, 56, 58, 59, 60, 63–4, 65, 66, 67, 68, 69, 71, 79, 80, 82, 84, 89, 95, 98, 101, 102, 110, 111, 112, 114, 115, 118–19, 121, 138
Enlightenment 18
European Community/Union law 9, 28, 54, 113–15, 121, 123, 140, 141
Ewing, KD 39, 61

Farquharson, Lord Justice 86, 87
Feldman, D 71, 104
Fordham, M 35, 89, 90, 93
Forsyth, CF 1, 29, 30, 31, 32, 33, 34, 35, 43, 45, 47, 48, 51, 55, 56–8, 64, 65, 66, 68, 69, 70–1, 79, 80, 85, 86, 87, 88, 96, 98–9, 102, 104, 111, 112, 113, 127, 134, 135, 138
freedom of movement 116
fundamental rights 116–18, 121, 123, 125, 139–40, 141
fusion of horizons 23–4, 25, 83

Gadamer, H-G 7–8, 9, 10, 11, 12, 13, 14, 15, 16, 17–18, 19–24, 25, 48–9, 52, 61–2, 83, 136, 137
Galligan, DJ 48
Gardner, J 50
gender discrimination 139
Giddens, A 17
Goldsworthy, J 50–1, 52, 120, 126–7
good faith 91, 92–3, 98, 105
Gordon, M 126

Gottlieb, A 77
Grondin, J 6, 12, 24, 25
group claims 99–100, 101

Habermas, J 9–10, 11, 18, 24
Hale, Baroness 54, 58, 84, 116, 117, 119, 124
Harden, I 78
Hare, I 32
Hart, HLA 8, 9, 22, 112
Hegel, GWF 77
Held, D 77, 78
Henley, K 7, 19
hermeneutics *see* philosophical hermeneutics
Himsworth, C 93, 98
Hoffmann, Lord 58, 61, 87, 116, 117
homosexuality 139
Hope, Lord 54, 83, 97, 119, 124
human rights 116–17, 125, 139–40
hybrid public authorities 85–6

immanent critique 2, 25, 73, 79–80, 104–6; comparison: theories and practice 84–104; (ouster clauses) 101–3, 106; (permission stage) 88–93, 105; (remedies) 103–4, 106; (scope of judicial review) 84–8, 105; (sufficient interest) 95–101, 105–6; (time limits) 93–5, 105; meaning of 77–9; values underlying the two theories 80–4
intention 72; collective 50–2; of Ministers 10; ouster clauses 63, 64, 67; philosophical hermeneutics: understanding and 7–10, 19, 48–9; *ultra vires* theory 29, 31–4, 35, 39, 43–4, 45, 46–7, 49–54, 63, 65, 66, 67, 72, 73, 81, 82
interpretation and application 10–16, 17, 21–2, 136

Jockey Club 88
Joseph, PA 35, 48, 53, 102
Jowell, JL 33, 34, 38, 44, 47, 52, 57, 80–1, 89, 116, 139
judicial review: common law theory *see separate entry*; constitutional legitimacy of 16, 30, 133–41; grounds 28–9, 37; meaning of 28; permission stage 88–93, 105; remedies 29, 69–71, 72, 103–4, 106; scope of 84–8, 105; sufficient

interest 95–101, 105–6; time limits
93–5, 105; *ultra vires* theory *see
separate entry*

Knight, CJS 61

Lakin, S 127
language: common law theory 45,
72, 81; philosophical hermeneutics
23–5, 83
Laws, Sir John 34, 46, 54, 61, 62, 63,
86, 110, 111, 113, 114, 116, 117,
121, 123, 126, 135, 141
Le Sueur, AP 89, 90, 91
legal certainty 71
legality principle 2, 71, 115, 117,
127
legislative sovereignty or supremacy *see*
parliamentary sovereignty
Lewis, N 78
Leyland, P 101
Ligere, E 99
Lindsay, A 95
Lloyd, Lord Justice 86, 87
locus standi 95–101, 105–6
Loughlin, M 128

MacCormick, N 119–20
McGarry, J 58, 63, 99, 110
McVeigh, S 14–15
Mance, Lord 114
Marshall, G 126
Marx, K 77
Meszaros, G 93
Miles, J 101
Millett, Lord 127
Mills, A 99
monopoly powers 56–8, 73, 85, 88,
105
Montesquieu, Baron de 60
Moules, R 117
Mountfield, H 139
Mustill, Lord 13–14, 60, 67

national security 123
negligence 36
Neuberger, Lord 114, 124

objective/subjective dichotomy 16
Oliver, D 1, 28, 36, 37–8, 86, 87
ouster clauses 49, 53, 62–8, 72, 135,
141; common law theory 63, 67–8,
72, 101–3; immanent critique

101–3, 106; limited time 35,
62, 63, 64, 102, 111, 113, 119;
parliamentary sovereignty as a
principle 110–11, 112–13, 115–16,
119, 121; total 62–3, 64, 101–2,
111, 119, 140; *ultra vires* theory 47,
53, 63–7, 69, 71, 72, 101–3, 106,
110

Panel on Take-Overs and Mergers 56,
94
Pannick, D 57, 86, 87
parliamentary sovereignty 2–3, 10,
15–16, 23; common law theory
36, 38, 39, 42, 43, 44–5, 46,
47–8, 52, 54, 72, 81, 82, 84, 140;
conceptions of 42–55; constitutional
fundamentals 54–5; Dworkinian
principle 44, 106, 110–30, 135,
140; (potential criticisms) 124–9;
Dworkinian rule 42–4, 72, 81,
106, 110, 135, 140; European
Community/Union 9, 54, 113–15,
121, 123, 140, 141; ouster clauses
47, 49, 53, 63, 64–5, 67, 72, 102,
110–11, 112–13, 115–16, 119,
140; *ultra vires* theory 30–1, 39, 42,
43–4, 45–7, 48, 49–55, 59, 64–5,
69, 72, 81, 82, 84, 110
parliamentary sovereignty as a principle
44, 106, 110–30, 135, 140; access
to the courts 111, 112; anomalous
cases 129; competing principles
118–19, 121, 122, 125, 128,
130, 134; fluidity 119–20, 125;
fundamental rights 116–18, 121,
123, 125; legality principle 127;
modification of a rule 111–12;
ouster clauses 110–11, 112–13,
115–16, 119, 121; political fairness
120–1; potential criticisms 124–9;
public support or hostility 127–8;
theory and practice 126; value
choice 128–9; weight, dimension of
113–18, 127, 130, 134
Phillips, Lord 70, 116, 127–8
philosophical hermeneutics 3, 6–25,
83; application and interpretation
10–16, 17, 21–2, 136; completeness
of text 15, 19; double hermeneutic
17; Gadamer and Dworkin 19–23;
language 23–5, 83; practical and
technical knowledge 13–15; tact,

146 *Intention, Supremacy and Judicial Review*

philosophical hermeneutics (*cont.*)
taste and judgement 14–15, 136–7;
  tradition and prejudice 16–18,
  19, 137–40; understanding and
  intention 7–10, 19, 48–9
planning decisions 95, 105
Plato 15, 77
Poole, T 35
positivism 58, 59–60, 62, 73
precedent 16
prejudice and tradition 16–18, 19,
  137–40
principle of parliamentary sovereignty
  see parliamentary sovereignty as a
  principle
principles, rules and policies 20–3,
  42–3, 59, 110
public authorities 85–6
public contracts 95, 105
public interest claims 98–9, 100, 101

quashing orders 29, 69, 70, 71, 94

R-Toubes Muñiz, J 22
race discrimination 139
Radin, M 50
Raz, J 22, 125
Reed, Lord 69, 99
Reid, Lord 29, 47, 62, 63, 115
religion 57
Ringhand, LA 1, 38, 65, 119
Rodger, Lord 119
Rose, Lord Justice 87, 88, 95, 98,
  100
Royal prerogative 28, 56, 103
Rozenburg, J 63
rule of law 20, 23, 53, 55, 137; access
  to the courts *see separate entry*;
  common law: principles fundamental
  to 114; common law theory 20,
  35, 38–9, 58, 59, 62, 72, 73, 80–4,
  92, 96, 137; ouster clauses 64–5;
  permission stage of judicial review
  89; *ultra vires* theory 20, 29, 33,
  38–9, 45, 52, 56, 58–62, 64–5,
  72–3, 80–1, 82–4, 92, 96
rules, principles and policies 20–3,
  42–3, 59, 110

Saunders, C 60
Scarman, Lord 61, 89, 90, 115
Sedley, Sir Stephen 36, 47, 92, 116,
  117

self-incrimination 118
separation of powers 60–1; *ultra vires*
  theory 58, 60, 61, 62, 73
Shelpse, KA 50
Simmonds, Lord 46–7, 48, 115
Simon Brown, Mr Justice 87
Singh, R 28
Socrates 77
South Africa 66
sovereignty *see* parliamentary
  sovereignty
sports governing bodies 57
standing 95–101, 105–6
Steyn, Lord 36, 53, 54, 63, 119, 120,
  124, 126, 135
subjective/objective dichotomy 16
Sunkin, M 90, 91, 93, 95, 137
surrogate standing 99, 100

tact, taste and judgement 14–15,
  136–7
Taggart, M 37, 65, 85, 111
Templeman, lord 45
terminology: parliamentary
  sovereignty 2; supervisory
  jurisdiction 28
themes of the debate 15, 18, 72–3;
  conceptions of parliamentary
  sovereignty 42–55, 72; ouster
  clauses 47, 49, 53, 62–8, 72; review
  of non-statutory power 55–8,
  73, 88; rule of law 58–62, 72–3;
  structural coherence of *ultra vires*
  theory 68–71
time limits 93–5, 105
Tomkins, A 60
tort law 36
tradition 48; and prejudice 16–18, 19,
  137–40

ultra vires theory 2, 10, 15, 23,
  25, 29, 30–4, 36, 133–6, 138;
  immanent critique 73, 77, 79, 80–1,
  82–4; (ouster clauses) 101–3, 106;
  (permission stage) 88–93, 105;
  (remedies) 103–4, 106; (scope of
  judicial review) 84, 85, 88, 105;
  (sufficient interest) 95–101, 105–6;
  (time limits) 93–5, 105; intention
  29, 31–4, 35, 39, 43–4, 45, 46–7,
  49–54, 63, 65, 66, 67, 72, 73, 81,
  82; non-statutory power 56–8, 73,
  85, 88, 105; ouster clauses 47, 53,

63–7, 69, 71, 72, 101–3, 106, 110; parliamentary sovereignty 30–1, 39, 42, 43–4, 45–7, 48, 49–55, 59, 64–5, 69, 72, 81, 82, 84, 110; query need for 54–5; review of non-statutory power 73; rule of law 20, 29, 33, 38–9, 45, 52, 56, 58–62, 64–5, 72–3, 80–1, 82–4, 92, 96; separation of powers 58, 60, 61, 62, 73; structural coherence of 68–71; summary 38–9; written constitution 30

United States: Constitution 30, 32; Supreme Court 30, 32

Wade, HWR 1, 30, 34, 35, 45, 64, 65, 69, 79, 80, 87, 88, 96, 98–9, 102, 113, 121, 122, 126, 138
Wadham, J 85
Waldron, J 9, 10, 50, 129
Warnke, G 13, 14, 19
Warrington, R 14–15
Weinsheimer, J 12, 24
Whittle, L 32, 51, 56
Wilberforce, Lord 98
Williams, RA 67
Woolf, Lord 48, 54, 57, 61, 63, 70, 83, 88, 89, 95, 122
Woolf, Sir Harry 86, 91, 137